# Reading
# Aids
## through the grades

### A Guide to Materials and 501 Activities
### for Individualizing Reading Instruction

# Reading Aids
# through the grades

A Guide to Materials and 501 Activities
for Individualizing Reading Instruction

### Fourth Edition by
## ANNE MARIE MUESER

## David H. Russell and Etta E. Karp

Teachers College, Columbia University
New York and London
1981

Published by Teachers College Press, 1234 Amsterdam Avenue, New York, NY 10027.

Library of Congress Cataloging in Publication Data

Russell, David Harris, 1906–1965.
  Reading aids through the grades.
  Includes indexes.
  1. Individualized reading instruction.  2. Reading—Aids and devices.  3. Activity programs in education.  I. Karp, Etta E., joint author.  II. Mueser, Anne Marie.  III. Title.
LB1050.38.R86 1981      372.4′1      80-23048
ISBN 0-8077-2609-5

Manufactured in the United States of America

92  91  90  89  88  87          3  4  5  6  7  8  9

To my daughter Ánna Máire,
whose arrival coincided with the
production of this edition of **Reading Aids,**

and to George Verrilli,
whose wit, skill, and ability to encourage
enabled me to deliver a book and a baby
during the same summer. . . .

# Contents

Introduction    1

Acknowledgments    3

SECTION ONE
Arranging Reading Environments    5

What Is Individualized Reading Instruction?    6
Diagnostic-Prescriptive Use of Materials    8
How Can One Teacher Do It All?    9
Modifying Materials to Meet Individual Needs    14
How to Modify Materials    17
Feedback to the Learner    21
Structured Response Sheets    22
Progress Plotting    24
Making Materials Self-Directing    30
Reading Room Arrangement and Management    34
Where Should It All Lead? Books, Books, and More Books    36

## SECTION TWO

### Activities for Reading Readiness   39

Auditory Discrimination   **40**
Visual Discrimination of Letters and Words   **52**
Alphabet Knowledge   **60**
Conceptual Vocabulary for Reading   **71**
Interest in Books, Story Sense and Sequence,
and Attention to the Reading Task   **75**
Following Directions   **82**
Language Arts and Learning Readiness   **94**

## SECTION THREE

### Basic Reading Skills   97

Basic sight Words   **98**
Grapheme-Phoneme Relationships (Phonics)   **120**
Word Structure   **145**
Easy Things to Read   **155**
Remediation of Specific Difficulties   **176**

## SECTION FOUR

### Advanced Reading Skills   187

Vocabulary Development   **188**
Things to Read and Comprehension Skills   **216**
Reference Skills   **230**
Survival Reading   **239**

## SECTION FIVE

### Published Reading Materials   255

How to Use This List   **256**
Guide to Published Materials   **295**
Publishers' Address List   **305**

Instructional Planning Index   **309**

# Introduction

The Fourth Edition of *Reading Aids Through the Grades* is divided into five major sections:

- Arranging Reading Environments
- Reading Readiness Activities
- Basic Reading Skills
- Advanced Reading Skills
- Published Reading Materials

Section One presents a rationale for individualized, diagnostic-prescriptive reading instruction and some procedures for making it happen in your classroom. If you are going to sit down and read any part of this book thoroughly, we suggest that you read Section One. The rest of the book has been designed for use as a reference source to be consulted as specific needs arise.

Section Two is devoted to reading readiness activities. It contains subsections on visual discrimination, auditory discrimination, alphabet knowledge, vocabulary for reading, interest in books and story sense, and following directions. Each subsection begins with a brief description of the skill area and behavioral objectives for the activities.

Section Three contains activities for basic reading skills. These activities are designed so that many of them can be used with older remedial readers as well as with young children. The subsections in this section are sight vocabulary, grapheme-phoneme relationships (phonics), word structure, easy things to read, and remediation of specific difficulties. Behavioral objectives precede each of the skill areas listed.

Section Four is devoted to advanced reading skills, although many of the activities can be prepared with lower-level content and used with younger or less able readers. Vocabulary development, things to read and comprehend, reference, and survival reading skills make up this section. Each subsection begins with the behavioral objectives for the activities.

Section Five consists mainly of an annotated listing of books and various other published materials for use by or with children. The materials are listed alphabetically by title and identified by publisher. A complete list of addresses for all publishers cited follows the descriptions of the materials.

This new edition of *Reading Aids Through the Grades* has 501 activities, 61 more than the previous edition. Once again, we have paid special attention to organizing the material for easy retrieval by a busy classroom teacher. This is especially important in a personalized learning environment where many different activities are going on at a given time.

The Fourth Edition of Reading Aids contains two different indices. The Instructional Planning Index beginning on page 309 lists the activities numerically and indicates the type of grouping for which each is suited and whether the activity requires teacher presentation or special preparation of materials. This chart also identifies activities that are especially helpful for classroom management on "rainy days and Friday afternoons." The Guide to Published Materials beginning on page 295 tells for which types of learners a given material might be appropriate. Using these two indices in combination should enable you to find the right activities and materials for a given learner without having to reread each section.

Throughout the book, the activities are numbered consecutively from 1 to 501. Within each of the book's three major sections, the objectives are numbered consecutively. With the exception of Jan Gibson's cartoons in Section One, most of the illustrations were done by the present author whose experience in the classroom included no formal training in art. We've done the best we could, and feel sure that the children will understand. Note that many of the illustrations are designed to be traced. This should give you courage help you prepare materials more easily.

# Acknowledgments

Many people contributed to making the Fourth Edition of *Reading Aids* a reality. I would especially like to thank:

—my Irish setters, Cinnamon and Puppily, and my horses, Bijou, Snowman, and Cuckoo, who kindly refrained from consuming the revised manuscript and artwork . . .

—Harry Chester and his gang, for making all the pieces fit and designing a wonderful cover . . .

—Jan Gibson, whose cartoons are still worth thousands of words . . .

—John Olson of Kachina Typesetting, for speedy and fine work . . .

—S. Alan Cohen, for the *Cohen Word Lists* and *Noall-Cohen Test of Word Analysis,* as well as for his friendship and support . . .

—Marianthi Lazos and Lexi Pinckney, whose editing and proofreading efforts found many of the mistakes, and John Mueser who finished the job . . .

—Moira Leahy, for trying out activities in her classroom . . .

—and perhaps most important,

—all the good teachers (especially Ánna Máire's grandmother), who have through the years anonymously contributed their ideas to classroom practice.

# Arranging Reading Environments

Materials for reading instruction have changed considerably in the more than four decades since *Reading Aids through the Grades* was first published. The earliest editions of this manual offered collections of reading activities intended primarily for use by the remedial reading or classroom teacher in efforts to meet the needs of students who had failed to keep up with the more successful members of their group. In the days when a basal reader was the major material of reading instruction, devices and activities designed to meet individual needs or to remediate problems were considered "supplementary" to the basic program. The first edition of *Reading Aids* was a pioneer among published collections of "supplementary" activities. Many a teacher had only ingenuity and a copy of *Reading Aids* as sources of extra activities in a basal program.

In 1975, a completely revised and updated edition of *Reading Aids* pointed out that dearth of available published materials was no longer a problem in the educational world. Publishers by that time had indeed responded to the need for materials to personalize reading instruction. The old-type basal readers still existed, but the marching of entire groups of children through level after level of the same books could no longer be justified—either on pedagogical or on economic grounds. Many schools seemed at last to be committed to personalized instruction for all.

The dawn of the 1980s saw the educational marketplace virtually flooded with materials. The materials to meet a wide variety of educational needs did in fact exist. These days, however, brought with them new problems. Rising costs coupled with budget cuts meant that many items teachers would have liked to purchase never made it to the classroom. In many settings, teachers once again had to fall back on their own resources to meet the needs of students.

This Fourth Edition of *Reading Aids* is offered with the economic as well as educational realities of today's world clearly in mind. The section on materials modification should be of special interest to those with inadequate materials budgets. The section on advanced reading skills has been expanded to include suggestions for teaching "survival reading" skills using a wide assortment of items readily available in the real world. The annotated list of published materials has been completely revised, and great care has been taken to include products that can help stretch your educational dollar.

## WHAT IS INDIVIDUALIZED READING INSTRUCTION?

What do we mean by individualized reading instruction? We mean that each learner is working at his or her own level and pace and, perhaps most important, that the *content* of what the learner is doing is precisely what is needed at that point in time. Merely permitting a learner to work at his or her own rate is not sufficient. Assigning a person to one particular level only tends to obscure the fact that each learner functions at a multiplicity of levels. What is needed is a way to permit each learner to work on the specific reading behaviors that are personally necessary—the activities for which might span a number of the traditionally labeled levels. For example, a student might have particular difficulty with a specific sound-symbol correspondence and require very easy material in that skill area until it has been mastered. That same student might be able to do some things that others who appear in general to be better readers can't do. The most efficient and effective reading environment is one designed to permit each student to work on his or her own unique combination of needs in a way that is personally best.

### Learning Style

Some efforts to individualize instruction have included attempts to identify a pupil's "learning style" and as a result of such diagnosis to prescribe a program and select materials accordingly. When this practice results, as it sometimes does, in assigning "auditory learners" to Program X, and "visual learners" to Program Y, then it is no more a means to individualizing than the assignment of a group of students with the same achievement test score to a grade level. Diagnosis must be continuous—not simply a one-shot identification of a learner's preferred modality or general level. A given learner's behavior in reading situations is simply not that predictable. In reading, which requires integration of visual and auditory stimuli, learning style seems to be more task-specific than general and is directly related to level of difficulty of each task. Attempts to link a learner's style of operating with one major approach to reading instruction may prove less fruitful than a continuous presentation of a variety of tasks with both auditory and visual inputs represented.

When you find that a learner is having trouble on a task, try to make that task easier. For example, if it is a discrimination task, make the differences in the stimuli more gross until the learner catches on; whatever the task, provide a model of the correct response. If you are sensitive to a learner's responses to a given set of learning stimuli and adjust the task level so that the learner can find success in that task, your instruction will more nearly suit his or her learning style than if you follow a general prescription based on a label.

## Sequence of Skills

Predetermined sequence of skills is another notion that often gets in the way of real individualization of instruction. Yes, there is a "best" sequence of reading skills. The problem is that that sequence varies from learner to learner. Not all learners need the same things in the same order. The sequence for a given student should be determined by what he or she needs. High-quality instruction is really like a continuously branching program—what comes next is determined by what is happening *now,* not by a predetermined sequential presentation.

## DIAGNOSTIC—PRESCRIPTIVE USE OF MATERIALS

Individually prescribed instruction requires pre-assessment of many different behaviors, to see which the learner needs to work on. Many commercially prepared sets of criterion-referenced tests (i.e., tests of whether a learner can or can't perform a specific task) are now available. However, you can devise your own set of assessments for each task if necessary.

Arrange all your learning materials so that activities which behaviorally do the same thing are together. The tasks for a given behavior should be arranged from easiest to most difficult. (The materials that go together can either be located physically in the same place, or identified—e.g., on a list or chart, or in a card file—as belonging together.) For each such set of activities, label one representative activity "pretest" and another one "post-test." The remaining activities can be used for instruction. If you use for your tests representative samples of the activities, those that are neither unusually difficult nor unusually easy, then you know that your learning activities will be behaviorally consistent with the assessments you are using. The most effective commercial diagnostic-prescriptive systems now on the market derived their criterion tests from the exact formats of the correlated learning activities. You can do it too.

Here are three specific examples of the above procedures using commonly available materials.

1. Take a review card at the end of each section of the *Durrell–Murphy Phonics Practice Program* and administer it as a pretest. If the student does well, skip the section. If the student needs help, go back and assign the cards in the section related to the review card. Use the same card or a second review card for that section as a mastery test after instruction.

2. Take a copy of each level of *Using the Context* from Barnell Loft. Pick a lesson from each to use as the pretest. If the student gets all the items in the Booklet A pretest correct, try a selection from Booklet B, and so on until you find the level in which the student can comfortably work and learn something (not less than 70 percent correct). Pick another lesson from each booklet as the post-test.

3. Take the seven booklets from the Random House *Practicing Reading* program. Beginning with a level at least a grade or two below what you think the student can handle well, let the student do one selection from each level as a pretest until you find the appropriate book for that student. Then when the student is working on lessons within that level, pay careful attention to the nature of any specific items missed and prescribe further work on that skill. For example, a student who consistently misses main idea items should be assigned work that specifically deals with finding the main idea of the material read. You might give the student work in *Getting the Main Idea* (Barnell Loft) or *Spotlight on Reading, Main Idea* (Random House). Be sure that the reading level of work in a skill in which the student may have difficulty is low enough so that the assigned work can be successfully completed.

The student response sheets supplied with *Practicing Reading* are coded to make continuous diagnosis of specific skill needs easy. You can develop your own record-keeping devices for many programs to accomplish the same aims. A model is provided in the material on Student Response Sheets, page 23.

You can follow the same types of procedures for many different materials and develop a diagnostic system right in your own classroom.

## HOW CAN ONE TEACHER DO IT ALL?

How can one teacher effectively individualize instruction for all the students? Materials are the key. Learner-directed and learner-corrected materials, *not* the teacher, must provide the bulk of presentation in the basic reading skills for each student. No teacher can simultaneously present thirty or more individual reading lessons and feedback to as many students. But materials can. And in reading instruction this is an advantage. Reading, by definition, is a print-mediated activity. CHILDREN LEARN READING BY DOING IT!

## P-Ratio: Measure of an Effective Classroom

Perhaps the most significant variable in reading achievement is the amount of on-task behavior. As a general rule, the higher the level of involvement, the greater the achievement. The Participation Ratio (P-Ratio) is a measure of the level of involvement. It is the percent of clock time actually spent in prescribed learning activities and is an indicator of how well your individualized program is going. Average classrooms employing group instruction in reading operate at a P-Ratio of about 35 to 45 percent. A successful individualized program may show a P-Ratio as high as 85 percent.

Measuring the P-Ratio in a classroom is easy to do. Randomly select ten students to observe. Write their names (or identifiable features—e.g., blue shirt, blonde braids) in the column at the left of the sample P-Ratio chart shown here.

Begin with the first student. Look at him or her for an instant. If the student is engaged in a prescribed reading activity, mark a P (for participation) in the first box. If the student is *not* engaged, mark an N. If the student is in transition between tasks (e.g., going to get an answer key to check his or her work) mark a T. If the student is directly under the control of a teacher while in transition between tasks (e.g., waiting for a new assignment), mark TX in the box.

Go on to the second student on the list. Look for an instant. Record. What you see is what you write down. It's not fair waiting a bit longer in hopes that a wandering student will return to the task. Be precise. Do the third student, and so on until you have finished the round. It doesn't take long. Then wait until it's two minutes from when you began student one. Begin a new round. Begin again after four minutes, six minutes, and so on until you have completed ten rounds of observations.

Total the P-Ratio for each student: multiply the number of N's by 10 and subtract from 100 (*or:* count the P, T, and TX marks and multiply by 10). For the P-Ratio for the whole class, all you have to do is count all the N's and subtract from 100 (*or* count all the P, T, and TX boxes). You can also calculate the P-Ratio for each round of observations.

Students from about grade 5 on can be trained to gather these data if you wish. And letting the learners in on the secret of what you are after helps too!

This observation scheme can give interesting insights. For example, in a class with lots of TX scores, students are having to wait too long for things to do. Try prescribing a variety of activities for a student and be sure that every student knows what to do while he or she is waiting for further instruction. (Read a book!) For a student who gets lots of N's, observe exactly what activity is involved when he or she *is* participating. Find what is working with this student and what isn't. Does it take the students in your class a long time to get going? Or do they start strong and give up too soon? The P-Ratio can help you answer these questions.[1]

---

[1]For a more detailed description of the possibilities in the P-Ratio observation scheme, see S. Alan Cohen, "The Taxonomy of Instructional Treatments in Reading: Its Uses and Its Implications as a Classroom Analysis Scheme," *Journal of the Reading Specialist,* October, 1971.

# P-RATIO CHART

CLASS_____

DATE_____TIME_____

OBSERVER_____

| Name | 2 | 4 | 6 | 8 | 10 | 12 | 14 | 16 | 18 | 20 | T O T A L |
|------|---|---|---|---|----|----|----|----|----|----|-----------|
|      |   |   |   |   |    |    |    |    |    |    |   |
|      |   |   |   |   |    |    |    |    |    |    |   |
|      |   |   |   |   |    |    |    |    |    |    |   |
|      |   |   |   |   |    |    |    |    |    |    |   |
|      |   |   |   |   |    |    |    |    |    |    |   |
|      |   |   |   |   |    |    |    |    |    |    |   |
|      |   |   |   |   |    |    |    |    |    |    |   |
|      |   |   |   |   |    |    |    |    |    |    |   |
|      |   |   |   |   |    |    |    |    |    |    |   |
|      |   |   |   |   |    |    |    |    |    |    |   |
| TOTAL |  |   |   |   |    |    |    |    |    |    |   |

P-RATIO
FOR
EACH
PUPIL

P-RATIO FOR EACH ROUND OF OBSERVATIONS

CLASS
P-RATIO

## MODIFYING MATERIALS TO MEET INDIVIDUAL NEEDS

Years ago, meeting individual needs in reading instruction was more difficult than it is today. Many a teacher had to rely solely on ingenuity to create the varied materials and activities needed. During recent years, however, publishers have made available a wide variety of materials that lend themselves to reading instruction geared to the personal needs of each individual learner. Schools that persist in pushing group after group through the levels of the same basal reader series can no longer justify such practice by claiming that suitable materials for individualizaton are unavailable. A combination of commercially prepared materials such as those described in Section Five of this book and teacher-created activities as suggested in Sections Two, Three, and Four can permit the teacher, even with thirty or more pupils, to individualize reading instruction in a feasible and cost-effective manner.

Many commercially prepared materials need some modification for optimum classroom use. Often, the utility of even those products specifically designed for individualized reading instruction can be improved. A publisher is in business to make money by selling a program or piece of material to as many classrooms as possible and may not necessarily, therefore, encourage the most cost-effective use of these products. Moreover, a teacher's manual for a given product is likely to describe that product in isolation, not as part of an instructional system that includes the materials of many other publishers as well.

### Why Modify Materials?

The specific purposes for modifying published materials fall into three general categories: economic, pedagogical, and procedural. An ideal piece of instructional material is durable and reasonably priced, pedagogically sound, and easy to use. Sometimes minor modifications can bring less-than-perfect published materials closer to the ideal.

*Modifications for economic reasons* enable you to operate your classroom in the most cost-effective manner. These modifications are specifically intended to—

- make consumable materials nonconsumable (i.e., reusable).
- make all materials more durable wherever possible.
- permit larger numbers of students to have access to a piece of material designed for single student use.
- permit larger numbers of classrooms or school units to have access to a piece of material designed for single room use.

*Modifications for pedagogical reasons* facilitate individualized instruction in the classroom and increase achievement. These modifications are specifically intended to—

- make materials self-directing.
- make materials self-correcting.
- maximize intrinsic motivation.
- facilitate the use of materials in a diagnostic-prescriptive manner.

*Modifications for procedural reasons* facilitate the use of materials by students and staff. These modifications are specifically intended to—

- organize materials for ease of storage.
- organize and label materials for ease of retrieval.
- arrange the learning environment with a place for everything and everything in its place, while at the same time maintaining feasible traffic patterns.

A more detailed outline of the different types of materials modifications follows.

## Modifications for Economic Reasons

The cost of maintaining the variety of materials necessary for optimum instruction can be prohibitive unless maximum potential mileage is obtained from published items. Here are some basic considerations to keep in mind:

- Consumable materials should be modified to make them nonconsumable (e.g., a student can mark responses on a transparent overlay rather than directly on a workbook page).
- Nonconsumable materials such as cards can be made more durable by laminating them or placing them in clear acetate folders.
- Parts of materials that tend to wear out (e.g., index tabs of folders, holes in loose-leaf pages, etc.) should be reinforced *before* they are demolished by heavy use.
- Materials designed for group instruction (e.g., kits with multiple copies of cards) can be divided among several classrooms.
- Some materials designed for use by one person (e.g., a workbook) can be disassembled to permit different students to use different pieces of the material at the same time.

## Modifications for Pedagogical Reasons

To permit individualization of instruction, the reading materials used must minimize the teacher's role as presenter of lesson and feedback, and maximize each learner's personal interaction with the appropriate activities. Such use of materials is the only way that one teacher can simultaneously provide as many different lessons as there are students. A high level of student involvement in reading activities leads to high achievement. To maximize task involvement, materials should be modified so that each student can correct his or her own work and chart progress toward specified goals.

While modifying materials to enhance their pedagogical utility, keep the following points in mind:

- Materials should be self-directing. After learning the basic procedures of how to use a piece of material, the student should be able to use it without continuous teacher intervention. The directions for a given task should be at a level as easy as or easier than the task itself. A flow chart describing procedures for using a piece of material is a handy reference.

- Materials should be self-correcting. This is absolutely crucial to optimum learning. The student should have access to the correct responses for each learning task. This feedback should be immediate and not require teacher input.
- Each piece of material or each set of related learning tasks should have a progress plotter.
- Materials should be arranged to facilitate their use in diagnosis and prescription. A student's performance on a learning task should help determine what he or she will do next.
- The objectives for a given task should be clear to the learner as well as to the teacher.
- Record-keeping procedures should be manageable and should keep both the student and teacher informed of continuous progress.

## Modifications for Procedural Reasons

Any classroom with an adequate variety of reading materials must be carefully organized to facilitate the retrieval and storage of these materials by the students and staff. Here are some points to keep in mind:

- Every piece of material should be labeled with the same name as the piece of material is listed on a student's prescription or contract.

- Pages or cards within a kit should be numbered or color coded or otherwise identified so that they can easily be removed for use and then accurately refiled. Don't assume that all published programs have already taken care of this. Some haven't.
- Cards with similar appearance from different kits should be coded in some way to facilitate refiling.
- Symbol or color coding can be used to link materials with the part of the room in which they belong.
- Corresponding components of a multimedia program (e.g., a tape cassette and its worksheets) should be identified for easy matching.
- Procedures for locating, using, and replacing materials should be appropriate for the age of the students using them (e.g., don't ask a five year old to find the fourth of six lessons on the same side of a cassette).
- Materials requiring continuous availability to all (e.g., answer keys and flow charts) should be posted on a wall or bulletin board.

## HOW TO MODIFY MATERIALS

Much of the remainder of Section One is devoted to specific suggestions for implementing modifications according to the general principles previously outlined. Here you will find—

- lists and descriptions of supplies you will need and suggestions for what to do with them.
- an occasional source we have found helpful when personal scrounging or local suppliers have not been enough.
- step-by-step procedures for the most important materials modifications.

## Things to Recycle

Always keep your eyes open for materials you can use in the classroom. Here are some things that you might find helpful:

- shoe boxes (for word banks).
- egg cartons (for sorting letter cards, etc.).
- large packing cartons (don't throw out the boxes books come in).
- shirt cardboards (if there's a laundry around that still uses them).
- old poster board (try your local political office *after* the election).
- large juice cans.
- washed X-ray film (use for transparencies or to make lapboards).

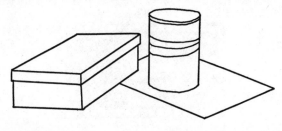

## Things You Probably Have to Buy

- Magic Markers in many colors (permanent for color coding things and making charts, washable for other uses).
- Scotch tape
- masking tape
- Mystic Tape in colors (it's pretty, it's strong, and it stays put).

## Lapboards

When we refer to a lapboard in this book we mean a firm backing of some sort that is fitted with a transparent acetate sheet. The student puts a worksheet between the acetate and the backing and writes on the acetate to do the work. (See our suggestions on Things to Write With, page 19.) The worksheet, therefore, is not consumed and can be used by others. After the student's work is corrected and recorded, the acetate is wiped clean to be used again.

You can make your own lapboards using acetate sheets, folders, or washed X-ray film, and clipboards or other backing material. Some published programs (*Random House Reading Program Orange,* for example) supply acetate sleeves that can be used in this manner.

## Acetate Sheets

To make workbook pages nonconsumable and more durable, you can enclose each page in an acetate folder. These can be purchased in bulk (500 to a carton) from most large stationery supply firms.

These folders are punched for three-ring loose-leaf use. Each contains a black construction paper backing sheet, which must be removed if you want both sides of a workbook page to show through the clear acetate. Unfortunately, the black paper is unsuitable for mounting pages (when you glue a page to the black sheet, large smudges tend to show through).

The same quality acetate sheets minus the black paper and holes can be ordered from most large stationery wholesalers. The price for these is lower, and you don't end up with a pile of black construction paper; but you'll have to punch your own holes if you want them. Unpunched acetate-covered pages can, of course, be numbered and stored in a kit.

## Individual Chalkboards

Modern technology has now brought you the old schoolroom slate, reborn as a lightweight, unbreakable, plastic chalkboard. These chalkboards have many uses and are an interesting alternative to pencil and paper. They are inexpensive enough for each student to have his or her own.

This is Annie's chalkboard

## Things to Write With

Finding writing tools suitable for use on acetate or laminated paper is not always easy. You want someting that goes on easily, stays put until the student is finished, and then is readily removable. The best procedure is to take a piece of acetate with you when you shop. Here are some points to remember:

- Mechanical grease pencils (fine lead) are OK but not neat. Red ones are not as messy as black ones. Pieces of all of them end up ground into the floor.
- Paper-wrapped grease pencils (china markers) are a poor choice. Marks made with them are hard to clean off; and besides, many are unwrapped but few are used to the end.
- On the relatively few occasions when you want to use felt markers of the permanent kind, be *very* careful. Few things in this world last as long—on acetate, on your clothes, on the walls.
- Some water-base felt-tipped pens are OK. The ink in others beads up and disappears before the word is finished. Try before you buy.
- Markers designed for writing on transparencies for overhead projectors are a good bet for writing on acetate.
- Easy-Off Crayons (by Binney and Smith, the Crayola people) were designed to wash off walls easily. They work just as well on acetate.
- Ordinary crayons work well too. Any crayon needs sharpening often to permit fine line writing.
- Wax or grease buildup on acetate can be removed by an occasional application of Fantastik or similar household cleaner. However, this is a job for the *teacher,* not the student, because Fantastik, like most cleaning fluids, is toxic.
- Writing tools tend to disappear rapidly. You might need to have a check-out box in which each student has to deposit his or her grease pencil before going home.

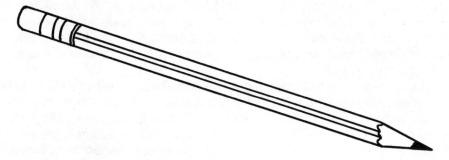

## Things to Fasten Things With

Units of work (e.g., a series of acetate-covered worksheets on a specific skill or objective) can be fastened together using brads, loose-leaf rings, or simply pieces of string. All these are serviceable, but each has a limitation. Brads don't permit the pages to open flat and lie flat on the desk. Loose-leaf rings are expensive and too large for only a few pages. String may not stay tied. If none of these appeal, try the "chicken rings" described next.

## Chicken Rings

"Chicken rings" are small curls of flexible plastic. A poultry person uses them to label the members of his or her flock. You can use them as a cheap, effective means of holding things together. And because they come in many different hues, you can use them for color coding as well.

Chicken rings are best ordered straight from the source. Try Kuhl Poultry Corporation, Flemington, N.J. Or, if you live in a rural area, your local Agway or other farm supply outlet may carry them. Ask for half-inch leg bands (No. 11) in assorted colors, or pick your favorites.

## Workbooks to Kits

Workbooks, both those that accompany basal readers and those that are published separately, are a much-maligned source of skill drill material. The problem with workbooks is often not their content but the fact that all too frequently the same bound set of 120 or so pages is given to every member of a group of children, and every child is then expected to go through these pages in order. Used more wisely, workbooks can be a good source of materials.

For both pedagogical and economic reasons, workbooks should be converted to kits. Even though we all know that not every child in the class needs every page of a given workbook, somehow too many of us seem to feel there is something irreverent about skipping pages in a workbook. Disassembling the workbook and making a kit solves the problem. If the pages aren't bound together, it's easier to assign to the student the pages he or she needs and only those.

To prepare the pages, you will need to devise ways of making them durable as well as reusable. You can mount them on stiff paper or cardboard; you can enclose them in acetate folders; possibly you can have them laminated. See also our suggestions about Preparing Worksheets for Lapboard Feedback on page 21.

To arrange the workbook pages in a kit, put all those that do the same thing together, in order of difficulty, with the easiest pages first. Clearly label them in some way for easy retrieval and storage. Color code sections of the kit (e.g., blue for beginning consonants; red for ending consonants, etc.). Color code each page and section dividers as well.

Skip the labels such as Primer and 2-1 Reader. These labels provide no useful information. (What level is a beginning blend, anyway?) Such labels may offend older students who need basic skills work. Just arrange the pages by *behavior;* they will be more serviceable. To make sure that your coding system is the one the students will follow in taking and putting away materials, remember to obliterate the page designations or other things that were necessary when the pages were between their original covers, and recode the pages according to your new arrangement.

Packing cases that books come in are excellent for kit files. Your local liquor store is another good source of boxes. You can depend on the sturdiness of boxes that once held a dozen full bottles. Cover the boxes with contact paper or paint them.

# FEEDBACK TO THE LEARNER

In an individualized learning environment where each student is working on his or her own thing, it is necessary for the materials to be self-correcting. It is no more possible for one teacher to present personalized feedback to every student than it is possible to present thirty or more individual lessons at a time.

Immediate feedback after responses is crucial to learning. Remember that you want the students to learn to make the appropriate responses to tasks. The best way to make this happen is to arrange for students' active participation in tasks and to give immediate feedback.

What about cheating? A student may consult the feedback in advance (i.e., "cheat") when he or she does not know the answer. So what? What you want is for that student to make the correct response the next time a similar item is presented. Seeing a model of the correct response is one of the best ways for someone to learn what an expected response is. Letting a student see the correct answer can be very instructive. Consulting an answer key when one doesn't know something is not cheating. Actually, it's intelligent learning behavior.

What about the student who doesn't bother to try to make the responses before heading for the answer key? First check to see if the work is too difficult for that student. An appropriate-level task is, in most instances, more interesting than simply copying something from an answer key. If the task level is appropriate, point out to the student that the required skill may not be learned if the items are not done.

The check on whether the skill has been learned is the post-test (mastery test) on each set of activities. If the student passes this checkout, he or she can be assumed to have learned what was expected. If such learning has occurred by means of what we used to call "cheating," the student has still learned what was expected . In most cases, however, if the activities have been correctly prescribed, the student will need to *do* them in order to pass the mastery test. This is usually sufficient incentive for the student.

Don't get caught in the trap of making a big deal out of cheating. The more you distrust students, the more they will fulfill your expectations. Keep remembering that a learning task should be just that—a learning task. The *test* is *your* check. All *learning* tasks should make feedback available to the *learner*. Make the learner responsible for his or her own learning. You want the student to learn, not to concentrate on beating the system. So don't create a system a learner feels the need to beat. Keep reminding yourself of the difference between learning tasks and tests. All learning tasks should make feedback available to the learner. Tests do not.

## Preparing Worksheets for Lapboard Feedback

The acetate-covered lapboard, an excellent device for making materials nonconsumable, also provides a mechanism for giving feedback to the learner.

You need four copies of a workbook to convert every page for lapboard feedback use. Disassemble the workbooks. Paste two identical pages back to back on a piece of oaktag or construction paper. Be sure to line the pages up carefully so that one is exactly on the back of the other. On one side, complete the page as you would like to have the student do. This side becomes the answer key.

The student slides the page into the lapboard, answerless side up. He or she then does the work on the acetate top of the lapboard. When finished with the page, the student removes the card and turns it over. The responses, of course, have remained visible on the acetate. The student puts the card back in, this time with the answer key up and lines up the key with his or her own responses to check the work. Even young children can master this technique of correcting their work easily.

Worksheets prepared for this feedback procedure can, of course, be used in flexible acetate folders of the right size, as well as in lapboards.

## Other Devices to Provide Feedback

Many materials come prepared with answer keys ready for student use. Use them.

Often the teacher's manual of a workbook contains facsimile pages of the workbook completely filled in. These can be used by many students without modification.

Young children can easily use acetate overlays to check their answers. You can quickly prepare these. This is one of the few places where you really do want to use permanent markers.

The self-teaching booklet described on page 83 builds feedback right into the learning task. It has many uses and is very effective.

Many audio-source programs build feedback right into the cassette script. Use one of these programs as a model when you make your own cassettes. *Audio Reading Progress Lab* is an excellent example of a good cassette-based program that gives feedback to the learner in each lesson.

If you want to explain why one answer is better than another, or present some sort of explanation or detailed description of responses, you can prepare your own answer cassette for a given piece of material. Discuss the material just as if you were talking to a student who had just completed the exercise. Label the cassette and make it available to students. This helps you be in more than one place at a time.

Answer key cards such as those from the *Barnell Loft Specific Skill Series* can be posted on a bulletin board reserved for feedback materials. Attaching the answers to the wall prevents them from getting lost, while making them available to all as needed. Having the keys located in one place in the room necessitates going to consult them. This little walk is good for students; it programs into the hour some physical activity. It also quietly encourages the student to do the work and *then* go get the answers. Few students are eager to do their work standing in front of a bulletin board.

## STRUCTURED RESPONSE SHEETS

Our work with large numbers of learners has demonstrated that skills activities done on "official" structured response sheets seem to result in better overall achievement than the same types of exercises done on random pieces of paper. Apparently, making the exercise important enough to have its own structured response sheet enhances the instructional value of the activity.

In addition, having a supply of prepared response sheets for activities that require them helps provide an orderly system for organizing the variety of learning tasks available, and the completed sheets are a record of work done. When the work is done on acetate, the results must be permanantly recorded elsewhere—usually on a progress plotter—before the work is erased. Otherwise important information about how well the student did on a task is lost both to you and to the student.

Response sheets can be designed to record useful information about the task. For example, the response sheets that accompany *Practicing Reading,* from Random House, are coded to enable the student to keep track of ongoing performance on different reading skill items. The sample response sheet that follows is similar to the one that is used in this program. At a glance, both the teacher and student can identify a skill area in which the student is having difficulty.

| | 1 | 2 | 3 | 4 | 5 | 6 |
|---|---|---|---|---|---|---|
| 1. | i | d | d | d | d | i |
| 2. | d | d | d | d | d | d |
| 3. | d | d | i | m | d | m |
| 4. | d | m | m | v | d | s |
| 5. | d | s | v | i | m | i |
| 6. | m | v | v | d | i | v |
| 7. | s | d | s | s | i | v |
| 8. | i | i | m | m | v | d |

m = main idea
d = detail
s = sequence
i = inference
v = vocabulary

| | 11 | 12 | 13 | 14 | 15 | 16 |
|---|---|---|---|---|---|---|
| 1. | d | d | d | i | i | m |

# Response Sheet

NAME _____    TASK _____

DATE _____

|  | ✓ or X |  | ✓ or X |
|---|---|---|---|
| 1 _____ ◯ | | 1 _____ ◯ | |
| 2 _____ ◯ | | 2 _____ ◯ | |
| 3 _____ ◯ | | 3 _____ ◯ | |
| 4 _____ ◯ | | 4 _____ ◯ | |
| 5 _____ ◯ | | 5 _____ ◯ | |
| 6 _____ ◯ | | 6 _____ ◯ | |
| 7 _____ ◯ | | 7 _____ ◯ | |
| 8 _____ ◯ | | 8 _____ ◯ | |
| 9 _____ ◯ | | 9 _____ ◯ | |
| 10 _____ ◯ | | 10 _____ ◯ | |

## PROGRESS PLOTTING

Progress plotting is an effective way to make even dull tasks meaningful. A progress plotter for each set of learning tasks lets both the student and the teacher know what kind of progress is being made toward a goal. Knowledge of progress toward a goal is an essential ingredient in a learner's motivation. Several different progress plotters are suggested here. You may be able to think of others. The important thing is not so much what kind of a progress plotter is used but the fact that it *is* used. Don't skip this important step.

The efficacy of progress plotters as an aid in maintaining learning task behavior is supported by research. Progress plotting has been demonstrated to be as effective as money or other extrinsic rewards in situations where the learning tasks were appropriate to the learner. And, because the progress plotter is an integral part of the learning materials, its use in a school setting is often easier to defend than the use of an extrinsic reward system might be.[2,3]

## Line and Bar Graph Progress Plotters

Progress plotters in the form of line graphs or bar graphs (histograms) are excellent for keeping track of how well a student is doing on a given objective or set of tasks. The conversion chart on page 26 can be enlarged and put up as a big wall chart. This will make it easy for a student to plot percent of items correct regardless of how many items there were in all or how many he or she got right or wrong.

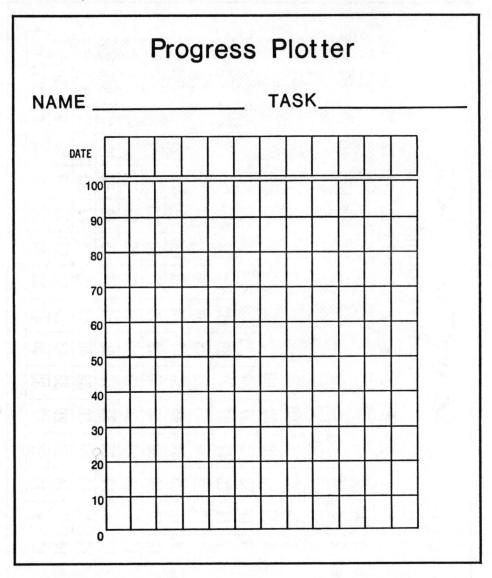

Progress Plotter

NAME _____  TASK_____

DATE

100
90
80
70
60
50
40
30
20
10
0

[2]D. E. P. Smith, D. Brethower, and R. Cabot, "Increasing Task Behavior in a Language Arts Program by Providing Reinforcement," *Journal of Experimental Child Psychology,* 1969, *8,* 45–62.

[3]A. M. Mueser, "Effects of Different Reinforcers and Operant Level on Reading Task Behavior of Black Kindergartners," unpublished doctoral dissertation, Yeshiva University, 1971.

If you are designing a progress plotter for a specific piece of material each exercise of which has the same number of items, the progress plotter can be designed with that number of items in mind and the raw score can be plotted directly. However, most pieces of material have variable numbers of items, and for that reason the conversion chart is a must.

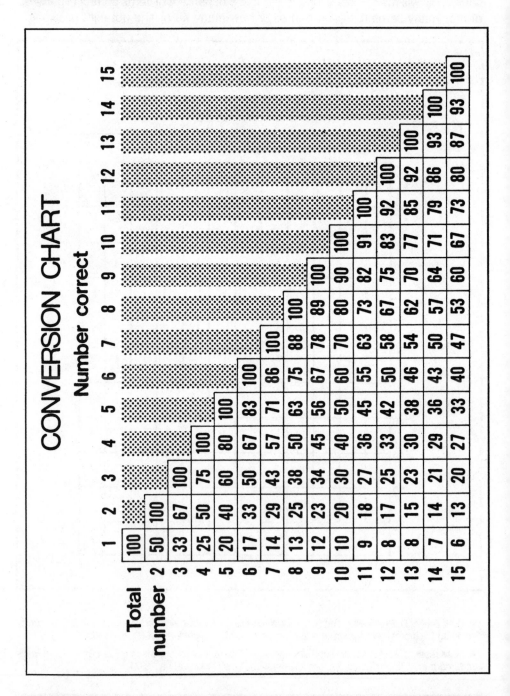

## CONVERSION CHART

| Total number \ Number correct | 1 | 2 | 3 | 4 | 5 | 6 | 7 | 8 | 9 | 10 | 11 | 12 | 13 | 14 | 15 |
|---|---|---|---|---|---|---|---|---|---|---|---|---|---|---|---|
| 1 | 100 | | | | | | | | | | | | | | |
| 2 | 50 | 100 | | | | | | | | | | | | | |
| 3 | 33 | 67 | 100 | | | | | | | | | | | | |
| 4 | 25 | 50 | 75 | 100 | | | | | | | | | | | |
| 5 | 20 | 40 | 60 | 80 | 100 | | | | | | | | | | |
| 6 | 17 | 33 | 50 | 67 | 83 | 100 | | | | | | | | | |
| 7 | 14 | 29 | 43 | 57 | 71 | 86 | 100 | | | | | | | | |
| 8 | 13 | 25 | 38 | 50 | 63 | 75 | 88 | 100 | | | | | | | |
| 9 | 12 | 23 | 34 | 45 | 56 | 67 | 78 | 89 | 100 | | | | | | |
| 10 | 10 | 20 | 30 | 40 | 50 | 60 | 70 | 80 | 90 | 100 | | | | | |
| 11 | 9 | 18 | 27 | 36 | 45 | 55 | 63 | 73 | 82 | 91 | 100 | | | | |
| 12 | 8 | 17 | 25 | 33 | 42 | 50 | 58 | 67 | 75 | 83 | 92 | 100 | | | |
| 13 | 8 | 15 | 23 | 30 | 38 | 46 | 54 | 62 | 70 | 77 | 85 | 92 | 100 | | |
| 14 | 7 | 14 | 21 | 29 | 36 | 43 | 50 | 57 | 64 | 71 | 79 | 86 | 93 | 100 | |
| 15 | 6 | 13 | 20 | 27 | 33 | 40 | 47 | 53 | 60 | 67 | 73 | 80 | 87 | 93 | 100 |

## Special Bar Graph for Graduated Levels

One thing a simple bar graph progress plotter does not take into account is the increasing level of difficulty of some materials. For example, a student who was reading easy material and getting 80 to 90 percent correct and has moved to more difficult material and still gets 80 to 90 percent correct has indeed made notable progress, even though the bar graph appears to show the same level of success. The following special bar graph was designed to show that a student who keeps the same level of proficiency at increasing levels of material is progressing.

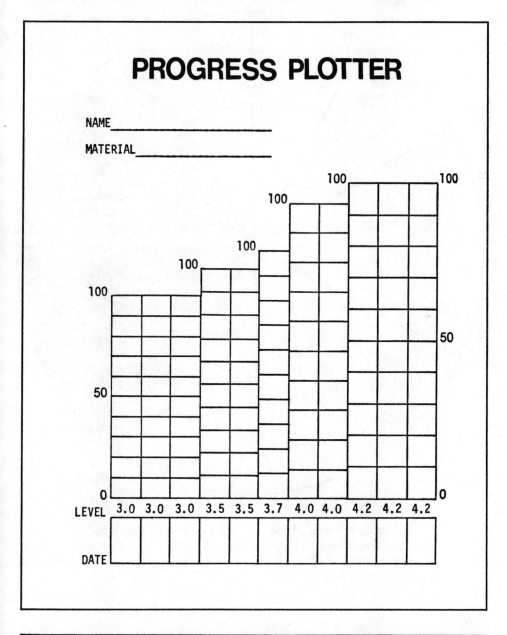

## Pie Graph Progress Plotter

A pie (circle) graph is useful for keeping track of how many of a particular set of things have been done and how many remain to be done. The circle is divided into a number of wedges, one for each task to be done. When each is completed, the student colors in a wedge. This type of graph is best for tasks that can be evaluated on an either/or basis (done or not done). It does not lend itself to expressing how well a task has been completed.

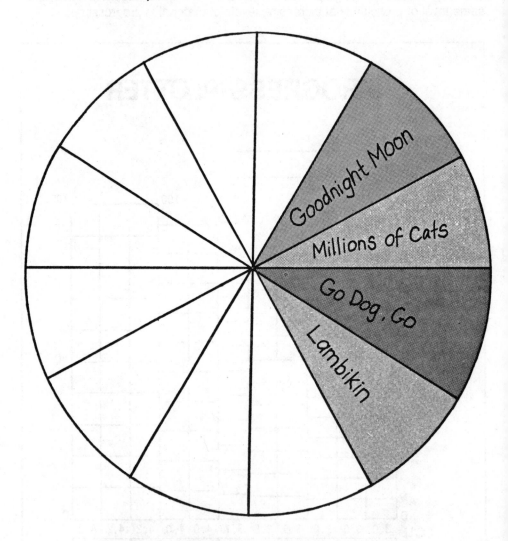

**Color in a piece of the pie every time you finish a book and talk to your teacher about it. Write the name of the book on each piece before you color it.**

## Stop Light Progress Plotter

For young children, a stop light progress plotter can work well. A student who gets all the items on an exercise correct colors the light green and goes on. A student who gets one or two wrong (out of ten) colors the light yellow or orange and goes on carefully. A student with more than two wrong, colors the light red and stops that particular exercise until after a personal meeting with the teacher. The criterion for what constitutes a green, yellow, or a red light can, of course, be adjusted to the needs of a particular student.

Originally, we used the regular three-light traffic signal for this progress plotter. The student was directed to color in the one correct light depending on the number correct. Very young children, however, seemed unable to resist coloring the whole thing, which made the device useless as a record of progress. The single signal light, to be colored in with green, yellow, or red as directed, seems better for young children. Older remedial readers, however, can do very nicely with the regular traffic signal. The idea may seem a bit juvenile to you, but kids seem to like it.

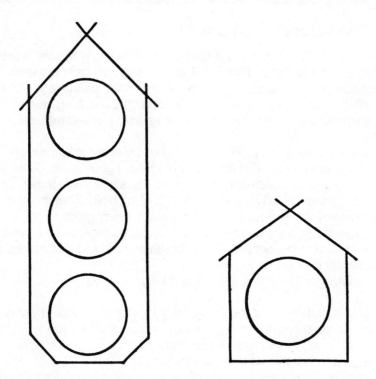

The traffic lights shown here are designed so you can trace them onto a stencil. Fifteen of the big ones or twenty of the small ones should fit on a standard page. Over each light on the page place a box in which the student can record the page and/or the date of the activity.

## MAKING MATERIALS SELF-DIRECTING

Many materials can be made self-directing with a few very simple modifications.

### Modify the Directions

If the directions at the top of a workbook page are not clear, rewrite them and paste a strip with the new directions on top of the old ones. This of course would not be feasible if you were going to let the students consume the workbooks. It becomes a reasonable task as soon as you make the decision to convert a workbook to a nonconsumable kit. Be sure the directions are at a reading level as low as that of the task to be done, or lower.

If you can't write the directions at a low enough level, try giving the student a model of the kind of response required. In many cases, it's very simple. Just do the first item or two on the page. Do the first one completely. Do the second one with a dotted line. Do the third one with part of a dotted line. The student will get the idea.

You can put some complicated directions for a given task on cassettes. This eliminates the problem of written directions that are harder than the task to be done.

### Flow Charts for Procedures

One of the best ways to make materials self-directing is to have a flow chart for each piece of instructional material. A flow chart graphically presents the procedures for doing a task, step by step. Some teacher's manuals give you flow charts for the materials. Most do not, which is really not such a bad thing after all. One of the best ways for you to learn how to operate a specific piece of material is to make a flow chart for it.

The flow chart for each piece of reading material should be available to all. A bulletin board (perhaps next to the answer keys) is a good place. Or the flow charts can be stored right with each piece of material. The student who forgets how to use a kit or specific program can refer to the chart to refresh his or her memory. A student using a piece of material for the first time has a ready guide.

If you want to follow the convention for flow chart design, use the symbols shown on page 31. These are not necessary, however. Anything that makes sense and looks good will do the job.

When making a flow chart, keep in mind the following:

- The starting point should be obvious. (Use the appropriate symbol, or a label such as "start here," or put a number one by the first step.)
- Arrows should clearly indicate where to go next.
- The written text should be kept very simple.
- You don't have to make a work of art, but a chart that looks nice has a better chance of being used than one that is a mess.
- The end of the process should be as obvious as the first step.
- The design of the chart should be appropriate for the level of the pupils who will use it. For example, a pre-reading child could use a chart with pictures, diagrams, or color coding, but not a chart in which essential information was written out.

Sometimes students can design excellent flow charts.

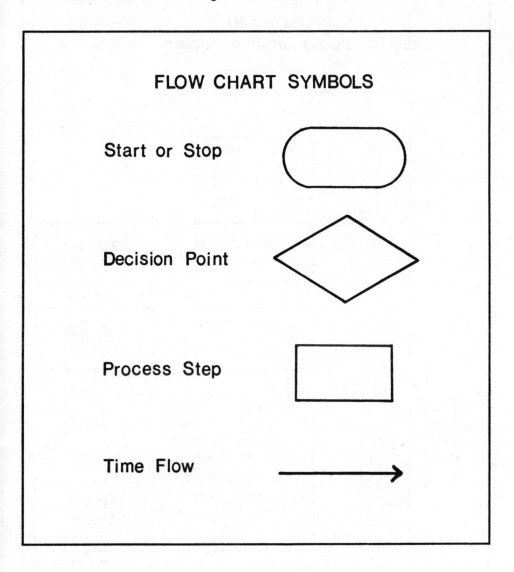

## Student "Experts"

Encourage a student to become an "expert" in the procedures for a given piece of material. A student who has difficulty should first consult the flow chart. Then, if he or she still has difficulty, the student "expert" should be consulted. Then and only then should the student be permitted to ask the teacher. Help students to become independent learners. This will give you more time to do the things that are really important and creative. Time spent reminding a student that the green and blue cards in *Random House Orange* are done *after* the book, or that the answer key for *Getting the Facts* is on the bulletin board, isn't good for you or good for the learners.

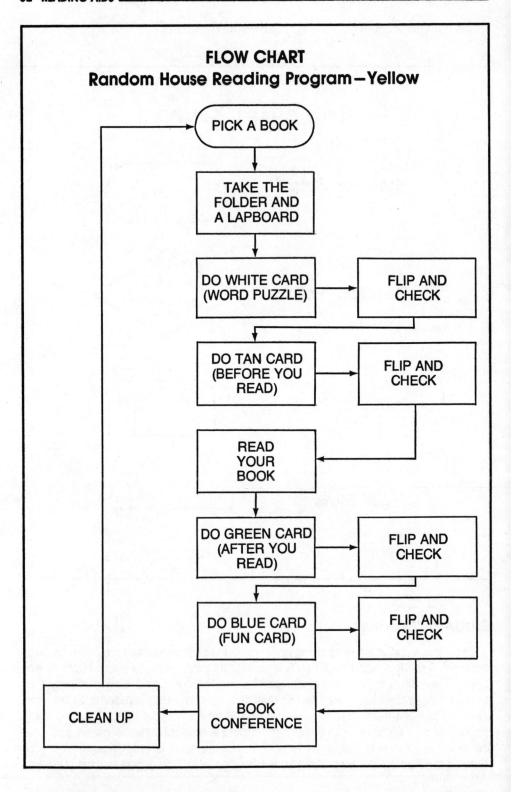

**FLOW CHART**
**Random House Reading Program—Yellow**

PICK A BOOK

TAKE THE FOLDER AND A LAPBOARD

DO WHITE CARD (WORD PUZZLE) → FLIP AND CHECK

DO TAN CARD (BEFORE YOU READ) → FLIP AND CHECK

READ YOUR BOOK

DO GREEN CARD (AFTER YOU READ) → FLIP AND CHECK

DO BLUE CARD (FUN CARD) → FLIP AND CHECK

CLEAN UP ← BOOK CONFERENCE

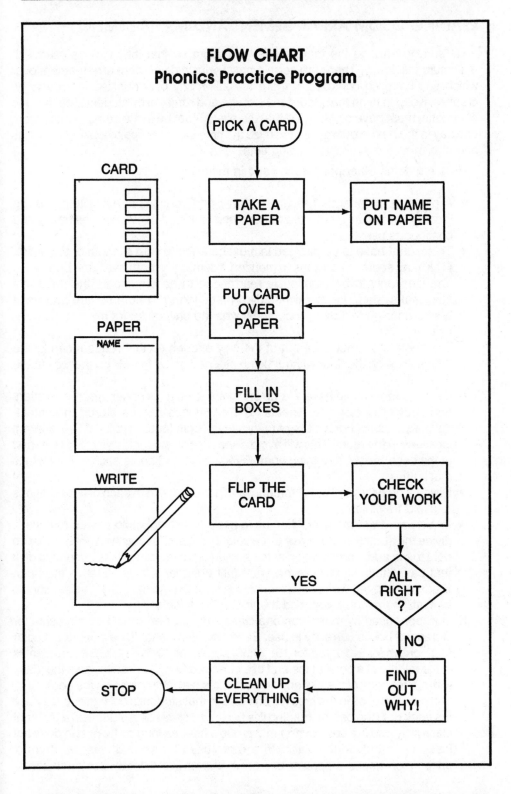

# FLOW CHART
## Phonics Practice Program

PICK A CARD

CARD

TAKE A PAPER → PUT NAME ON PAPER

PAPER
NAME ———

PUT CARD OVER PAPER

FILL IN BOXES

WRITE

FLIP THE CARD → CHECK YOUR WORK

ALL RIGHT ?

YES

NO

FIND OUT WHY!

CLEAN UP EVERYTHING

STOP

# READING ROOM ARRANGEMENT AND MANAGEMENT

Be sure to arrange the materials in your room so that they can be used with maximum efficiency. There are certain basic principles of room arrangement over which you have no control, but there are still many opportunities for you to be creative. Keep in mind that for orderly storage and retrieval by students, each piece of material must have a place and that the place must be in the same location from one day to the next. You want to minimize the time students spend looking for things and maximize the available reading time.

Here are some other pointers to keep in mind:

- A piece of material that receives heavy and continuous use should not be located immediately next to another piece of material that receives heavy and continuous use.
- Things that have to be plugged in must be within a cord's length of the outlet. (This may seem too obvious to mention, but many a room has been beautifully arranged only to be laboriously rearranged to accommodate the building's electrical system. In my own study, I managed to fill up an entire bookcase before noticing that directly behind it was the only outlet for my electric typewriter.)
- The book nook should be out-of-the-way enough so that readers can locate themselves on the floor without being stepped on by friends on the way to the SRA Kit.
- Each student should have a large envelope to hold his or her progress plotters and structured response sheets. The envelopes can be stored in contact-covered cartons. For a class of thirty, file the envelopes in at least five different locations in the room. This will avoid a line of thirty students trying to get started at the beginning of a reading hour. Five lines of six people each will not waste much time.
- Divide a heavily used set of material and store half of it in each of two locations to avoid traffic jams.
- In a class where many children have assignments to audio source materials, divide the students into two or three color groups. Students with green must go right to the audio prescription at the beginning of the class if they intend to do it that day. Students with yellow wait until a signal is given later in the hour. Students with red wait until a machine is free. On the next day, the last should be first, the middles last, and the first in the middle.
- In a room used by more than one class a day, a box should be set aside for storage of books currently in use. Each class hour should be assigned a color (e.g., green for 9–10; red for 10–10:50; purple for 10:50–11:35). If a student is in the middle of a book at the end of a class session, he or she marks the place with a bookmark of the assigned color, writes his or her name on the bookmark, and puts the book in the box. No one else in that student's color group may use the book until the person reading it is finished. However, a student in a different class may use the book during that group's hour as long as he or she does not lose the first student's place. In a room used by several classes, it is not uncommon to see a popular book with four or five different bookmarks in it.

## Directory of Materials

Each reading classroom should have a directory (large wall chart) of all the materials in the room. List the materials alphabetically and include abbreviations you use on the students' prescriptions. In addition, you should color code the materials according to location. For example, list everything in the northwest corner of the room in blue. Identify each material by a symbol as well, so the student doesn't look for a kit when he or she is assigned to tasks on a cassette.

It helps to place, whenever possible, all the kits in one location, all the audio source materials in another, and so on. In addition to labeling materials by type, color coding and listing them on a master directory, you should have a subdirectory for each section of the room (in the appropriate color). This small directory can hang like a mobile from the ceiling right over the spot in which the materials are stored. Be sure to list the materials on both sides.

Easy-to-copy symbols for different kinds of materials are shown here.

To make the master directory, it's best to begin with a large piece of oaktag or chart board. Instead of writing directly on the oaktag, write the name of the material on a small strip of oaktag. Cut slits in the large chart to hold the smaller pieces of oaktag, each with one material listed on it. You will then be able to move the items on the list to keep them in alphabetical order even when new materials are added to the room. Flexible charts permit you to rearrange the room without doing the entire set of charts over. And, if you make a mistake on the last line of a list, you don't have to begin the whole thing over again.

## WHERE SHOULD IT ALL LEAD?
## BOOKS, BOOKS, AND MORE BOOKS

The overall goal of effective reading instruction should be to develop independent readers who can and do read widely for their own private as well as required purposes. If your students can read and don't, you have only accomplished part of your job.

Perhaps the best way to develop readers is to make reading real books an essential ingredient of the reading environment right from the beginning. Even the pre-reading child can have a successful and productive experience with literature through audio source read-alongs. Right from the start, the student should be permitted to select the books he or she wants to hear or read. In order for this opportunity to be a genuine choice, you must have many books available.

### How to Build a Classroom Library

- Buy paperbacks and more paperbacks.
- Use your basal reader allotment to buy hard-cover children's trade books.
- Go to the public library and take out as many books as they will permit you to carry through the door. Change your clothes, put on dark glasses, and go back for another batch.
- Encourage your students to go to the library.
- When library books have to be returned, get another set.
- Try your local rummage sales. Excellent children's books often sell for as little as a dime or a quarter apiece.
- Encourage your students to join paperback book clubs. Some clubs give premiums (extra books) for large orders.
- Purchase, whenever your district will fund you, one or more of the excellent reading programs developed around children's books. These programs are identified in Section Five by a ■.

### Keeping Books Available

The classroom library should be a comfortable place where books are always available. Do not duplicate the storage and cataloging procedures of a regular library. Neatly cataloged books on shelves are not nearly as inviting as books displayed so that the potential reader can really see the bright attractive covers.

Here are some ways to display books:

- Spread some of them out on top of a table.
- Get racks like the ones for paperbacks in your local candy store. The racks display the books *cover* out, rather than spine out.
- Try storing piles of paperbacks in large plastic laundry baskets (not much more than a dollar or two at a bargain-type store).
- Put paperbacks in a shoe bag with clear plastic pockets. A number of these can hang on hooks or on a coat rack.

## Helping Students Select Books

The reader should select his or her own books. Self-selection is an important part of reading real books. Don't spend lots of time computing readability levels of books. Let the reader be the primary judge of whether or not he or she can read the book. A reader's interests play an important part in how well a given book can be read at that time.

If a student consistently picks books that are very much too hard or very much too easy, you can help by delimiting the array from which he or she may choose. For example, you could place twenty books that seem to be suitable on a table and encourage the student to pick from there. The element of choice should always be permitted.

Color coding can help keep books arranged roughly by level. We suggest no more than three categories: easy, medium, and hard. A strip of colored tape on the cover of each book will help students put it back with others like it. If you are using the laundry basket method of storage, you can coordinate the tape and basket colors.

## Encouraging More Reading

A student who has read and enjoyed a book should be encouraged to suggest that book to one of his or her peers. Reserve a space on the bulletin board for notes from one student to another. For example:

Dear Ralph,

Why don't you read <u>All About Snakes</u>? There's a chapter in it that reminds me of you.

Love,
Peggy

Pat should read <u>The Cat in the Hat</u>. It's a funny book.

Mat

> Sue:
>
> You should try reading <u>Big</u> <u>Red</u>, because I think you should read at least one dog book for every ten horse books. It's time for a change. Try it, you'll like it.
>
> Sammy

## The Book Corner

Try to set aside a corner of your room for a book nook. Make it comfortable. Donations of pillows and carpet remnants help. Allow (encourage) the students to be comfortable when they read. (When was the last time you chose to read a good novel sitting up in a straight-backed chair at a desk?)

## Reward for Reading

If you are able to secure an abundance of paperbacks, you can let a student keep one for every ten books read. This has been one of the most effective motivators we have used in getting reluctant readers to read real books.

Avoid making a book report a consequence of reading a book. If the payoff for reading is drudgery, then reading will never become a preferred activity. Remember that the more a student reads, the better he or she will be able to read.

You should try reading some of the books in your classroom, too! Having a good book corner will give you a chance to revisit old favorites and catch up on all the good children's books you missed by growing up too soon.

SECTION TWO

# Activities for Reading Readiness

Getting ready to read is of crucial importance to a young learner, and the available time is brief. How does one get ready to read? A look at some commercial programs that claim to develop "reading readiness" will reveal a wide variety of activities, many of which have no apparent connection to the reading act. This lack of connection is probably as real as it is apparent. Activities such as distinguishing between mooing cows and honking horns, identifying the teddy bear facing to the left instead of to the right, and matching geometric shapes and pretty pictures may make engaging busywork for small children. However, such tasks do not constitute a direct path to learning to read. Teachers would do well, therefore, to concentrate on developing those skills and understandings most relevant to readiness for reading and to avoid the proliferation of peripheral activities that do not move the child along to becoming a person who reads.

Reading readiness does not simply arrive one day out of the blue. The child who is ready to read possesses a series of learned behaviors that relate to the reading act. Some children seem to acquire these behaviors quite incidentally as they interact with their environment. Other children must be taught these reading readiness behaviors quite specifically.

What are the important reading readiness behaviors? Donald Durrell, in his text *Improving Reading Instruction,* identifies four major background abilities as important to beginning reading. They are:

- Visual discrimination of word elements
- Auditory discrimination of word elements
- Interest in printed words and in books
- Ability to maintain attention to the reading task

In *Teach Them All to Read,* S. Alan Cohen lists seven reading readiness areas as being those most likely to lead to success in beginning reading:

- Letter knowledge
- Visual discrimination of letters and words
- Auditory discrimination of sounds in words
- Story sense and memory for sequence
- Love of books
- Vocabulary for reading
- Attention to the reading task

The reading activities that follow are organized according to the areas of ability that Durrell and Cohen suggest to be most important. In addition, there is a section of activities on following directions, which are designed to give the pre-reading student a repertoire of behaviors necessary to follow directions for the exercises in reading readiness skills. If you have students who do not have the entry behaviors required to perform reading readiness tasks, turn to the activities that begin on page 82.

A few popular readiness activities that do not directly relate to reading have been retained from the original edition of *Reading Aids* because they may have valuable outcomes other than preparing children to read. These activities, designed to contribute to oral language development and general learning readiness, can be found at the end of this section. They are included here with the clear admonition that, although they may do good things, they should not be belabored at the expense of activities more directly related to the reading act.

## AUDITORY DISCRIMINATION

Auditory discrimination of sounds in words is an absolutely essential reading readiness ability. A student who does not hear sounds in words will have difficulty associating sounds with their visual symbols.

Listed below are eight behavioral objectives for auditory discrimination skills.

**RR-1.** Given two or more spoken words, the learner indicates whether the words are the same or different.

**RR-2.** Given two or more spoken phrases (sentences), the learner indicates whether the phrases (sentences) are the same or different.

**RR-3.** Given two or more spoken words, the learner indicates whether the words begin with the same sound.

**RR-4.** Given two or more spoken words, the learner indicates whether the words end with the same sound.

**RR-5.** Given two or more spoken words, the learner indicates whether or not the words rhyme.

**RR-6.** Given two spoken lines of verse, the learner indicates whether or not the words at the end of the lines rhyme.

**RR-7.** Given a spoken word, the learner indicates whether a specified sound comes at the beginning or end of the word.

**RR-8.** Given two or more spoken words, the learner indicates whether the words have the same medial sound.

## 1. Same or Different Words

Say two words. The student should indicate whether they are the same or different. The student can make the responses on a prepared worksheet, circling one thing if the words are the same and something else if the words are different. The worksheet might look like the one shown here.

The words can be dictated by the teacher or, for individualized self-instruction, the words and the feedback can be recorded on a cassette.

The same type of worksheet can be used for other auditory discrimination activities.

## 2. Same or Different Word Pictures

Prepare a worksheet with pairs of pictures. Some rows should have pictures with the same name. Others should have pictures with different names. The task for the student is to say the name of each picture in the row and then indicate if the pictures have the same name or different names.

Note that the pictures with the same names should not be visually identical. This is to aid the student in responding to the *sound* of the name and prevent answering on appearance alone.

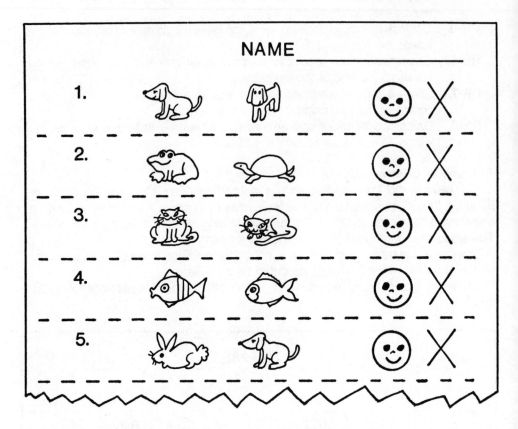

### 3. Same or Different Phrases and Sentences

This activity is done the same way as Same or Different Words (Activity 1), except that the auditory stimuli are phrases and sentences, not words. The same worksheets can be used.

Some sample sentences:

I can fly. I can cry.
Go up the tree. Go up the tree.
See the dog. See the dog.
Go home now. Get home now.

Some sample phrases:

over the hill——over the hill
to hear him talk——to hear him talk
in the park——in the dark

If the sentences are put on cassette, the students can work independently on this activity. Feedback should also be put directly on the cassette. (For example: "Listen again. I can fly. I can cry. They are not the same. You should have circled the sad face and the X.")

## 4. Beginning Sounds

Prepare a worksheet on which students can record their responses. For the response symbols to be marked, use pictures of an animal's head (its front part). The same response sheet can be used for other activities involving the beginning (front) sounds of words.

Say two words. If they begin alike, the student circles the two heads. If they don't begin alike, the student circles the head and the X.

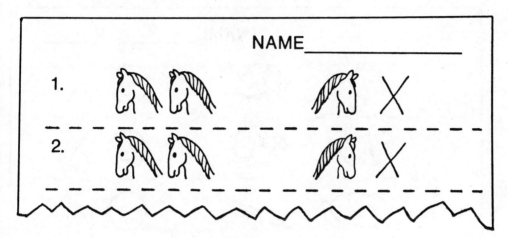

Here are some sample pairs of words:

| | |
|---|---|
| bat, ball | horse, house |
| star, bread | dog, ditch |
| rat, cat | truck, tramp |

If a cassette is used, don't forget to build in feedback to the learner. Or, provide an acetate overlay so the student can check the work independently.

## 5. Name Game

One useful device to get children to pay attention to initial sounds is to pair or group students whose names begin with the same sound. For example, Jerry, John, and Joan; Betty, Brian, and Bob; Alan, Anne, and Alice; Rita and Ronnie; Willie, Wendy, and Walter. After as many children as possible have been matched, the others can try to find an object in the room whose name begins like theirs. The teacher should look through all the children's names in advance to make sure that each child can find a match—either with another child, with an object in the room, or with a posted picture of an object. However, if a name is absolutely impossible, be prepared to deal with that and make it a learning experience too. For example, say to Ursula, "Your name is so special that we can't find another thing in this room that begins the same. You can be in charge of the game today. You can help me tell if the other children have made the right match."

### 6. Beginning Sound Picture Worksheet

Prepare a worksheet containing rows with pairs of pictures. The student is to indicate if the names of the pictures in the row begin with the same sound. Behaviorally, the task for the learner is quite similar to Activity 4. However, in this instance the learner produces his or her own auditory input by saying the picture names out loud.

### 7. Beginning Sound for a Day

Name an object. Each student must find in the room another object whose name begins with the same sound as the object named. Or the student can be asked to bring from home something whose name begins with a given sound. For example, if you decide that Tuesday is to be "banana day," then students might bring in things such as bat, ball, bottle, beanbag, book, or belt.

### 8. Drawing Beginning Sound Pictures

Prepare a worksheet with one picture at the top of the page. The rest of the page is divided into fairly big boxes. The task for the student is to draw in each box an object whose name begins with the same sound as the object at the top of the page.

### 9. Another Beginning Sound Worksheet

Prepare a worksheet containing an object in a box at the top of the page and a number of other pictures. The task for the student is to circle each picture whose name begins like the name of the picture in the box.

## 10. Beginning Sound Picture Cards

Make a set of cards similar to the Rhyming Picture Cards (Activity 20). Cut pictures from magazines and paste them on oaktag. Use 25 or 30 cards for one game. For example:

boat, bat, bear
house, horse, hand
whale, wheel
goat, gate
flower, flag
yarn
mouse, man
car, cow
shell, shower
zebra, zipper
duck, doll, dog
raincoat
water, woman, witch

Code the backs of the cards with colors and/or shapes so that the cards whose names begin alike also have matching backs. This makes the game self-correcting; students can check the accuracy of their own matching by turning the cards over.

The cards for the beginning sounds game can be stored in a labeled box. To identify it more clearly as something involving beginning sounds, paste an animal's front half on the box top. Games with ending sounds will have the back half of the same animal to identify them.

### 11. Ending Sound Picture Cards

Make a set of cards such as those used in the Beginning Sound Picture Cards game (Activity 10). This time code the backs of the cards so that ending sounds match. Pictures you might use could include:

car, star, bear, chair
dog, pig, log
needle, turtle, table
boat, coat (or jacket)
book, sink, truck, rake
mouse, horse
broom, loom
tree, bee
bread, head
mop, top

The cards can be stored in a labeled box that has the back (ending) half of an animal pictured on it to identify it as Ending Sound Picture Cards game.

### 12. Ending Sounds

Prepare a worksheet familiar to that for Beginning Sounds (Activity 4). This time, however, use the back half of the animal to indicate ending sounds.

Say two words. If they have the same ending sound, the student circles the back halves of the fishes. If they do not have the same ending sound, the fish and the X are to be circled.

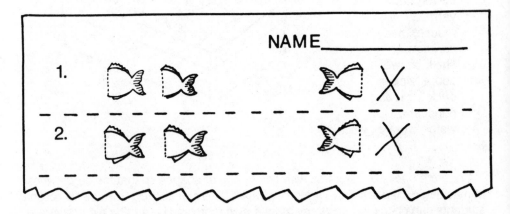

If the words are presented on cassette, the cassette should give the student feedback as well. An alternative to having the feedback on the cassette is to have an answer key that the student can use for the worksheet. (An acetate overlay works well.)

### 13. Ending Sound Picture Worksheet

Prepare a worksheet containing rows with pairs of pictures. The student is to indicate whether the names of the pictures end with the same sound. Behaviorally, the task for the learner is quite similar to Activity 12. However, the learner in this instance produces his or her own auditory input by saying the picture names out loud.

### 14. Ending Sound for a Day

Name an object. Each student must find in the room another object whose name ends with the same sound. Or the student can be asked to bring from home something whose name ends with a given sound.

### 15. Another Ending Sound Picture Worksheet

Prepare a worksheet containing a pictured object in a box at the top of the page and a number of other pictures. The student is to circle each picture whose name ends with the same sound as the name of the picture in the box.

### 16. Drawing Ending Sound Pictures

Prepare a worksheet with one picture at the top of the page. The rest of the page is divided into good-sized boxes. The task for the student is to draw in each box an object whose name ends with the same sound as the object at the top of the page.

### 17. Rhyming Words

Use the response sheet you prepared for Activity 1.

Say two words. If they rhyme, the student circles the pair of smiling faces. If they do not rhyme, the student circles the sad face with the X.

This activity can be dictated by the teacher or put on cassette. Don't forget to make provisions for feedback to the learner.

### 18. Rhyming Pictures

Prepare a worksheet with pairs of pictures. The task for the student is to indicate whether or not the names of the pictures rhyme. The learner response is virtually the same as that required in Activity 17. However, in this activity the learner is required to be the auditory source by first saying the picture names aloud.

### 19. More Rhyming Pictures

Make a worksheet with rows of pictures. In each row, the student is to circle every picture whose name rhymes with the name of the first picture.

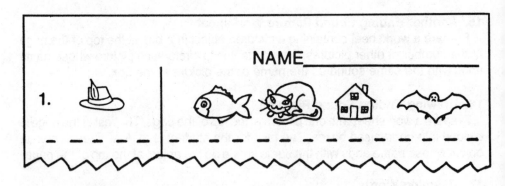

### 20. Rhyming Picture Cards

Make a set of picture cards for a rhyming game. Cut pictures from magazines and paste them on oaktag. Approximately 25 cards make a satisfactory number. There should be about eight to ten sets of rhyming words and also some words that do not rhyme with any other cards in the deck.

A sample set:

| | |
|---|---|
| mat, hat, bat, cat | horse |
| man, pan | cow |
| duck, truck | boat, goat |
| mouse, house | fish, dish |
| pail, tail, whale | well, shell, bell |
| wheel, seal | car |
| bug, rug | |

Note that the sample list of words contains some words with more than one rhyme and some with no rhyme at all.

The student has to match the rhyming cards. Code the backs of the pictures that rhyme with the same color and/or shape. For example, the *pail, tail,* and *whale* cards could each have a green stripe on the back. This makes it possible for the student to check his or her own rhymes.

An easier version of this game would have fewer cards in the deck and each card would have one and only one match.

## 21. Rhyming from Pictures

Draw on the chalkboard pictures of objects with names that rhyme, such as a pie and a fly, a pan and a man, etc. Point to the first picture and ask what it is. "Yes, it's a pie. Who can name another picture that rhymes with it?"

As an alternative to using the chalkboard, try holding up a picture from a magazine and ask a student to give as many words that rhyme with the picture's name as possible. (This second version of the activity is easier for those of us who don't draw well.)

## 22. Non-Rhyming Words

Pronounce a series of words that rhyme and include one word that does not rhyme. Have the students clap their hands when they hear the non-rhyming word. For example, say, "Right, fight, light, sight, see, might." Sometimes a series will have to be presented twice.

## 23. Rhyming Verse

Say a two-line verse. The student has to tell you whether or not the words at the ends of the lines rhyme.

Here are some examples. They should give you courage.

Have you ever met Polly
Waiting for a trolley?

The three little kittens
Lost their stockings.

Twinkle twinkle little star,
How I'd like to buy a car.

### 24. Guessing Rhyming Game

Ask the students questions that will elicit rhyming words. For example, you might start by saying, "This little boy is Bill (or Phil)." Point to a child or a picture of one. "He lives in a house on a very high _____. Who can tell where Bill's (or Phil's) house is? It is a word that sounds like Bill (or Phil). Yes, it is hill. Hill rhymes with Bill (or Phil). Now let's try another word that rhymes with Bill (or Phil). Bill (or Phil) likes to sit on the window _____. Now who can say another word that rhymes with Bill (or Phil) and hill and sill?"

### 25. Choral Speaking

Choral speaking of nursery rhymes or other simple poems and verse can help call students' attention to rhyming words—and also to the rhythms of language. This is an especially helpful activity to the child who lacks the confidence to speak alone in front of a group.

### 26. Beginning or Ending Sounds

Read a list of words and ask the students to indicate whether a specified sound is at the beginning or at the end of the word. For example, the words for the sound of *t* could be *tall, Ted, bat, sit, fat, tell, Tammy, tin, ten, terrible, tender, terrific.*

The students can respond orally or on a worksheet. The worksheet should be designed so that the student circles one thing if he or she hears the specified sound at the beginning of the word and another thing if the sound is heard at the end. On the sample worksheet below, the student would circle the dog's head if the sound is heard at the beginning of the word and the dog's tail if the sound is heard at the end. Be sure to have the dog facing the left margin of the page.

NAME_____

1.

2.

3.

This activity can be made completely self-directing and self-correcting by putting the words and the feedback on cassette.

## 27. Rhymes

Have the students say a word to complete very short rhymes that you present to them. For example:

I have fun                   Mom will buy
When I _____.               An apple _____.

Some of the students may be able to make up rhymes for others to finish.

## 28. Medial Sounds

Use the worksheet prepared for Activity 1.

Say two one-syllable words. If they have the same medial sound, the student circles the smiling faces. If they do not, he or she circles the sad face and the X. These words can be dictated by the teacher or put on cassette. Don't forget the feedback.

Here are some pairs of words:

sun, cup          bird, fern
fit, fat          pen, pin
box, rock         run, ran

## 29. More Medial Sounds

Prepare a worksheet containing pairs of pictures. The task for the student is to indicate whether or not the names of the pictures in a row have the same medial sound. This task is similar to Activity 28, except that the student is his or her own audio source. In designing the worksheet, you are, of course, limited to those things you can draw or cut and paste from prepared sources.

## VISUAL DISCRIMINATION OF LETTERS AND WORDS

Visual discrimination of letters and words is an essential reading readiness ability. Students who have difficulty in telling one letter from another visually have three strikes against them even before they are asked to attach meaning to those symbols.

Here are five behavioral objectives for visual discrimination. Note that the behaviors suggested all refer to letters and words, not to non-letter shapes.

**RR-9.** Given a letter visually, the learner indicates which of X choices matches the given letter.

**RR-10.** Given a letter cluster (blend, digraph) visually, the learner indicates which of X choices matches the given letter cluster.

**RR-11.** Given a word visually, the learner indicates which of X choices matches the given word or locates the word in context.

**RR-12.** Given a phrase (sentence) visually, the learner indicates which of X choices matches the given phrase (sentence), or locates the phrase (sentence) in context.

**RR-13.** Given a letter or letter cluster, the learner identifies the letter or cluster wherever it appears on a page.

### 30. Simple Letter Matching

Prepare a worksheet with a letter in a box at the top of the page. Instruct the student to circle that letter wherever it appears on the page.

For beginning learners, small pages with one stimulus letter per page would be best. You can prepare one standard size ditto (8½″ × 11″) that contains two exercises, but cut it in half before giving it to the student.

A correctly completed copy of the worksheet pasted on the other side makes the activity completely self-correcting if used in a lapboard (see p. 21). Giving the student immediate feedback is the key to success.

### 31. Self-Teaching Book for Letter Matching

A booklet that provides immediate feedback can easily be constructed for letter matching—and for other tasks too. This particular format has proved to be extremely effective (better than 95 percent success rate in one study[4]) in teaching visual discrimination of letters.

Use about 20 pages, each with a letter discrimination task. The pages should be about half of a standard 8½″ × 11″ sheet. The research study used pages from the *Michigan Language Program, Reading Letters 1 and 2.* You can make your own like the model on the following page. Exact directions for doing this appear on page 54.

---

[4]A. M. Mueser, "Effects of Different Reinforcers and Operant Level on Reading Task Behavior of Black Kindergartners," unpublished doctoral dissertation, Yeshiva University, 1971.

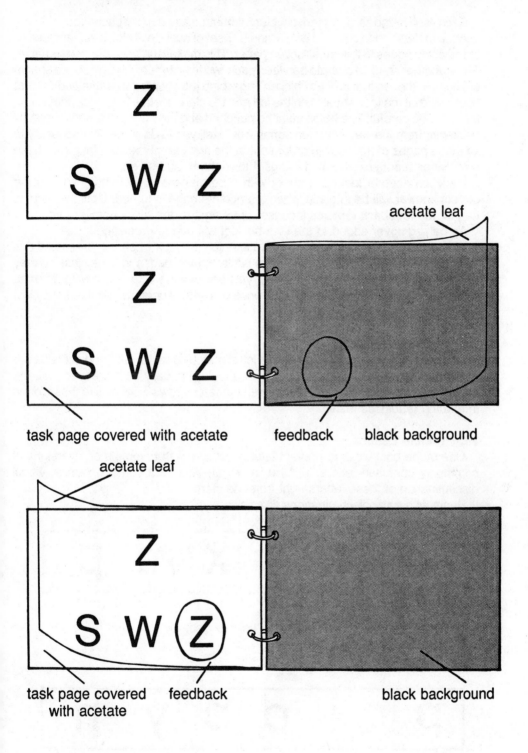

task page covered with acetate      feedback      black background

acetate leaf

task page covered with acetate      feedback      black background

Each task page is mounted on black construction paper (packaged with the acetate folders), then covered with a single sheet of acetate, which is either glued or taped at the edges to the construction paper. This makes the page nonconsumable. Place another sheet of acetate between each two task pages. These acetate sheets will contain the feedback. With chicken rings, bind the sheets into a little booklet that opens so that the task sheet is on the left and the clear acetate feedback sheet is on the right. Be careful! The holes must be punched and the book put together exactly backward from the way common sense would tell you to do it. This is necessary to keep the pages of the book in order so that the first turn presents a task sheet, the next brings feedback, the next brings a task sheet, and so on.

Mark the acetate feedback sheet with a permanent black marker so that the correct answer will be in place when the acetate page is turned. Until the page is turned, the feedback remains inconspicuous against the black background.

An oaktag cover added to the little booklet will add to durability.

Why go to all this trouble? Kids seem to enjoy the task when it is presented this way. They learn to discriminate letters while turning pages in order just as they would when reading a real book. So, you are dealing with two crucial reading readiness skills at the same time. And, once you get the books assembled, they last a long time.

### 32. More Letter Matching

When the student can handle simple letter matching tasks, with one stimulus per page, the complexity of the page format should gradually be increased until the student is working on matching tasks with numerous rows of items like those found in reading readiness tests.

### 33. Problem Letters

One of the best ways to prevent later difficulties with reversals or inversions of commonly confused letters (p, b, d, q, w, m) is a thorough program in visual discrimination of these letters right from the start.

Begin with easy discriminations, like this:

| p | z   o   x   m   p |
|---|---------------------|

Gradually increase the difficulty of the exercises by including more and more choices similar to the stimulus letter.

For example, this is a fairly difficult exercise:

| p | l   d   p   y   h |
|---|---------------------|

This is even more difficult:

| p | b d q p g |
|---|---|

Remember! The key to getting a student to learn these tasks is to provide immediate feedback on performance. The self-teaching booklet (see Activity 31) is ideal for doing problem letters.

## 34. Fixing Problem Letters

The p-b-d-q reversal/inversion problem may in some cases be due to the vertical element of the letter appearing so important to the child that he or she fails to focus on the location of the rest of the letter.

An exercise format that reduces the intensity of the vertical stimulus can aid the student in processing the rest of the letter and hence make p-b-d-q discriminations easier.[5]

It's simple. Just make the looks of the letters darker and/or thicker than the vertical lines.

For example:

NAME_____

| p | b d q p |
|---|---|
| b | d b q p |
| d | b q q d |

[5]J. S. Hyman, "Effects of the Vertical Element in b, d, p, and q on Reading Reversals of Kindergarten Children," unpublished doctoral dissertation, Yeshiva University, 1971.

### 35. Matching Letters Card Game

Prepare cards each having one letter of the alphabet. Each letter being used should be represented from two to four times, giving a total number of cards from about 50 to about 100 depending on how difficult you wish to make the game. The student is to find the cards that are exactly alike and put them together. This game may be played by two or more. The one who can match the most cards correctly wins. Time can be kept. If two students have a tie score, the one whose time was faster is the winner.

### 36. Big and Little Letters

Prepare sheets with short rows of lower-case and capital letters. Instruct the student to put a circle around—or draw a line through—the big letters—or the small letters.

One of the sheets might look something like this:

```
                AAaa     aaaA     AAAa     aaAA
   CCC    Ccc     ccC  CCcc    ccc      CCC      cCCC
       B  B  B  B     bbBBBB    b  b  b  b     BbBbb
       D  d  DDD     D  ddd      DDd      D  D  D  dd  d  d
       SSS  S  s  s  s  sSS     SS      s  s  s      SS  Ss  sS
```

### 37. Simple Word Matching

Prepare a worksheet with a word in a box at the top of the page. Instruct the student to circle that word wherever it appears on the page. Start with small pages with one stimulus word per page. Work up to more difficult formats gradually.

This is the same type of worksheet used in Activity 30. However, words are used instead of letters.

Don't forget to provide feedback for the learner.

### 38. More Word Matching

When the student can handle simple word matching tasks, with one stimulus per page, the complexity of the page format should gradually be increased. The difficulty of the discriminations to be made should also be increased. Be sure to include lots of work on commonly confused words (for example, was, saw; on, no; every, very, ever).

### 39. Matching Words Card Game

Prepare word cards containing words that have a generally similar appearance. These can be words with which many students tend to have configuration confusions. Or, for an easier version of the game, select words that are grossly different.

Each word appears on two cards. The student has to pair the matching cards correctly. If two students play, scores can be kept. Or one student can play against time, trying on each run through the deck to match the words correctly faster than the time before.

### 40. Airplane Game

Draw a spiral path on a large sheet of oaktag. Divide the path into sections and print a word on each section. If you cover the oaktag with clear contact paper before you write the words, then you can later use different word lists with the same basic game board. Make two sets of cards, each with the same words as are on the path. Give each student a pack of words and a paper airplane. You can trace the plane shown below to make the marker for each student.

The game begins with both airplanes at the far end of the path (runway). Each student has a pack of cards, well shuffled, placed face up. The first student looks at the word on the top card and compares it to the first step on the runway. If there is a visual match (i.e., if the words are the same), the student can move the plane one step. If there is not a match, the card goes on the bottom of the pile. Then the other student takes a turn. The first student to move his or her plane into the hangar is the winner.

If a student still needs to work on visual matching but is tired of moving a jumbo jet to a hangar, try the same game with horse to barn, car to garage, cat to mouse, or child to school.

The difficulty of the game can be varied by choosing different words for the path. The word list in the illustration provides a fairly easy game because the differences are quite gross. A much higher-level task can be provided by using a list in which there are many commonly confused words and words that look alike. For example, a list for a difficult game might include these words:

> big, pig, on, no, when, where, were, there, then, boy, bog, dog, well, will, was, saw

A word list for a given pair of students can be prepared according to their particular needs.

Note that this exercise in the visual matching of words can easily become a reading sight word game and word drill. All that is necessary is to have each player say each word aloud as the plane lands on it.

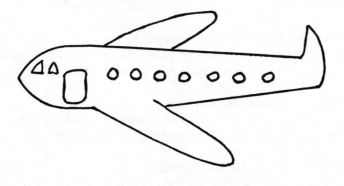

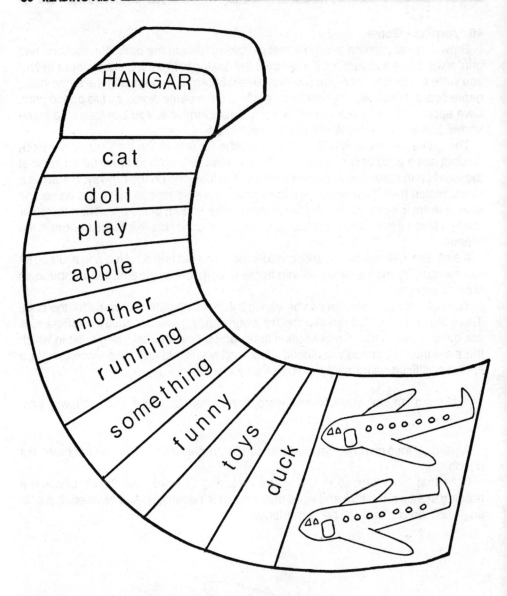

HANGAR

cat
doll
play
apple
mother
running
something
funny
toys
duck

### 41. Self-Teaching Book for Word Matching

The Self-Teaching Book works just as well for words as for letters. Follow the instructions for Activity 31 and substitute words for the stimuli and choices.

### 42. Simple Letter Cluster Matching

Follow the instructions for Simple Letter Matching, Activity 30. Use a letter cluster (blend or digraph) for the stimulus instead of a single letter.

### 43. Self-Teaching Book for Cluster Matching

Use the Self-Teaching Book format described for Activity 31 to work on letter combinations.

## 44. Simple Phrase and Sentence Matching

Prepare a worksheet with a phrase or a short sentence in a box at the top of the page. Instruct the student to circle the phrase or sentence wherever it appears on the page. Start with small pages and one stimulus per page. Gradually increase the level of difficulty.

## 45. Phrase-Matching Game

Give each student a card with a simple phrase printed on it. Write on the chalkboard a duplicate of each phrase handed out. Each student finds on the board the phrase that matches the one on his or her card and stands in front of the place where the phrase appears. The objective of this activity is behaviorally identical to the same task done on a worksheet (Activity 44), but this version permits the students to move about. It is a good rainy day game.

## 46. Finding Phrases in Sentences

At the left of a card or paper, two or three phrases of similar appearance are printed. On the same line with each phrase is a sentence using the phrase. The student is told to underline in the sentence the phrase that appears opposite it.

For example:

| | |
|---|---|
| white horse | Willie has a <u>white horse.</u> |
| white house | Willie had a <u>white house.</u> |
| white mouse | Willie saw a <u>white mouse.</u> |
| | |
| big pig | The big pig is in the yard. |
| big dog | The big dog is in the yard. |

## 47. Matching Phrases

A more difficult version of Activity 46 is one in which the given phrase is not in the same row as the sentence that contains that phrase. The student has to draw a line from each phrase to the sentence in which that phrase occurs.

For example:

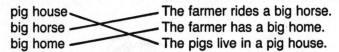

pig house         The farmer rides a big horse.
big horse         The farmer has a big home.
big home         The pigs live in a pig house.

## 48. Finding Word Elements

Give the student a quantity of printed materials such as magazines, newspapers, posters, leaflets, or old books. Have the student circle a specified word element (letter or letter cluster) wherever it is found in the printed material. For example, if the element being studied is *sh,* the student might find it in the words *shut, show, push, crushed,* or *shampoo.*

The difficulty level of this task depends not only on what the student is asked to find but also on the context in which he or she is asked to find it. For example, a very easy version of this activity might ask the student to locate a single letter in matter consisting solely of large-type newspaper headlines.

## ALPHABET KNOWLEDGE

Knowledge of letter names has generally been an excellent predictor of success in beginning reading. In the past, those children who came to school knowing the alphabet tended to be the higher achievers at the end of grade 1. Now, perhaps as a result of television programs such as "Sesame Street" and "The Electric Company," many more children seem to come to school knowing letter names. Although letter name knowledge is not a guarantee that a given child will learn to read, those children who don't know their letters should be helped to master them.

There are good reasons for teaching children the names of the letters. If a student knows the letter names, then you can refer to the letter by name in reading lessons or in giving directions. Most of the letter names contain one major sound of the letter. Naming the letters is, for many children, the first experience with grapheme-phoneme (symbol-sound) relationships.

Here are our objectives for alphabet knowledge.

**RR-14.** Given visually a letter in upper or lower case, the learner will say the name of the letter.

**RR-15.** After hearing a letter name, the learner will select from choices the letter named.

**RR-16.** After hearing a letter name, the learner will write that letter in upper- or lower-case form as directed.

**RR-17.** Given visually an upper-case letter, the learner will select its corresponding lower-case form from X choices.

**RR-18.** Given visually a lower-case letter, the learner will select its corresponding upper-case form from X choices.

### 49. Initials

When letter names are being learned, let each child use initials for a few days instead of his or her name. Each child should wear a little tag with the correct initials and must not answer to his or her name, only to the initials.

For example, if Willie says "Hi, Annie," she should ignore him. He should say instead, "Hi, A.M." Annie must then reply, "Hello, W.L."

## 50. Alphabet Song

One of the first experiences many children have with the letter names is the alphabet song—A, B, C, D, E, F, G, and so on—sung to an approximation of the melody of "Twinkle, Twinkle, Little Star."

Even if *you* can't *stand* it, let them sing it. Why deprive kids of the opportunity to begin getting the letter names with the right letters? Of course, someone has to be there to point to each letter as its name is sung.

## 51. Letters All Around Us

When teaching letter names, be sure to use letter names that are commonly found and heard in the learner's everyday environment. For example:

A & P
B & G, R.C. Cola
TWA
NBC, CBS, ABC
IRA, ESP
A.C., D.C.
U.S., U.S.A., U.S.S.R.
UN, NAACP
A.M., P.M.
Call letters of local radio and TV stations

## 52. Alphabet Objects

Here is a list of nouns to illustrate the alphabet. The "A is for apple" routine may be as old as the hills, but it still works.

**A** is for apple.

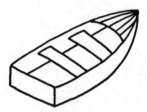

**B** is for boat.

**C** is for car.

**D** is for duck.

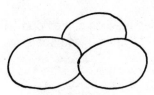

**E** is for eggs.

**F** is for fire.

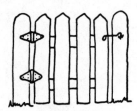

**G** is for gate.

**H** is for house.

**I** is for ice cream.

**J** is for jar.

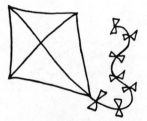

**K** is for kite.

**L** is for lion.

**M** is for man.

**N** is for nest.

**O** is for orange.

**P** is for pig.

**Q** is for queen.

**R** is for rat.

**S** is for sun.

**T** is for turtle.

**U** is for umbrella.

**V** is for valentine.

**W** is for witch.

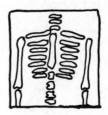

**X** is for X ray.

**Y** is for yarn.

**Z** is for zebra.

These are just suggestions. Of course, you can select any objects you wish. These were picked because they were relatively easy to draw. You may trace these illustrations if you wish.

## 53. Little Letter Stories

To help students differentiate letters frequently confused, try these little letter stories with or without pictures to illustrate.

This is b.
b is on the line.
b is tall like a building.
b looks to the right.

This is d.
d is on the line.
d looks to the left.

This is p.
p is down below the line.
p is long on the bottom.
p looks to the right.

This is m.
m is on the line.
m has two little hills.

This is n.
n is on the line.
n has one little hill.

This is s.
s is on the line.
s is like a snake.

This is t.
t is on the line.
t has a little hat.

This is w.
w is on the line.
w can hold water.

This is z.
z is on the line.
z goes zig zag.

### 54. Letter Names for a Day

To teach the students that each letter has a name, assign a letter name to each child. Let the child be that letter all day. He or she should wear a sign with the letter and be addressed as Mr. B or Ms. K as the case may be, rather than by his or her own name.

### 55. Letter-Name Practice

Worksheets with multiple-choice items for alphabet knowledge can be constructed for student use. The sheets can either be used under teacher direction, or the instructions can be put on cassette so the students can work quite independently. Here is part of an easy worksheet for alphabet knowledge.

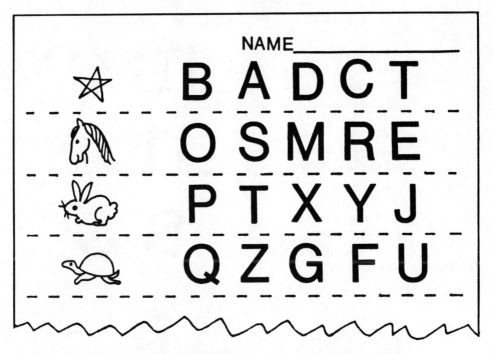

The script for the worksheet would be:

Find the row with the star. Circle the *D* in the row with the star.
Find the horse. Circle the *M* in the row with the horse.
Now find the rabbit. Circle the *P.*
Now look at the turtle. In that row circle the *F.*

You can make a number of different worksheets to go with the same cassette. This saves much recording time and gets the maximum value from one tape. The same cassette can also be used with worksheets containing lower-case letters or a combination of upper and lower case. The example above gave practice on easy discriminations among capital letters. Here is part of a worksheet, using the same audio, to give practice on more difficult discriminations among lower-case letters.

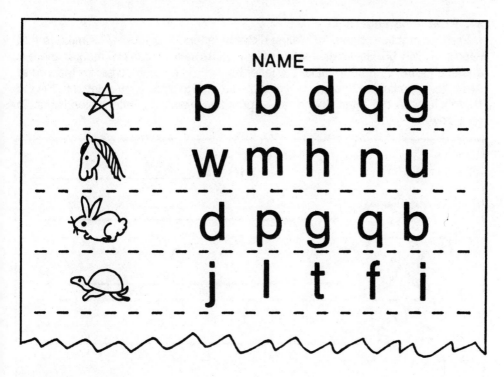

NAME_____

p  b  d  q  g

w  m  h  n  u

d  p  g  q  b

j  l  t  f  i

### 56. Erase a Letter

Draw an outline of a familiar character or animal on the chalkboard. It really doesn't matter what you choose, so pick something you can draw well. Print all the alphabet letters, randomly arranged, within the outline.

Send a student to the board to "Find an A," "Find a W," "Find an S," and so on. As quickly as possible, the student erases each letter as it is located. If a mistake is made, the student sits down. Replace the erased letters for the next player. The winner is the one with the largest number of correctly erased letters. If more than one child erases all the letters, the one who does this the fastest is the winner.

### 57. Producing Letters

Prepare practice sheets for writing dictated letters. The format is similar to that used in Activity 55. However, instead of four letters next to each row marker, there is a space for the student to make the letter himself. The audio script, for teacher or cassette, is similar too. Instead of telling the student to circle a given letter it tells the student to write that letter. Space can be provided to write the letter several times in each row.

NAME_____

The script for this worksheet would be:

Find the row with the star. Make a D on the line. Now make 3 more D's.
Find the horse. Make an M on the line. Make 3 more M's.
Now find the rabbit. Make a P on the line. Make 3 more P's.
Now look at the turtle. Make the letter F on the line. Make 3 more F's.

### 58. Lower- and Upper-Case Letters

To aid in identification and matching of corresponding upper- and lower-case letters, use illustrations of the same object in various sizes.

I am little b.　　　　　　　　I am big B.
I am little.　　　　　　　　　I am big.
My name is b.　　　　　　　　My name is capital B.
My sound begins　　　　　　　My sound begins

## 59. Matching Upper- and Lower-Case Letters

Be sure you have a chart somewhere in the room that displays each capital letter along with its lower-case form. If you wish, the chart can be illustrated with the "letter words" suggested in Activity 52.

## 60. More Upper- and Lower-Case Matching

Make a worksheet with columns of letters. The task for the student is to match the capital letter with its corresponding lower-case form in the other column, by drawing a connecting line.

Be sure to make the activity self-correcting. Use lapboards or acetate overlays.

## 61. Still More Upper- and Lower-Case Matching

Here is simply another format for doing the same thing as the previous activity.

NAME_____

| M | w | m | j | x | y |
| W | m | w | p | z | s |
| Q | q | o | p | r | z |
| a | X | W | C | B | A |

Don't forget the feedback to the learner.

## 62. Alphabet Pretzels

Here is a recipe for alphabet pretzels. It was developed and tested by Merrily Hansen's fifth grade class, P.S. 9, in Brooklyn, N.Y. You can use the pretzels as rewards for students learning letter names. If a student can name the letter, let him or her eat it. (This is immediate feedback at its best!)

> 1 cup 85° F water
> 1 cake active yeast or
>   1 pkg. dry yeast
> ¼ tsp. sugar
> 4½ cups all-purpose flour
> ¾ tsp. salt
> 2 tsp. sugar
> 1 egg yolk beaten
>   with about 1 tbs. water
> coarse (kosher) salt

Combine water, yeast, and sugar. Let stand until yeast is dissolved. Combine flour, salt, and sugar. Add mixture to yeast mixture to form a stiff dough. Knead the dough on a floured counter for 8 to 10 minutes. To knead, fold the side of the dough farthest from you toward you. Then push the fold into the rest of the dough with the heel of your hand. Turn the dough and repeat the motion. You will know that the dough has been properly kneaded when it is no longer sticky but smooth and elastic.

Oil a large bowl and put in the dough. Turn the dough so the surface becomes slightly oiled and will not dry out. Cover the dough with a clean damp towel and let it rise in a warm place until it is double in size.

Punch down the dough with your fist. Grease a cookie sheet and shape the dough into letters and place on the greased pans.

Use a pastry brush to paint each pretzel with the egg yolk mixture; then sprinkle the pretzels with salt.

Preheat the oven to 475°F. Let the pretzels rise again in a warm place until they are almost double in size. Bake for about 10 minutes or until they are golden brown and firm.

## 63. Accordion Alphabet Book

To make a sturdy accordion-type alphabet book, cut oaktag into long strips about six inches high. Fold each strip accordion style into even sections about three inches wide each. Tape strips together until there are 27 sections—one for each letter of the alphabet and one for the cover.

Each page of the book has a letter of the alphabet and an appropriate picture to illustrate it. These pictures can be created by the student or cut from a magazine.

The accordion-style booklet format can be used as an alternative to a traditionally assembled volume for a variety of purposes.

# CONCEPTUAL VOCABULARY FOR READING

If one accepts "getting meaning from the printed page" as a definition of reading, then it is clear that the child who is taught to decode the squiggles on a page and pronounce the word must link that word in some way with previous experience. Saying the word is not enough. The learner must know what it means. For this reason, vocabulary development aimed at ensuring understanding of words the child will meet in beginning reading experiences is an ingredient of a good reading readiness program. Note that the stress should be on those words that the child will meet in books. General vocabulary enrichment has much to recommend it. However, it may not directly pay off in beginning reading skill achievement. The reading readiness program therefore should concentrate on giving children essential concepts and labels needed to make their beginning reading experiences meaningful. Once children have begun to read, they have at their fingertips one of the most powerful vocabulary builders possible—lots of reading in a variety of books.

Vocabulary development as part of the reading readiness program should concentrate primarily on the following overall objective:

**RR-19.** Given a spoken word, the learner will match that word with its appropriate meaning.

Remember to concentrate on the words and concepts necessary to prepare children for what they will be asked to read.

## 64. Building Vocabulary

The students form a circle. Each student is asked a question designed to focus on a word meaning. If a child cannot answer the question, he or she leaves the circle and moves to the outside to begin forming another circle. The winner is the student left in the middle of the circle made by everybody who has missed a question. Before terminating the game and moving on to another activity, each student can be given another chance to answer the question previously missed.

Here are sample questions suitable for this game:

What is a baby cow called? (calf)
When you drop a rubber ball, what does it do? (bounce)
If you heat water long enough, it will (boil)
What do you do to water to make ice? (freeze it)
What do you have when you put food between two slices of bread?
(a sandwich)

## 65. Props for Playing

An effective way to teach useful sight vocabulary to young children is to use readily identifiable items as props for play. For example, a housekeeping corner in the classroom could include empty containers such as cereal boxes, cans (with top safely removed) and similar items. Encourage the children to refer to the items by name. The child who serves the doll *corn flakes* from the appropriate box will soon come to recognize the words *corn flakes*.

### 66. Concepts for Word Perception

The child who begins to read must discriminate between words that look some-what alike. In guiding the child to make these discriminations, the teacher will probably use words such as *same, different; smaller, larger; big, bigger,* and *biggest; up* and *down; tall* and *short; high* and *low; right* and *left; over* and *under.*

These concepts and their labels can be developed in a variety of games. For example, to develop the notion of up and down, right and left, the children can play the game "Simon Says," using directions such as Simon Says, "Thumbs up," "Thumbs down," "Right hand on head," "Left hand down," "Stamp right foot," and so on.

Pictures can also be used to develop these concepts. (See Activity 71.)

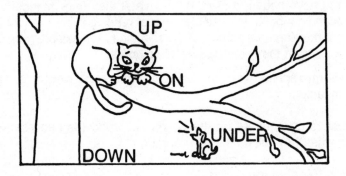

### 67. Pictures for Basic Concepts

The teacher can present for discussion pictures of items that the child will meet in the books used for beginning reading instruction. This will help clarify new concepts and make sure that the child uses the correct labels for the concepts he or she already has. For example, if the word "pony" is going to be taught, the child should be able to call the appropriate animal a pony, not a horse or something else. In many cases, the child has quite a clear concept of the thing in question. It is often the correct label that is missing.

### 68. Classification of Pictures

Collect pictures of various vehicles, foods, household articles, clothes, animals, etc. Mount each picture on oaktag for durability. The student can classify the pictures according to use, size, or some other specified characteristic.

The family-type magazines available at the supermarket checkout counter are an excellent source of pictures for this activity. A number of these games can be made at different levels and stored, each in its own envelope or box, for individual student use.

For example, an easy level of this activity might contain 20 to 30 pictures of pets and household articles. The student would separate the cards into "animals" and "things." On the back of each card write its category and color code it so that the student can easily check his or her own work.

A more difficult level of this activity might present 30 different foods that the student could classify into hot and cold, or main course and dessert.

This is the type of game that can successfully be student-constructed. On a rainy day, turn your students loose with magazines and scissors.

## 69. Analogies and Opposites

Ask the students to listen to and complete items such as these:

Pickles are sour; candy is _____.
An airplane is fast; a bike is _____.
The sky is above; the ground is _____.

This type of procedure can be used to elicit relationships. For example:

A dog runs on its legs; a car runs on its _____.
Rabbits have fur; birds have _____.
The sun rises in the east; it sets in the _____.
The sun sets in the evening; it rises in the _____.

This exercise can be done at many different levels of difficulty, depending on the needs of individual students. Picture cards can be prepared and used as aids in explaining a number of analogies at basic levels.

## 70. Descriptive Word Game—Objects

Hold up a familiar object in order to elicit descriptive words such as *round, heavy, shiny, rough,* etc. Show the object and ask: "What is this?" "What shape is it?" "Touch it. How does it feel?"

## 71. Descriptive Word Game—Pictures

To illustrate abstract words such as *above, under, on, off,* pictures can be used. For example, after showing the following picture, the teacher would ask, "What do you see?" "Where is the cat?" (on the table) "Where is the mouse?" (under the table) Suitable pictures can be found in magazines, or perhaps you can draw them.

## 72. Shoe Box Concept Game

Before playing this game, each student must have a shoe box that opens at one end. To prepare the shoe box, cut two of the corners (A) with scissors or a mat knife so that one end of the box can be folded out flat. When the box is in use, the cover should be on and the end flap folded down to leave a doorlike opening (B). To store the box, remove the top, fold the flap to its original closed position, replace the top, and secure it with a large rubber band (C).

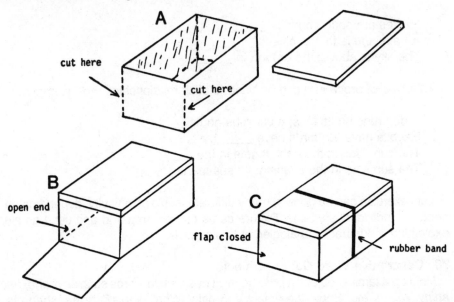

Each student should collect a variety of objects with different characteristics for his or her shoe box. The objects should be lots of different sizes, shapes, and textures. Some of the things that go well are bottle caps, small fabric samples, paper clips, erasers, rough and smooth pebbles, sandpaper scraps, a small rubber ball, tiny toys, etc.

To play the game each student opens the end of the shoe box as in (B) above. Without looking into the box, the student reaches in and pulls out an object or objects in response to directions such as:

- Find something soft.
- Bring out one big thing and one little thing.
- Get an object that is rough.
- Bring out five things.

The responses should be discussed, and students can be encouraged to challenge another's example of the concept asked for. Although this is an engaging enough activity without organized competition, the game can be played competitively if you wish. Award five points to the first student who supplies a correct object; three points to the second student; and one point to each other student who responds correctly within ten seconds.

## 73. Interpreting Pictures

Show a picture to a group and have the children discuss it. Questions about the picture's main idea and specific details can be asked. Picture interpretation can be a useful activity to start children making inferences from context and to teach the difference between the main idea and specific details. However, discussion of pictures is given far more importance in some basal programs than it deserves. Don't let this activity assume more time than it's worth.

# INTEREST IN BOOKS, STORY SENSE AND SEQUENCE, ATTENTION TO THE READING TASK

The classroom environment should be a constant source of interest in books. Children need to have lots of colorful (and high-quality) children's books around, and a teacher who is enthusiastic about literature.

"Story sense" and understanding of story sequence can be developed while introducing the learner to children's literature. Attention to the reading task and left-to-right sequence can also be developed using real books, as well as games and exercises.

One important thing to keep in mind while developing interest in books and maintaining attention to the reading task is that giving children things worth being interested in and worthy of their attention will go a long way toward ensuring success.

Here are some learner behaviors that are worth developing. For the pre-reading child, the first "reading" experiences will be listening to stories. As the child learns to read, substitute reading for listening in these objectives.

**RR-20.** Given an environment containing a number of suitable children's trade books, the learner will choose to listen to a story in preference to other activities.

**RR-21.** Given a number of children's books, the learner will select the one he or she wants to hear.

**RR-22.** After selecting a book and hearing it read, the learner will be able to find that same book again for rereading.

**RR-23.** After listening to a story, the learner will retell the story, recalling the important details in sequence.

**RR-24.** After listening to a story, the learner will draw an appropriate illustration.

**RR-25.** Given a picture, the learner will create a story about it.

**RR-26.** Given a series of pictures, the learner will arrange them in order to tell a story that makes sense.

**RR-27.** Given a reading skill task on a page, the learner will approach it from left to right.

**RR-28.** Given a book, the learner will follow the story as it is read aloud.

### 74. Following a Story

One of the best ways to develop attention to the reading task is to have a child following along in the book while a story is being read aloud. For this activity, short picture books are best. Well before being able to follow the exact words of the text, a child can be taught to hold the book and turn the pages at a given signal. Soon most children will be doing more than following the pictures. They will begin picking out words, and eventually they will follow along exactly.

You can select and record stories on your own. Use a little bell to signal the page turn. Or, if funds are available, you can avail yourself of the many excellent commercially prepared cassettes. The advantage of these is high quality of production and things such as sound effects and background music, which you might find difficult to supply. One advantage of doing your own is that you can pick out whatever stories you wish; another is that some students enjoy the familiarity of the teacher's voice on the tape.

### 75. Choosing a Story

Right from the beginning, young children should be permitted to select the story they want to hear.

A number of read-along books with their cassettes should be on display each day. Each student should be encouraged to select the story he or she wants and to listen to it. Ideally, each beginning reading classroom should have a minimum of six cassette playback units so that several children can listen to their favorites at the same time.

Selecting a book with its cassette is one of the first experiences the young learner should have with locating instructional material, using it, and putting it back.

### 76. Books on Cassette

For very young children, it's best if possible to have only one book recorded on a cassette. Finding the book and its matching cassette is a sufficiently difficult task by itself. For a pre-reading child, finding the place where one book ends and another begins on the tape (or perhaps even finding the right side of the cassette) is a bit difficult at first.

Identify the cassette and its book clearly. Don't expect the student to match the book title with the tiny type on the label of the cassette. A color symbol code would be helpful.

### 77. Storing Books and Cassettes

A heavy-duty business-size envelope can be cut in half and pasted to the book cover to hold the cassette for that book. Use strong masking tape to reinforce it.

### 78. Another Way to Store Books and Cassettes

Take a large manila envelope, big enough to hold both the book and its cassette. Cut a window in one side of the envelope, large enough to display the book cover. Cover the window with an acetate sheet. Store both the book and the cassette in the envelope. As an alternative to the acetate window, if the book has a paper jacket, you can paste the jacket to the outside of the envelope. Cover it with clear contact paper to preserve it.

Book covers were designed to entice the reader. Be sure to display each book in a way that makes the child want to go to it.

### 79. Retelling a Story

After listening to a story, a child should be encouraged to retell it and keep the details in their correct sequence.

Many children like to record their own versions of a story on an audio cassette, which can then be played back and compared to the original.

### 80. Story Sequence Pictures

Divide a large piece of drawing paper into four sections. Number the sections from 1 to 4.

After listening to a story, the task for the student is to draw four events from the story in correct sequence. (Four is not a magic number. Some children may need to begin with two. Others may be able to handle five, or six, or more.)

### 81. Check for Story Comprehension

After a child has listened to a story, you can check his or her comprehension with a multiple-choice picture exercise. Here are some sample questions for the popular children's book *Peter Rabbit,* by Beatrix Potter.

Where did Peter go after his mother told him not to?
Where did Peter hide from Mr. MacGregor?
What did Peter's mother give him when he got home?
What did Peter's sisters get?

These questions are read to the child, or they can be put on cassette. The responses are made on the following type of worksheet:

### 82. Picking the Main Idea Picture

After listening to a story, the student can be asked to select from choices a picture expressing the main idea of the story. This is a preliminary activity to having the student draw his or her own main idea picture.

### 83. Drawing the Main Idea

After listening to a story, the student can be asked to draw a picture illustrating the main idea of the story.

### 84. Storytelling—Picture Stories

For this activity the teacher holds up a picture and the students make up a story about it. Picture postcards, illustrations from magazines, and travel posters are good sources of material.

A variation of this activity uses a book jacket from a children's picture book as the stimulus. After the children have made up their own story, they can listen to the original and compare.

### 85. What Next?

The teacher needs three or four lines of a story unknown to the students, who then supply endings. The story may be original or one that will be read at a future time. For example, the teacher reads, "Peter was a very sleepy little rabbit. He usually fell asleep while the other little rabbits were working or having fun. One day Peter fell asleep under a large cabbage plant. Suddenly he woke up with a start. Close by stood . . .." An alternative to having the child tell what he or she thinks happens next is to have him or her draw a picture predicting the outcome of the story.

### 86. Round Robin Storytelling

The students sit in a circle. Either the teacher or a student begins the story with an opening sentence. For example, "Once there was a greedy little dog." Students are called on in turn or in random order. Each supplies a suitable next sentence until the story is completed.

### 87. Sequence-Watching Game

The teacher or a student performs a short series of acts such as tapping on the desk, lifting a book, and then picking up a piece of chalk. A student then tells what was done and in what order *or* is called upon to repeat exactly the demonstrated sequence.

### 88. Pictures in Sequence

Rule a sheet of oaktag into four or six boxes. A 9″ × 12″ sheet is large enough and it readily divides into the desired number of boxes. Each box contains a picture. The pictures, in sequence, tell a story. Now prepare another sheet identical to the first. Leave one intact (A). Cut the other one into parts (B). The student assembles the individual pictures to tell the story on the larger sheet.

This activity, in which the student simply matches story cards with a given sequence, sets the stage for more difficult tasks involving story sequence. Later on, the student will assemble cards in sequence without the completed story available as a model.

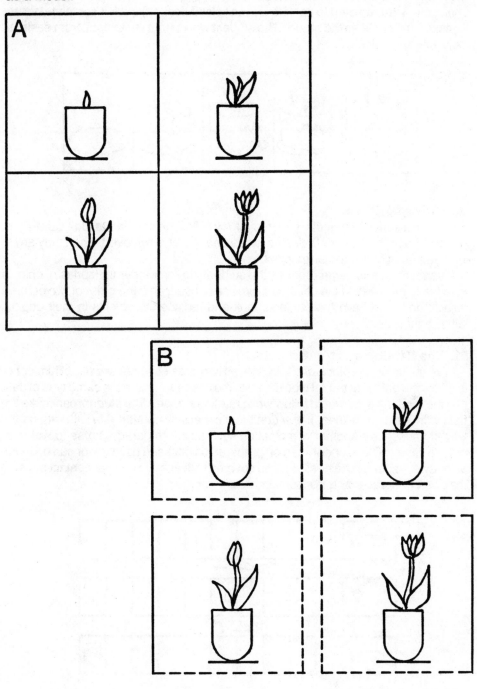

### 89. Completing Pictures

Figures, objects, designs, letters, or words are drawn at the left on a sheet of paper. Each of these completed drawings is followed by a double line. Alongside this line is a series of the same objects, each one slightly less complete from left to right. The student is instructed to complete (and color if desired) each incomplete picture to make it the same as the model. The student works from left to right, from easier to more difficult tasks.

### 90. Guessing Game

Line up a series of objects, pictures, or toys. Tell the children to look carefully at the row. Have them cover their eyes while one object is removed. Then they are to look and identify the missing object.

A variation of this game requires the students to remember the series of objects from left to right. While the children's eyes are closed, shift the order of two or three objects and then have the students look and replace the objects in their original left-to-right order.

### 91. The Rat Game

Give the student a piece of paper divided into lines of boxes and direct him or her to follow the path that the rat would take to the cheese. (This is the same type of path that the reader's eyes would follow while reading a page.) The student can make the path with X's or with lines. If you don't feel especially comfortable with rats on the way to cheese, try another combination such as car to garage, horse to water, or child to candy. These sheets can be prepared on ditto and used up, or can be made on heavier paper such as oaktag, and covered with acetate or clear contact paper to make them durable and nonconsumable.

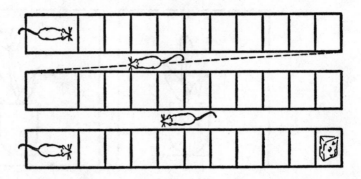

## 92. Dot and Circle Game

Give the student a sheet of paper that has a green (for GO) margin at the left and clusters of circles, triangles, or other shapes drawn in rows to the right of this margin. Direct the student always to start at the green margin and to put a dot in each circle (or triangle, or whatever).

An even more effective version of this worksheet uses letters instead of shapes. For example, the student can be instructed to begin at the green margin and to put dots over short vertical lines (dotting their *i*'s) or to put crossmarks through vertical lines (crossing their *t*'s). Like the Rat Game, this activity can be prepared on consumable ditto paper or on permanent contact-covered sheets.

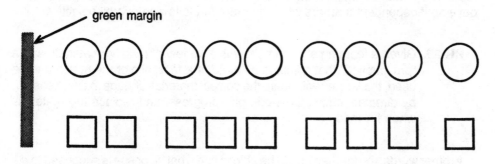

## 93. Line Game

The Line Game is a variation of the previously described Dot and Circle Game. Sheets of paper (or permanent contact-covered cards) are arranged with a green margin at the left and with rows of vertical lines in groups of varying number. Instruct the student to begin at the green margin at the left and to draw a horizontal line through the center of each cluster of lines, making sure that the lines do not extend beyond the outside vertical lines of each cluster.

To heighten interest, games of this kind can be timed.

## 94. Sequence of Letters

Hold up a card containing letters or words covered with a marker or a sheet. Move the marker slowly to the right, so that letters are exposed in proper sequence. The task for the student is to say the letter names (or the words) as they are revealed. This may help get the student used to reading from left to right.

## FOLLOWING DIRECTIONS

Throughout the grades, the ability to follow oral and written directions seems to be directly related to success in reading achievement. With emphasis on individualized learning environments in which the tasks are learner-directed and learner-corrected, the importance of following directions accurately becomes even more critical. As part of their reading readiness program, children at the pre-reading stage should be prepared to engage in the task behavior required in beginning reading instruction.

Children are not born knowing how to follow the directions for learning how to read. They must be taught. The goal of instruction in classroom procedures is to develop independent learners who can meet the following overall objective:

> **RR-29.** Given a learning environment with a variety of reading materials and a "prescription" that contains a key to or a facsimile of the material to be used, the learner will locate the correct material, engage in task behavior as directed, check the work, plot progress, and replace the materials when finished.

In other words, the learner should be able to find what he or she is supposed to do, do it, and put everything back when the job is done—hopefully with a minimum of teacher intervention. The mechanics of working on skills material should be simple enough for the child that these procedures do not become an impediment to learning.

Here are some specific objectives for following directions:

> **RR-30.** Given spoken directions and a page with a picture (letter, shape, word, or numeral), the learner will mark the picture as directed. (For example, circle it, make an X, draw a line through it, underline it.)
>
> **RR-31.** Given spoken directions and a page with more than one picture (letter, shape, word, or numeral), the learner will mark the specified picture (top, bottom, middle, left, right, big, little) as directed.
>
> **RR-32.** Given a page with pairs of matching pictures (letters, shapes, words, or numerals), the learner will draw a line from each one to its exact match.
>
> **RR-33.** Given a page containing items in rows, each identified by a familiar picture, the learner will locate each row and mark it according to spoken directions.
>
> **RR-34.** Given a page containing items in rows, each identified by a numeral, the learner will locate each row and mark it according to spoken directions.
>
> **RR-35.** Given a color, the student will select its match from choices.
>
> **RR-36.** Given a page, the student will write (print) his or her name on the page as directed.
>
> **RR-37.** Given a page with items to be marked in a specified way, and one or more items completed as a model, the student will finish the page as directed.

**RR-38.** Given an appropriate level task with built-in feedback, the learner will do the task, consult the feedback, and know whether he or she was right or wrong.

A child who is able to follow these directions is well on the way to being able to function independently in a learning environment.

Note that in the formats we suggest for practice materials in following directions, the lowest levels of these activities use pictures instead of letters and words as stimuli. This is the one major exception to the rule that reading readiness activities should deal directly with reading-related tasks that involve letters and words. Familiar pictures are used in introducing the child to the basic directions so that focus can be on the procedures to be followed, rather than on the nature of the stimulus. As soon as the learner can follow the directions with pictures, similar tasks should be presented with letters and words.

## 95. Circling an Item

When your students are directed to circle something, do they know what to do? They will know how to circle an item if they complete the following programmed booklet on making a circle.

Begin with a little booklet containing ten pages, each with one picture on it. Use a picture of a familiar object or animal. Sample pages are shown below. At the right of each page is the script (what the teacher is to say). This can be an entirely teacher-directed lesson, with the teacher giving the feedback for each response, or the booklet can be prepared with acetate interleaves (see Activity 31) so that feedback is available from the material as well.

Page 1. Look at the picture. What is it? (horse) Put your finger on the horse. Turn the page.

Page 2. Here is a circle around the horse. Now you trace the circle.

Page 3. Here there is almost a whole circle around the horse. Now you finish the circle.

Page 4. Finish the circle.

Page 5. Finish the circle.

Page 6. This picture has no circle around it. You make a circle around it.

Page 7. Now circle this picture.

Page 8. Here is a different picture. Circle it.

Page 9. Now circle this picture.

Page 10. Now circle this picture. That's good. Now you know how to make a circle around a picture.

### 96.  Circling a Letter or Word

You can make a follow-up exercise to the one above by having the student circle a sequence of letters or words.

### 97.  Circling a Numeral

One way to sneak in a little practice on the names for the numerals is to use numerals in one of these little booklets. If there is only one numeral to a page, and you refer to it by name, you will be helping the student to identify it.

### 98.  Making an X on an Item

The exact sequence of programmed steps in Activity 95 can be used to teach the student to make an X on an item. Begin with a page with a familiar picture. Demonstrate the desired response. Then lead the child from tracing the X to finishing the incomplete X's, to making the X independently. Use the same script as for making a circle, but say *Make an X on* instead of *Make a circle around.*

### 99.  Making a Line through an Item

The same steps can be used to teach the student to make a line *through* an item. Keep stressing that the line is to go right through the picture.

### 100.  Making a Line under a Picture

After a child can make a line through a picture, use the same steps to teach underlining. Keep stressing that the line is to go *under* the picture. This is a hard notion to get right. Feedback after each response is essential.

### 101.  Getting It All Together

After your students have been taught to make all of the above responses (Activities 95 to 100), prepare a little booklet containing examples of each to see if mastery really has occurred. Follow the format for the Self-Teaching Book for Letter Matching described for Activity 31. Give the child practice in switching from one response to another. Then give a test to see if all the different directions have been learned. If more practice is still needed, send a child back to the self-teaching booklets for another go at it. Here is a sample test:

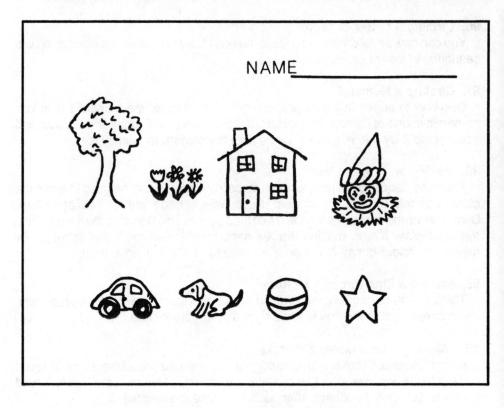

NAME_____

Make an X *on* the tree.
Put a line *under* the flowers.
Put a line *through* the house.
Circle the car.
Make a line *under* the dog.

Draw a line *through* the ball.
Make an X *on* the clown.
Circle the star. Now put a line *under* it.
Circle the picture of the tree.

Actually, you should try giving this test to the students *before* putting them through the series of self-teaching booklets. For those students who already can make the responses as directed, don't waste their time and yours on more exercises.

## 102. Top and Bottom of Page

To teach the student where the top of the page is and where the bottom is, design a series of pages each with two pictures, one at the top and one at the bottom. Through a series of directions to be followed, the student will learn to begin work at the top of the page.

Here are sample pages for a booklet. Once again, you can make the tasks entirely teacher-directed, or you can add feedback from the materials as well.

Each booklet should have about ten pages following this format. Stress the words *top* and *bottom*. Have the child point to the top or the bottom of the page each time. Always direct the student to the top of the page first.

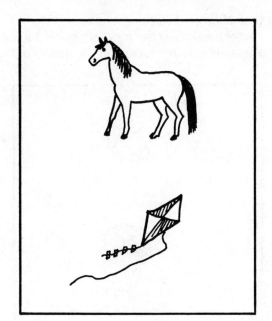

Make an X on the horse at the *top* of the page. Now circle the kite at the *bottom* of the page. Where is the horse? (top) Where is the kite? (bottom)

Draw a line through the tree at the *top* of the page. Put an X on the face at the *bottom* of the page. Where is the tree? (top) Where is the face? (bottom)

You should follow this exercise, as well as those for middle of page, and left and right, with a similar exercise in which you give the directions in terms of "the picture," instead of naming the items specifically. In other words, instead of saying, "Circle the horse at the top of the page," say "Circle the picture at the top of the page."

### 103. Middle of Page

After the student can find the top and the bottom of the page, prepare another set of exercises with a picture in the middle of the page as well.

Circle the dog at the top of the page.

Now make an X on the cat in the middle of the page.

Draw a line under the tree at the bottom of the page.

### 104. Same and Different

To understand the directions for tasks involving matching, the student must know the labels "same" and "different." To teach these labels, try a series of simple animal pictures such as two cats and a dog. Have the child point to "the one that is different."

Most children have a good notion of the *concepts* of "same" and "different," at least at a gut level. If you don't believe that, try offering a child two stones and an ice cream cone and see which one he or she wants. The child knows which one is different. What a number of young children lack, however, is the correct *labels* for the concepts "same" and "different." They need experience in following directions requiring them to pick out the ones that are the same or the ones that are different.

### 105. Matching Pictures

When you are sure that students can follow the direction to mark "the ones that are the same," provide practice in matching pictures in columns. In this exercise the students should draw a line from the picture to the one that is the same. Provide a model for the first one.

If the student gets immediate feedback after these responses, mastery of this type of task should happen very quickly. Don't belabor these exercises. Remember, what you want the student to learn is how to draw a line between the things that are the same. This won't take very long.

## 106. Matching Letters or Numerals

As soon as the child can draw a line from a picture in one column to the one in the other column that is the same, use letters or numerals as stimuli.

These exercises are more directly related to the directions he or she will have to follow in later tasks.

## 107. Pages with Rows of Items

After students can make the desired respones (circle, X, etc.) on activities having a single stimulus, it is necessary to teach them to deal with activities with more items. Many exercises and reading readiness tests identify rows of items with familiar pictures. (Activity 55 is an example of this.) Students must be taught to follow the directions for each row, beginning with the row at the top. Here is a very simple worksheet to develop this ability. Use it as a model.

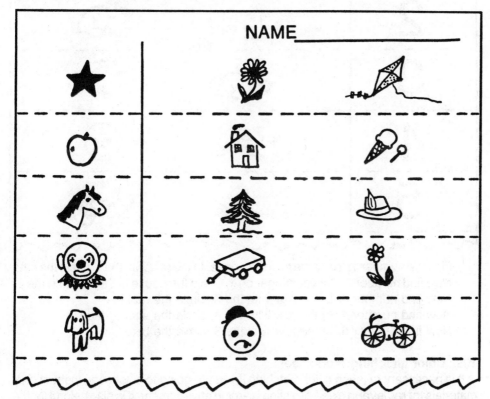

NAME_____

Find the star. Put your finger on the row with the star and then circle the kite.
Find the apple. In the row with the apple, circle the house.
Find the horse. In the row with the horse, circle the tree.
Find the clown. In the row with the clown, circle the flower.
Find the dog. In the row with the dog, circle the bike.

For the first experience with this activity, some children may find a marker helpful. Be sure to watch carefully as the student does each step. Feedback is essential for each step when the task is new and strange.

### 108. Pages with Numbered Rows of Items

After students can locate a row identified by a familiar picture, they should be taught to perform the same behavior when the row is identified by a numeral. This requires them to know the names for the numerals, which really isn't very difficult. Give lots of practice and feedback. Always make sure that a student starts at the top of the page and works down.

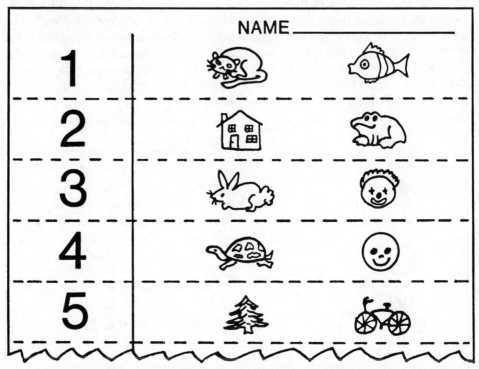

Find the number 1. It is at the top of the page. In the row with the 1, circle the cat.
Now find number 2. Put your finger on it. Circle the house in the row with the 2.
Now find number 3. In the row with the 3, circle the rabbit.
Now find number 4. In the row with the 4, circle the smiling face.
Now find number 5. In the row with the 5, circle the bike.

### 109. Color Matching Worksheet

It is necessary to teach color matching if you are going to color code instructional materials for retrieval in a self-directing learning environment. It is also helpful for the students to know the names for the colors. These exercises, however, deal with the matching of colors whether or not the student can name each match.

Make a worksheet with two columns of shapes. Color the shapes in one column. Color the other column in mixed-up order. The task for the student is to draw a line from one color to its match in the other column. If you don't have a Xerox machine that reproduces colors, you will have to color each of these sheets by hand. Unless coloring little shapes is really a pleasure for you, we suggest making the sheets nonconsumable.

## 110. Color Symbol Matching

Give the student a worksheet with rows of shapes. The shapes should be in various colors. In this exercise, the task involves responding to two cues: the color and the shape. The student should draw a line from each one to its exact match. Don't expect a child to do this more difficult task until he or she has mastered the simple color matching.

## 111. Color Matching with Crayons

Give the student a worksheet with rows of shapes. One in each row is already in color. The student should have one crayon for each color on the worksheet. The task is to color the other shape in the row the same color as its mate.

## 112. Writing the Name

Right from the very beginning of the school experience, a child should be encouraged and required to identify his or her own work by name. Provide practice in writing the name on a page. Each worksheet used should have a special line or box for the student's name to remind the child to put it there. If very young students are taught to begin every worksheet with a name, perhaps the upper grade teachers will receive fewer anonymous papers.

For a child who is having trouble writing his or her name, a private worksheet prepared just for that child will help. Begin with the name written in dotted lines for the child to trace. Gradually provide fewer and fewer clues until the child is writing the name completely independently.

## 113. Marking According to a Model

Most of the previous activities rely on spoken directions for explaining the task to the student. This is essential to get the learners off to a good start. The next step is to provide the student with one or two items on the page marked as you wish them marked, and then have the students complete the page according to the model items. In other words, if you circle the correct response in item one, the student should not mark the rest of the page with X's. Any of the exercises suggested in the previous pages can be used for teaching this behavior. Simply do the first item or two the way you want it done. Remember that feedback for each response is necessary.

## 114. Feedback from Materials, Answer Key

When the teacher is there to tell the student if an answer is right or wrong, there is usually little doubt in the student's mind about how he or she did on a given item. However, in an individualized learning environment, the student will often be asked to check his or her own work. For very young children, the Self-Teaching Book format (Activity 31) or an acetate overlay for each worksheet should be used. If a child can use a completely separate answer key format, you shouldn't be wasting time with these low-level matching exercises. Show the child how the correct answer on the acetate lines up with his or her own response. You can demonstrate this with a worksheet containing one or two incorrectly done items that the child should check using an overlay.

## LANGUAGE ARTS AND LEARNING READINESS

The following are language arts and learning readiness activities. Although they are not directly related to reading instruction, and behavioral objectives are not presented for them here, these activities may be useful for other classroom purposes. Use them wisely!

### 115. Dramatization

Read a story to the children. Encourage them to dramatize it, giving simple lines to the parts. Or have them supply lines to a familiar story. For example, they can be the wolf in "Red Riding Hood," the gingerbread man in "The Gingerbread Man," or one of the bears in "The Three Bears."

### 116. Show and Tell

Encourage the students to bring to class objects such as toys, souvenirs, collections, unusual pieces of junk, or other prized possessions, which need not be expensive—just interesting. The student shows what he or she has brought to the class and tells the class about it.

This language arts activity has, in many cases, been both overworked and misdirected. Used judiciously, however, it can help the students develop ability in oral expression and speaking before a group. Keep remembering that the goal of the activity is oral expression. Encourage the quality of what the child has to say, for that is the purpose of the activity. Avoid the temptation to reward a youngster for the extravagance of the props. It is what there is to tell, not what there is to show, that is of primary importance. Show and Tell should never be permitted to deteriorate into bring and brag.

### 117. Picture Puzzles

Take two duplicate pictures. Mount each one on oaktag and laminate them if possible for durability. (If you can't laminate, just accept that this particular product will be short-lived.) Cut one of each pair of pictures into pieces. Mount the other one on the outside of a manila envelope. Store the pieces inside the corresponding envelope.

The student has to take the pieces from the envelopes and reconstruct the picture on the outside. These puzzles can be very easy (two or three simple pieces) or very difficult (many complex pieces.).

Some students will be able to make their own puzzles.

### 118. Similarities

Have a large oaktag chart with symbols on it. Give the student duplicates of the symbols or shapes and have them match these to the shapes on the chart.

If the symbols and shapes used happen to be letters and words, then this becomes a real *reading* readiness activity.

## 119. Seeing and Drawing (Visual Memory)

Draw on the chalkboard a large symbol that will be easy to reproduce. Let the students look at it for ten seconds. Then cover it or erase it and have the students reproduce it on paper as accurately as possible.

This becomes an activity relevant to reading if the symbols and shapes used are letters and words.

## 120. Finding Missing Parts

Use pictures from old readers, textbooks, magazines, or newspapers. Cut each picture and mount it on oaktag for durability. Cut off a part of each picture. The student have to find the missing parts. For example, cut the fender off a car, the wing off a jet, the tail from a horse or dog.

## 121. Sounds Round About

Have the students close their eyes and be as quiet as possible. Ask them to listen for and remember all the sounds they can hear inside the room. After 30 seconds or so, the students should tell what they heard. For example, they might report a foot shuffling, a jet passing overhead, someone coughing, a child on the playground.

This activity will do approximately nothing for a child's reading. However, it is a good activity to quiet things down on a rainy day. It can contribute to classroom management, but it should be used sparingly when needed.

## 122. Tapping Game

Have the students listen while you tap loudly on the chalkboard, faintly on the desk, then very loudly on the chair. Have a student repeat the tapping exactly.

A variation of this activity is to have the students listen and count the taps. They must then tell you how many taps they heard.

This is another good rainy day activity that has nothing to do with reading.

## 123. Original Word-by-Word Stories

The students sit in a circle. The teacher or one of the students begins by giving a word that could start a sentence. The next student adds another word to the first and says them both. For example, if the first person said "Oscar," the second might say "Oscar went," the third might say "Oscar went into," and so on until the sentence is complete. When the students become adept at constructing meaningful sentences in this way, entire little stories can be attempted.

## 124. Finding Similar Shapes, Colors

Cut folded pieces of construction paper into various shapes and sizes. Fold the paper into quarters before cutting. This will give you four of each thing you cut. Four thicknesses still can be cut easily. Use various colors of paper and make squares, circles, rectangles, stars, crescents, etc. Give the student a set of these shapes and ask him or her to classify them according to shape. The same shapes can be classified according to size or color as well.

### 125. Symbolo

This game is similar to dominoes. Use colored symbols instead of dots. The children are to match the symbols. Some suggestions for symbols to use are blue star, red circle, purple hexagon, yellow square, green triangle, orange crescent, and brown X. The simplest version of the game would have all the dominoes made with just one symbol on each half. Make the dominoes out of oaktag. Use markers or crayons to make the symbols. A more complex version of the game can combine as many as six symbols on each side of the domino.

The symbols below can be traced and used as models for the dominoes you make.

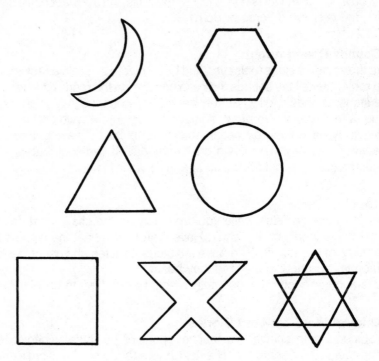

# Basic
# Reading
# Skills

This section of *Reading Aids Through the Grades* is devoted to those basic reading skills that readers need in their efforts to learn to get meaning from squiggles printed on a page. Some reading people call this stage "learning to read," as distinguished from "reading to learn."

The activities in this section are divided into five categories:

Basic Sight Words
Grapheme-Phoneme Relationships (Phonics)
Word Structure
Easy Things to Read (From Phrases to Stories)
Remediation of Specific Difficulties

Although this section is labeled Basic Reading Skills, we do not intend to imply that it is only for young children. Many of the activities described in these pages are quite necessary and effective for older learners who are experiencing difficulties in learning to read.

The subsection on remediation of specific difficulties, beginning on page 176, contains numerous suggestions that will be helpful with learners who are having problems. Many of these activities can be used in preventive as well as remedial situations. Teachers of learning disabled children should find them especially useful.

A number of these activities can, if designed with more difficult vocabulary or content, be used with more advanced readers. And most of the activities suggested in Section Four, Advanced Reading Skills, can be used with beginning and remedial readers if the materials are prepared using basic vocabulary words. The graded vocabulary list with words arranged by parts of speech is helpful for preparing easy-to-read materials. This list, Activity 256, will be found beginning on page 155.

## BASIC SIGHT WORDS

A wide variety of word drill activities and games is presented here, to give the student as much practice as possible in instant recognition of essential basic sight words. To avoid tedium, the same words can be drilled in a variety of different ways.

The overall objective for these activities is:

**BR-1.** Given a word visually, the student will pronounce that word correctly on sight.

The words you select for a given student should, of course, vary with the personal needs of that student. To assist you in making the selection of words for a beginning reader, we have included here the Cohen Basic Word List, made up of 712 words that are essential to the beginning reading vocabulary. The list includes the words from the Dolch 220 Basic Sight Words, which are identified by an asterisk on the Cohen List.

### 126. Cohen Basic Word List

The Cohen Basic Word List is reprinted, with permission, from *High Intensity Learning Systems—Reading* (New York: Random House, 1972). There are more than 700 words in this list. The starred items are the 220 words in the Dolch Basic Sight Vocabulary.

The checklist format may be used, both for beginning readers and for remedial students, to keep a cumulative record of words mastered.

# COHEN BASIC WORD LIST

NAME _____ DATE _____

**A**

_____ ★a
_____ able
_____ ★about
_____ above
_____ across
_____ add
_____ afraid
_____ ★after
_____ afternoon
_____ ★again
_____ against
_____ age
_____ ago
_____ ahead
_____ air
_____ airplane
_____ alike
_____ ★all
_____ almost
_____ alone
_____ along
_____ already
_____ also
_____ ★always
_____ ★am
_____ ★an

_____ ★and
_____ angry
_____ animal
_____ another
_____ answer
_____ ant
_____ ★any
_____ anything
_____ apple
_____ ★are
_____ arm
_____ ★around
_____ ★as
_____ ★ask
_____ ★at
_____ ★ate
_____ ★away

**B**

_____ baby
_____ back
_____ bad
_____ bag
_____ bake
_____ ball
_____ balloon
_____ barn
_____ base

_____ basket
_____ ★be
_____ bear
_____ beautiful
_____ ★because
_____ become
_____ bed
_____ bee
_____ ★been
_____ ★before
_____ began
_____ behind
_____ being
_____ believe
_____ bell
_____ belong
_____ below
_____ beside
_____ ★best
_____ ★better
_____ between
_____ ★big
_____ bigger
_____ bird
_____ birthday
_____ bit
_____ ★black

| | | |
|---|---|---|
| _____ blow | _____ can't | _____ ★could |
| _____ ★blue | _____ cap | _____ country |
| _____ board | _____ captain | _____ cousin |
| _____ boat | _____ car | _____ cover |
| _____ book | _____ care | _____ cow |
| _____ ★both | _____ careful | _____ cried |
| _____ bought | _____ ★carry | _____ cross |
| _____ box | _____ cat | _____ cry |
| _____ boy | _____ catch | _____ ★cut |
| _____ brave | _____ caught | **D** |
| _____ bread | _____ certainly | _____ daddy |
| _____ breakfast | _____ chair | _____ dance |
| _____ bright | _____ change | _____ dark |
| _____ ★bring | _____ chicken | _____ day |
| _____ broken | _____ child | _____ dear |
| _____ brother | _____ children | _____ decide |
| _____ brought | _____ Christmas | _____ deep |
| _____ ★brown | _____ circle | _____ ★did |
| _____ build | _____ city | _____ different |
| _____ burn | _____ ★clean | _____ dinner |
| _____ bus | _____ climb | _____ ★do |
| _____ busy | _____ clock | _____ ★does |
| _____ ★but | _____ close | _____ dog |
| _____ ★buy | _____ coat | _____ doll |
| _____ ★by | _____ ★cold | _____ ★done |
| **C** | _____ color | _____ ★don't |
| _____ ★call | _____ ★come | _____ door |
| _____ ★came | _____ coming | _____ ★down |
| _____ ★can | _____ company | _____ ★draw |
| _____ candy | _____ cook | _____ dress |

_____ ★drink

_____ drive

_____ drop

_____ dry

_____ duck

_____ during

**E**

_____ each

_____ ear

_____ early

_____ easy

_____ ★eat

_____ edge

_____ egg

_____ ★eight

_____ either

_____ else

_____ end

_____ enough

_____ even

_____ evening

_____ ever

_____ ★every

_____ everybody

_____ everyone

_____ everything

_____ everywhere

_____ except

_____ excite

_____ explain

_____ eye

**F**

_____ face

_____ ★fall

_____ family

_____ ★far

_____ farm

_____ ★fast

_____ fat

_____ father

_____ favorite

_____ feed

_____ feel

_____ feet

_____ fell

_____ fence

_____ few

_____ field

_____ fight

_____ fill

_____ finally

_____ ★find

_____ fine

_____ fire

_____ ★first

_____ fish

_____ ★five

_____ fix

_____ floor

_____ flower

_____ ★fly

_____ food

_____ foot

_____ ★for

_____ forget

_____ ★found

_____ ★four

_____ friend

_____ frighten

_____ ★from

_____ front

_____ ★full

_____ fun

**G**

_____ game

_____ garden

_____ ★gave

_____ ★get

_____ girl

_____ ★give

_____ glad

_____ glass

_____ ★go

_____ ★goes

_____ ★going

_____ gone

_____ ★good

_____ ★got

_____ grand

_____ grass

_____ gray

_____ great

_____ ★green

_____ ground

_____ ★grow

_____ guess

**H**

_____ ★had

_____ hair

_____ half

_____ hand

_____ happen

_____ happy

_____ hard

_____ ★has

_____ hat

_____ ★have

_____ ★he

_____ head

_____ hear

_____ heard

_____ heavy

_____ held

_____ hello

_____ ★help

_____ ★her

_____ ★here

_____ hide

_____ high

_____ hill

_____ ★him

_____ ★his

_____ hit

_____ ★hold

_____ hole

_____ home

_____ hope

_____ horse

_____ ★hot

_____ house

_____ ★how

_____ huge

_____ hundred

_____ hungry

_____ hurry

_____ ★hurt

**I**

_____ ★I

_____ ice

_____ idea

_____ ★if

_____ I'll

_____ important

_____ ★in

_____ inside

_____ interest

_____ ★into

_____ ★is

_____ ★it

_____ ★its

**J**

_____ ★jump

_____ ★just

**K**

_____ ★keep

_____ kept

_____ kill

_____ ★kind

_____ king

_____ kitten

_____ knew

_____ ★know

**L**

_____ lady

_____ land

_____ large

_____ last

_____ late

_____ ★laugh

_____ lay

_____ learn

_____ leave

_____ left

_____ leg

_____ ★let

_____ letter

_____ ★light

_____ ★like

_____ line

_____ lion

_____ list

_____ listen

_____ ★little

_____ ★live

_____ lonely

_____ ★long

_____ ★look

_____ looked

_____ lost

_____ lot

_____ love

_____ low

**M**

_____ ★made

_____ ★make

_____ man

_____ ★many

_____ matter

_____ ★may

_____ maybe

_____ ★me

_____ mean

_____ meet

_____ men

_____ met

_____ middle

_____ might

_____ milk

_____ mind

_____ minute

_____ miss

_____ mistake

_____ money

_____ more

_____ morning

_____ most

_____ mother

_____ mountain

_____ mouse

_____ mouth

_____ move

_____ Mr.

_____ Mrs.

_____ ★much

_____ ★my

_____ ★myself

**N**

_____ name

_____ near

_____ neck

_____ need

_____ neighbor

_____ ★never

_____ ★new

_____ next

_____ nice

_____ night

_____ nine

_____ ★no

_____ noise

_____ none

_____ nose

_____ ★not

_____ nothing

_____ ★now

_____ number

**O**

_____ ★of

_____ ★off

_____ oh

_____ ★old

_____ ★on

_____ ★once

_____ ★one

_____ ★only

_____ ★open

_____ ★or

_____ orange

_____ order

_____ other

_____ ought

_____ ★our

_____ ★out

_____ ★over

_____ ★own

**P**

_____ page

_____ paper

_____ parade

_____ part

_____ party

_____ pass

_____ past

_____ pay

_____ pencil

_____ people

_____ perhaps

_____ pet

_____ ★pick

_____ picnic

_____ picture

_____ piece

_____ pig

_____ pink

_____ place

_____ ★play

_____ ★please

_____ pocket

_____ point

_____ poor

_____ possible

_____ practice

_____ present

_____ ★pretty

_____ probably

_____ ★pull

_____ puppy

_____ purple

_____ purr

_____ push

_____ ★put

**Q**

_____ question

_____ quick

_____ quiet

**R**

_____ rabbit

_____ race

_____ rain

_____ ★ran

_____ rang

_____ reach

_____ ★read

_____ ready

_____ real

_____ really

_____ reason

_____ ★red

_____ remain

_____ remember

_____ reply

_____ rest

_____ return

_____ ★ride

_____ ★right

_____ ring

_____ river

_____ road

_____ rode

_____ roll

_____ roof

_____ room

_____ ★round

_____ ★run

_____ running

**S**

_____ sad

_____ ★said

_____ same

_____ sand

_____ sang

_____ sat

_____ ★saw

_____ ★say

_____ school

_____ second

_____ ★see

_____ seem

_____ seen

_____ sell

_____ send

_____ sent

_____ set

_____ ★seven

_____ several

_____ shake

_____ ★shall

_____ ★she

_____ ship

_____ shoe

_____ short

_____ should

_____ shout

_____ ★show

_____ shut

_____ sick

_____ side

_____ sigh

_____ since

_____ ★sing

_____ sister

_____ ★sit

_____ ★six

_____ sky

_____ ★sleep

_____ slept

_____ slow

_____ ★small

_____ smell

_____ smile

_____ snow

_____ ★so

_____ soft

_____ ★some

_____ somebody

_____ somehow

_____ someone

_____ something

_____ sometimes

_____ son

_____ song

_____ ★soon

_____ sorry

_____ sound

_____ speak

_____ stairs

_____ stand

_____ ★start

_____ stay

_____ step

_____ stick

_____ still

_____ stone

_____ stood

_____ ★stop

_____ stopped

_____ store

_____ story

_____ straight

_____ strange

_____ street

_____ strong

_____ such

_____ suddenly

_____ summer

_____ sun

_____ sunshine

_____ suppose

_____ sure

_____ surprise

_____ swam

_____ swim

_____ swimming

_____ swing

**T**

_____ table

_____ tail

_____ ★take

_____ talk

_____ tall

_____ teacher

_____ teeth

_____ telephone

_____ television

_____ ★tell

_____ ★ten

_____ terrible

_____ than

_____ ★thank

_____ ★that

_____ ★the

_____ ★their

_____ ★them

_____ ★then

_____ ★there

_____ ★these

_____ ★they

_____ thing

_____ ★think

_____ third

_____ ★this

_____ ★those

_____ though

_____ thought

_____ ★three

_____ through

_____ till

_____ time

_____ tired

_____ ★to

_____ ★today

_____ toe

_____ ★together

_____ told

_____ tomorrow

_____ tongue

_____ tonight

_____ ★too

_____ took

_____ top

_____ touch

_____ toward

_____ town

_____ toy

_____ train

_____ travel

_____ tree

_____ tried

_____ trip

_____ trouble

_____ truck

_____ true

_____ ★try

_____ turn

_____ ★two

**U**

_____ umbrella

_____ uncle

_____ ★under

_____ understand

_____ unhappy

_____ until

_____ ★up

_____ ★upon

_____ ★us

_____ ★use

_____ usually

**V**

_____ ★very

_____ visit

**W**

_____ wait

_____ ★walk

_____ wall

_____ ★want

_____ ★warm

_____ ★was

_____ ★wash

_____ watch

_____ water

_____ wave

_____ way

_____ ★we

_____ wear

_____ weather

_____ week

_____ ★well

_____ ★went

_____ ★were

_____ wet

_____ ★what

_____ wheel

_____ ★when

_____ ★where

_____ ★which

_____ while

_____ whisper

_____ ★white

_____ ★who

_____ whole

_____ whose

_____ ★why

_____ ★will

_____ win

_____ wind

_____ window

_____ wing

_____ winter

_____ ★wish

_____ ★with

| | | |
|---|---|---|
| _____ without | _____ world | _____ ★yes |
| _____ woman | _____ ★would | _____ yesterday |
| _____ women | _____ ★write | _____ yet |
| _____ wonder | _____ wrong | _____ ★you |
| _____ wonderful | **Y** | _____ young |
| _____ wood | _____ yard | _____ ★your |
| _____ word | _____ year | |
| _____ ★work | _____ ★yellow | |

## 127. Rapid Presentation (Tachistoscope)

To provide flash presentation of words, it is not necessary to purchase expensive machines. For rapid presentation of sight words, certain homemade devices will suffice. Here are directions for making a simple tachistoscope.

Use a piece of oaktag or cardboard. Five by eight inches is a good size, although it can be larger or smaller if you prefer. Fold back about ½ inch along each of the long sides (A). These folds create a tray to hold cards on slips of paper with words printed on them. Cut a window opening large enough to expose the words or phrases you want to flash (B). Cut a piece of oaktag to serve as a shutter (C). Secure it at one end with a brass paper fastener, which should be tight enough to hold the shutter but not so tight that it cannot move.

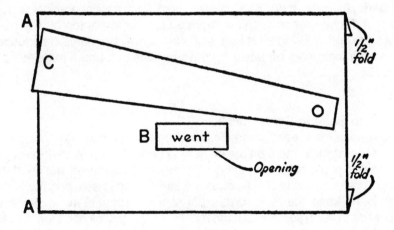

Words or phrases are printed one to a card (or one to each side of a card), so that when the card is placed in the little tray the print shows through the window. The shutter is used to conceal the word until you want to flash it. Hold the screen and the card upright with the left hand; the thumb holds the card against the screen. The right hand lifts the shutter and then lets it drop. The right hand is also used in changing cards to be flashed on the screen. (If you are left handed and want to construct a left-handed tachistoscope, just reverse right and left in the directions and diagrams.)

Expose each word or phrase for about ¼ to ½ second. If the word is missed, open the shutter and allow the student to inspect the word and try again.

This little tachistoscope could easily be made by students. Each student could make his or her own.

### 128. Word Bank

Every student at the beginning reading stage should have a word bank. A shoe box is a good container for a word bank. The box contains twenty-six envelopes (small letter size will do) each labeled with a letter of the alphabet. Each word the student learns is printed or typed on a small piece of index card. The student files this personal collection of words in envelopes labeled with the first letter of each word.

The word bank is a source for a number of activities. Filing the words gives practice in visual discrimination of letters and alphabetical order.

The word bank should contain words the student has learned. (One can't put something one doesn't have in the bank.) A twenty-seventh envelope may be added for words the student is working on but is not always sure of. Label it with a question mark.

### 129. Word Bank Challenge

A student's word bank contains words that he or she is supposed to be able to read at sight. Any student should be permitted to challenge any other student on a word in the latter's bank. If the challenged student cannot say a word in his or her own bank, then the word must be removed from its alphabetical envelope and placed in the special envelope designated for words not thoroughly mastered. It stays there until the student is sure of it. This activity promotes continuous practice on, and reinforcement of, basic sight words. It is fun, and it helps keep students interested.

### 130. Word Bank to Sentences

The word cards in each student's word bank should be small enough so that the student can arrange them on the desk to form sentences. A dark-colored piece of construction paper placed on the desk provides an excellent work surface for this activity. The contrasting color makes the cards easy to see, and the texture of the paper helps keep the little cards from slipping about. Two students can work together on forming sentences. One makes the sentences and then the other reads them. Students left to their word banks and their own devices will figure out lots of things to do with these words.

### 131. Fishing for Words

Fold word cards and pin the open ends together with a large steel pin, hairpin, or paper clip. Be sure to use pins or clips that will be attracted by a magnet. Some ordinary straight pins will not do.

If you want to take the time, make the cards in the shape of a fish. Stick the pin through the fish near the mouth. You can trace the model fish shown below.

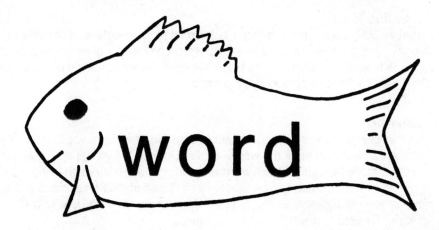

Place all the word cards in a fish tank (without the water) or other large container. A plastic wastepaper basket works well. (A metal one may draw the magnet.) Tie a fishing line (string) onto a small pole (stick) and use a magnet for a hook. The student fishes until a word is pulled out. If the student can read the word, the card is kept. A word that can't be read is thrown back. The student may keep a record of the words correctly read each day.

### 132. Self-Teaching Picture Cards

Cut oaktag into cards or use 3″ × 5″ index cards. Have each child illustrate a set of cards by drawing or cutting pictures out of magazines. A word or descriptive phrase is printed on the picture side of the card. The student, independently or with another student, practices the words and phrases using the picture side of the card until he or she knows them. The goal is to be able to read instantly at sight the sides of the cards with no pictures.

### 133. Picture Dictionary

Each student can make a personal picture dictionary or indexed scrapbook. Label the pages with both capital and lower-case letters. Illustrations can be obtained from old magazines, newspapers, and discarded readers, or the students can draw some of them. As soon as a word is learned, the student enters it and its picture on the appropriate page. Commercial picture dictionaries should also be available to your students. However, these homemade dictionaries have the advantage of being individualized, containing all the words—and only the words—on which the user is working.

### 134. My Word Book

The student can make a book containing sight words as they are learned. The student can create illustrations for these words or cut and paste from other sources.

"My Word Book" differs from the picture dictionary in that it lists words in the order in which they are learned, rather than alphabetically. There is no reason why a student who wants to can't have both.

### 135. Treasure Hunt

In front of the group, place a large box containing objects and/or pictures of objects. Along the chalkboard ledge set up word cards each of which names one object in the box. Each player closes his or her eyes, draws out an object or picture, and then tries to find the corresponding word.

### 136. Labeling

Label things in the classroom as an aid to enlarging the sight vocabulary of the students. A student who sees the words *Closet Door* on the closet door every day may be more apt to recognize these words in reading material than one who doesn't see them as often. Shelves can be labeled to indicate places for various supplies such as crayons and paste. Every possible opportunity for a student to match an object with its name in print should be provided.

### 137. Word and Picture Hunt

Give each child a reader or a picture book and a list of objects. The task for the student is to find a picture of each of the objects listed.

### 138. Matching Words with Pictures

Try making interesting worksheets for sight word drill using pictures. Pictures may be used to illustrate words other than nouns as long as you select the choice words carefully. The task for the student is to circle the word that goes with the picture. For example:

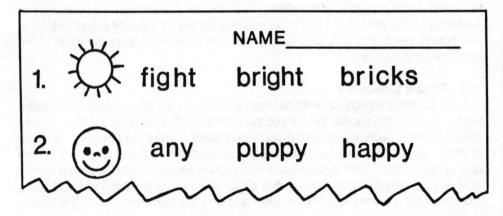

### 139. Wheel of Chance

Make a large oaktag clock face numbered from 1 to 12, or higher if you prefer. Use as many numbers as you wish. The face should be more like that of a roulette wheel than that of a clock. Attach one large movable hand to the center with a big paper fastener. On the chalkboard (or on a large sheet of oaktag for permanent list) print as many numbered words as there are numbers on the wheel.

Each student in turn spins the hand and reads the word or phrase corresponding to the number on which it lands.

### 140. Erase-A-Word Relay Race

This is a good rainy day activity. Divide the group into two teams. On the chalkboard write two lists of words, phrases, or sentences. There is one list for each team. Each list must have as many entries as there are players on a team.

At the signal, the first child on each team says the first word or phrase in the column for that team. If correct, the child runs to the board and erases the word read, then runs back and taps the next team member, who then reads the next line, and so on. The first team with an empty board wins.

### 141. Drawing from the Deck

This activity is for pupil teams or small groups. Put the words students need to practice on cards, one word to a card. Or, if you wish, use commercially prepared sight vocabulary cards. Shuffle the cards and place them face down on the table. Each student in turn draws a card and reads the word on it. If the word is read correctly, the card is kept. If a mistake is made, the card is placed face down at the bottom of the pile. When all the cards in the pile are gone, the student with the most cards is the winner.

### 142. Airplane Sight Word Game

Airplane can be a visual matching exercise as described in Activity 40. Or it can provide practice in sight vocabulary.

For practice in sight vocabulary, write the words to be drilled on the runway and on the cards. The game is played the same way as previously described, except that each player must read each of the words out loud correctly before moving the plane.

### 143. Word Race

Draw a chalk line on the floor for a starting line. Draw a second line parallel to the first and as many spaces away from it as there are words in the game. (For spaces you can use the floor boards, linoleum squares, or chalk lines.)

Each player uses a cardboard figure or a favorite toy as a marker. The figure may be numbered or named if desired. The players place their figures on the starting line. The teacher or pupil leader holds up a card with a word on it. If the first student can read the word correctly, the appropriate figure is moved one space. The student whose marker crosses the goal line first is the winner.

### 144. Finders

Finders is played somewhat like Bingo. Each player has a Bingo-like card ruled into 25 squares. The cards should be large; 9″ × 12″ oaktag is a good size. In each square a vocabulary word is printed. There is no free space in the middle.

The teacher or student leader has a duplicate set of cards. Be sure that every word on every pupil's card appears in this duplicate set. The duplicates should be made on different color card stock than the pupil cards.

Show one word card at a time to the group of players. The first student to find the word on his or her card raises a hand, pronounces the word, points to it, and then receives the word card to place over the matching word on the Finders card. The first student to have five words covered in a row or a column is the winner.

### 145. Sight Word Football

On a large sheet of oaktag draw a football field with sections to represent ten yards each. Place a cardboard football on the fifty-yard line. Shuffle a set of word cards. (This game is most useful if you have selected words that the two players need to practice.) Flip a coin to see who goes first. The first player reads the word on the first card. If the word is read correctly, the player moves the ball ten yards toward the opponent's goal. Incorrect reading of the word is a fumble and results in moving the ball back ten yards. A player who fumbles loses his or her turn. When a player crosses the opposing player's goal line, six points are scored. Correct reading of the next word adds a point to the score. After a touchdown and extra point try, the ball returns to the fifty-yard line and the other player moves.

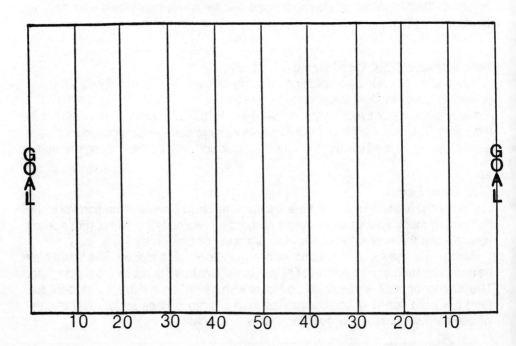

## 146. Matching Card Game

Use a set of printed word cards. There should be sixty in all. Each word should appear on four cards. Deal each player three or five cards (three for four or more players, five each for two or three players). Place five cards face up on the table.

Here is how the game is played. If the first player has in hand, for example, a card marked *horse,* and there is a card for *horse* on the table, that player may expose the card in the hand, pronounce the word, and then place the two *horse* cards face up at his or her place at the table. If a player does not have a card to match any of the exposed cards on the table, a card from the hand is discarded and another one picked from the deck. If the player has a matching card, but can't pronounce the word, the card is placed on top of its match on the table and a new card is drawn from the deck. A player who can make more than one match at a time may do so. Drawing a card from the deck ends a player's turn. The second player follows, with the added possibility of making a match with the other player's face-up cards as well a the cards in the center. For example, if the first player has taken *horse,* and the second player has a *horse* card, the second player may take the two cards for *horse* in front of the first player. Another player who has the fourth *horse* card may in turn claim the previous three from the second player.

Play continues until the cards run out. The player with the most cards is the winner.

## 147. Draw a Noun

Give each student (or student team) a large sheet of drawing paper and a box of crayons. Use a set of about twenty flash cards, each with a noun representing something students can draw. Present each card for about two to three seconds. Then have the students draw as many things as they can remember in ten minutes (or longer, if you prefer). Check by going through the words on the flash cards again.

Sample word list:

| | |
|---|---|
| horse | bat |
| cat | fence |
| hand | balloon |
| jet | bike |
| house | snake |
| bed | |
| man | |
| ear | |
| rabbit | |
| ball | |
| truck | |
| bird | |
| dog | |
| jar | |
| tree | |

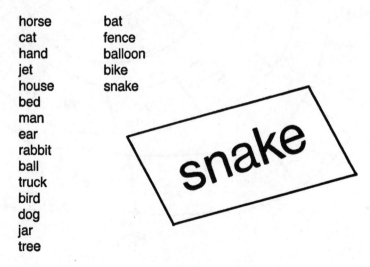

### 148. Say a Word

Make a spiral path marked off into spaces. On each space print a word, blend, digraph, or phonogram, as in the illustration below. Choose appropriate words or word parts according to the needs of the players.

To play the game, each player moves the number of spaces indicated by a throw of the dice or the spin of a number wheel. The player stays on the space reached if the word there is read correctly. If the space contains a word part rather than a whole word, the player must supply a word using that word part in order to stay. A player who fails to read or supply a word must move back until a space is found where he or she has success. The first player to reach the center wins.

If you don't feel up to drawing spiral paths, you might try making spaces around the edge of a large square or rectangle, somewhat like the lots on a Monopoly game board.

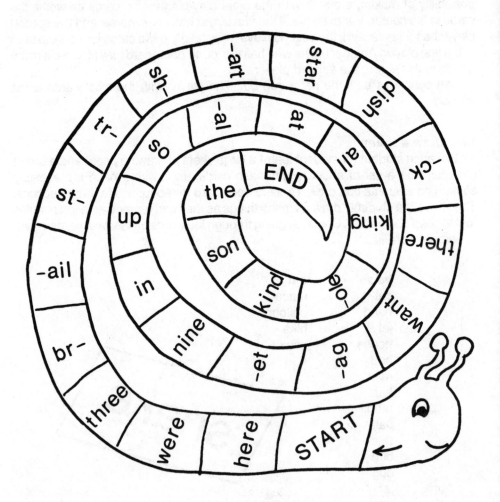

| | | |
|---|---|---|
| then | try | there |
| pig | frog | sun |
| boy | fell | girl |

Cards for Player O

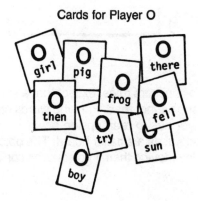

Cards for Player X

## 149. Sight Word Tic-Tac-Toe

Make a Tic-Tac-Toe board on a 5″ × 8″ index card or other suitable material. The board has nine words, one in each square. Each player gets a duplicate set of nine word cards, each with an *X* or an *O* on it.

The rules are those of regular Tic-Tac-Toe, but in addition to placing one's *X* or *O* in the desired square, the player must match and read the word correctly. In other words, to begin by placing an X in the upper right-hand corner of the board pictured here, the player must say "there" and place the X "there" card in the square. Three in a row, column, or diagonal wins the game.

### 150. Silent Movies

Take a large piece of bristol board or heavy cardboard (heavier than the light-weight oaktag). In the center of the board draw a rectangle about 10″ × 6″. The upper and lower sides of the rectangle are not single lines but are formed by two slits about ½″ apart as in A. The rectangle is the "screen" (C). The "film" is a long roll of paper (B). This roll should be wide enough to fill the screen space. On this roll are printed short phrases that tell a continuous story. The phrases are spaced on the roll so that only one phrase will show on the screen at a time. The "film" is pulled slowly through the slits, and the students read the story phrase by phrase.

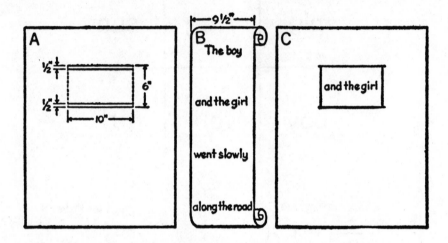

### 151. Sight Word Checkers

Sight Word Checkers follows the standard checkers rules, except that a student may not land checkers in any square he or she cannot read. Print the words on the board facing both ways, so that neither player has to read upside down.

A simplified version of Sight Word Checkers uses a smaller board. The object is simply to get one's pieces to the other side, by moving them into squares correctly read.

### 152. Picture Bingo

Picture Bingo is played with the same rules as regular Bingo. Instead of numerals on the cards, pictures are used. In order to maximize the utility of this activity, illustrations for vocabulary to be met in beginning readers and skills exercises should be used.

The teacher (or a student) calls a word from the master list. A student who finds the picture for that word on the card covers it with a marker. Bingo is the completion of any row from left to right (up to down, corner to corner, or the four corners can also be Bingo if you wish).

Ideal markers for players to use can be made out of small squares of clear acetate marked with an X in permanent color. These markers are visible while on the card, but they permit the student still to see the picture underneath.

| sns | uǝɯ | puɐl | ʇno |
|-----|-----|------|-----|
| sun | men | land | out |
| ʇuǝʇ | dnɔ | ɓıq | uı |
| tent | cup | big | in |
| sɐʍ | uɐʌ | pɐǝɥ | llıɥ |
| was | van | head | hill |

**Sight Word Checkers**

### 153. Sight Word Picture Bingo

The same rules and the same type of cards are used as for regular Picture Bingo. Each picture, however, is labeled with the corresponding word.

### 154. Sight Word Bingo

Sight Word Bingo is played just like regular Bingo except that there are words instead of numerals on the cards.

If you don't want to make your own Bingo cards, an excellent version of Sight Word Bingo using the Dolch Basic Sight Word List is available from Garrard Publishing Company.

### 155. Spelling Bingo

Spelling Bingo can be played just like any other Bingo game. Like Sight Word Bingo, it can be used to reinforce basic sight words. The major difference is that in Spelling Bingo each student prepares his or her own cards.

Give each student a blank grid and a word list containing twenty-five words. Each student copies the words onto the grid, one word per box. The order is up to the student, who can put the words in any available squares. When all the students have prepared their cards, play Bingo in the usual way.

If you have an especially weak student who really can't read the words well enough to prepare a card and play, let that student be the one to pick the words from the master list to be called. Pair the weak student with a very strong student who will then read each word. In this way, the poor student can play the game on a visual matching level while hearing each word said aloud for reinforcement.

| | | | | |
|---|---|---|---|---|
| doll | fish | kite | house | sun |
| star | cat | turtle | duck | candle |
| dish | flower | clown | tree | horse |
| face | dog | lamp | rabbit | cone |
| car | cup | ball | bat | moon |

**Sight Word Picture Bingo**

## 156. Crayon Colors

A basic box of eight big Crayola crayons is one way to give the student practice in matching color words with the appropriate shades. Each crayon has printed on its label the word naming its color. Call the students' attention to this. (Note beforehand whether the purple crayon is called purple or violet, and be sure to get it right!)

Crayons work as a source of drill on many colors until the students peel off the papers. Unfortunately, the students who keep their crayons intact are not always the ones who need to practice the words.

### 157. Color Cards

Prepare cards (or worksheets) each of which contains a black-and-white drawing outlining an object. The sheet should contain directions for coloring the object its characteristic color or colors. For example:

Here is a tree. Color it green and
brown. Make the apples red. Make
a yellow sun in a blue sky.

### 158. Number Words

To give practice in associating a numeral with its correct word, use worksheets that contain the numerals, pictures depicting numbers of objects, and the number words. The task for the student is to match the items that go together. These worksheets should be made self-correcting.

### 159. Number Word Flash Cards

Flash cards with a numeral on one side and the number word on the other can be used to give practice in recognizing the number words.

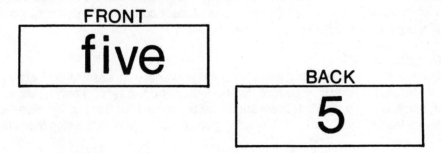

FRONT

five

BACK

5

# GRAPHEME-PHONEME RELATIONSHIPS (PHONICS)

In learning to read, regardless of whether the approach employed is primarily a code emphasis one or a meaning emphasis one, the learner must develop the ability to relate visual symbols to sounds. The activities and games in the following pages of *Reading Aids* are designed to give the student a variety of experiences with grapheme-phoneme relationships.

If each activity were described with all its possible variations, this section alone would fill the book. Keep in mind, therefore, that an activity described for beginning consonants, for example, might well apply to ending consonants or to beginning or ending digraphs or blends as well. The format of many of the specified activities can be used with different content than that used in the example. The formats suggested for a number of the readiness activities in Section Two can also be used in preparing worksheets for phonics activities.

Objectives for this section are:

**BR-2.**   After hearing a specified sound, the learner will correctly associate it with a letter (letter cluster, blend, phonogram, etc.) that represents that sound.

**BR-3.**   Given visually a letter (letter cluster, blend, phonogram, etc.), the learner will correctly associate it with the sound or sounds it represents.

In other words, given a sound, the learner should be able to match that sound with its visual symbol or symbols. Or, given a visual symbol, the learner should be able to match that symbol with its sound or sounds.

The activities in this section include work with beginning and ending consonants, beginning and ending digraphs and blends, medial consonants and vowels, short and long vowels, vowel digraphs, word families or phonograms, and silent letters.

The objectives above can and should be made specific by precisely specifying which sounds or visual symbols are to be given and the exact manner in which the student will be expected to respond.

## 160. Sound Dictionary

Use a scrapbook or loose-leaf pages in a binder. The edges of the pages can be cut so they can be thumb-indexed if desired. As a student studies a particular sound-symbol relationship, pictures can be found in magazines and pasted on the correct page of the sound dictionary. A word that goes with each picture can also be cut and pasted, or it can be copied. The student can then underline the letters for the particular sound involved. In this way, the student constructs a personal picture dictionary that can be used for reference.

## 161. I Hear a __?__

Here is a good rainy day game to provide practice in associating beginning consonant letters with their sounds. Every student needs a set of twenty cards, each with a consonant on it. The letters should be big enough so that you can see them from the front of the room. (Omit the *q,* to give you an even twenty which then make four nice rows of five on the student's desk.) Each player arranges the letters alphabetically on the desk. The teacher (or a good student reader) calls a word. Each player is to hold up the letter with which the word begins.

To play this game competitively, give one point to each student who holds up the correct letter within five seconds.

## 162. Alphabet Trip

Here is a little alphabet game that children have been playing on their own for years.

One student begins—"A, my name is Anne, I'm going to Albuquerque, and I'll take apples." The next student continues—"B, my name is Bob, I'm going to Bermuda, and I'll take bottles." Next—"C, my name is Carl, I'm going to California, and I'll take cucumbers." And so on, around the class, through the alphabet.

## 163. Consonant Trip

This game requires a little planning, because you have to have questions that can be answered by a word beginning with the correct consonant. Other than that, it's easy.

Begin by saying, "Let's take a trip to Florida (or wherever)." Then ask questions each of which must be answered by a word beginning with the letter *f.* For example:

> What car will I go in? (Fiat, Ferrari, or Ford)
> Who will go with me? (Florence or Fred)
> What will the weather be? (fair)
> What will we eat? (figs)
> How many days will the trip take? (five)

## 164. Another Consonant Trip

Here is another variation on the taking-a-trip game. Begin with *B.* Each student in turn names an object to take on the trip. Go on naming objects beginning with *B* until someone makes a mistake or can't think of any word at all. That person drops out and the others go on to the next consonant.

## 165. I Spy Something

The familiar game "I Spy" can be used to help the students review beginning or ending consonants.

The first player says, "I spy something that starts with *B.*" The others try to guess what the first one sees—e.g., ball, bat, balloon, bookcase, etc. The person who guesses the right thing is the next one to spy something.

## 166. Beginning Sound Day

Assign a beginning sound to a particular day. On that day, each student has to bring in an object the name of which begins with the designated sound. The objects are labeled and displayed until the next appointed day when the routine begins all over again with a different letter and sound.

### 167. Beginning Sounds Shoe Boxes

As an alternative to pictures arranged by beginning sounds, try a shoe box of small objects the names of which all begin with the same sound and the same letter. Each box (and item) should be labeled with the beginning letter. A "five and ten cent" store is a good source of little models of a variety of suitable objects. Here are some suggestions:

> B—balloon, bottle, boy, book, bow, boat
> C—candle, cork, car, comb, cap
> H—horse, house, handkerchief
> M—marble, map, man, mitten

### 168. Consonant Game

Here is a quiet rainy day game. Give each student a card with a consonant letter on it. At his or her turn, a student has to say a word beginning with that consonant and tell if the item named is animal, vegetable, or mineral. This can be played in preparation for Consonant Twenty Questions, Activity 169.

### 169. Consonant Twenty Questions

This game is played like regular Twenty Questions except that the initial clue contains the beginning letter of the object in question. For example, "I'm thinking of something that begins with M and is vegetable." The other players are given twenty questions to try to guess what the person has in mind.

### 170. Consonant Card Game

This game is played with picture cards and letter cards. Make a set of picture cards by mounting (or drawing) small pictures of objects, each one on a 3″ × 5″ index card. Cut index cards in half to make the letter cards, each of which should contain a beginning or ending letter of one of the words pictured. The game may be played with as few as seven pictures or as many as twenty. For each picture card there must be two letter cards—one for the beginning consonant and one for the ending consonant. You can make a number of different card sets for this game. Here is a sample game set using ten picture cards:

> Picture cards: girl, dog, cat, pig, jar,
> hat, bed, lamp, bird, book
> Letter cards: g, l, d, g, c, t, p, g, j, r, h, t, b,
> d, l, p, b, d, b, k

To play the game (best with two, possible for three or four) shuffle the letter cards and deal them face down to each player. The picture cards are arranged face up in the center. The first player takes the top card from his or her letter pile and places it by the appropriate picture card (to the left if it's the beginning consonant, to the right if it's the final). The next player takes the top card and places it. When a picture has both its beginning and its final sound correctly lettered, the player who put down the second letter gets the picture. The object of the game is to collect the most pictures.

### 171. Consonant Beanbag

Take a large sheet of oilcloth, at least two square yards in area. A light-colored plastic tablecloth will work nicely. Mark the cloth into one-foot squares using plastic tape. In each square write a consonant blend or digraph. Secure the cloth on the floor with masking tape. From about ten feet back, a student tosses a beanbag at the squares. The student must then name in one minute as many words as possible beginning with the letter combination on which the beanbag landed. The player with the highest number of words wins.

### 172. The Consonant Scene

When a particular beginning consonant is being studied, a student can draw a picture and try to include as many things in it as possible that begin with the specified consonant. Each of the objects in the picture should be labeled with the beginning consonant. For example:

### 173. From Sound to Symbol

The teacher dictates a series of lists of three or four words, with all the words in each series beginning with the same sound. For each series of words dictated, the students write the letter for the initial sound heard.

### 174. Naming Pictures by Consonant Substitution

Make a worksheet containing a series of pictures. Next to each picture have words differing only in beginning (or ending) consonants, blends, or digraphs. The task for the student is to select the word that goes with the picture.

The student can either circle the choice or, if the space is provided, write the correct word. This activity can be made self-correcting for use with a lapboard.

### 175. Rotating Wheel

Two circles, one smaller than the other, should be made from oaktag or other sturdy material. Fasten them together in the center, using a large brass paper fastener. The fastener should be tight enough to hold the circles together, but loose enough to permit them to turn.

Print initial consonants on the large circle. Print phonograms on the smaller circle. By turning the larger circle, different initial consonants can be combined with the same phonogram.

This wheel can also be used for beginning digraphs and blends. Simply substitute the desired digraphs or blends for the initial consonants on the outer wheel.

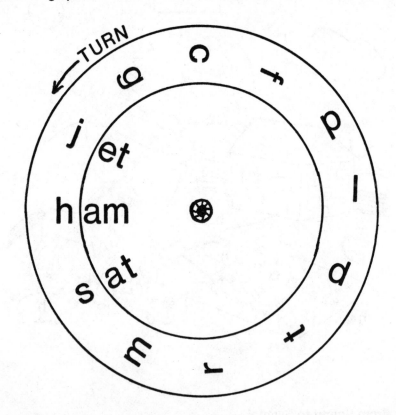

For ending consonants or blends, write the words the other way around, so that the ending consonants are on the outer wheel and the first parts of words (beginning consonants plus medial vowels) are on the inner one.

## 176. Same Beginnings

List words in rows on the chalkboard or a worksheet. The student should circle the words in each row that begin with the same sound. If a worksheet is used rather than the chalkboard, immediate feedback can be provided by means of an answer key for student self-checking. A sheet of oaktag with holes cut in the spaces for the correct answers is a good way to check this kind of worksheet.

## 177. Pick a Word

Place on the chalkboard edge a number of cards with words printed on them. The teacher (or an able student) should say a word. A student then goes to the board and selects a card containing a word that begins with the same sound as the one pronounced.

## 178. Letter Circles

To give practice on making words with vowel combinations, try diagrams like these:

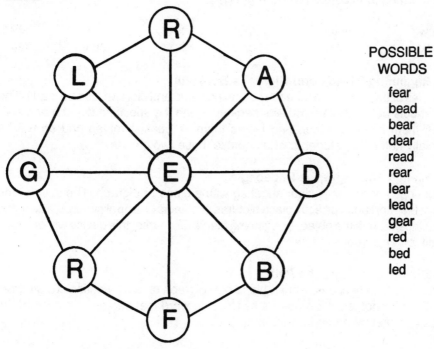

POSSIBLE
WORDS

fear
bead
bear
dear
read
rear
lear
lead
gear
red
bed
led

The purpose is to make as many real words as possible by moving from one letter to another. A letter may be used more than once.

## 179. Pick a Letter

List initial consonants such as *g, h, p, s, m, f,* etc., on the chalkboard or on a chart. The teacher (or a student) says a word, and a student then points to the letter with which the pronounced word begins. This same activity can be done with initial digraphs and blends and final consonants and blends.

### 180. Word Sorting

Put a list of assorted words on the board or on a worksheet. Have the student copy them according to word families or beginning sounds as directed. For example, the list:

| | | |
|---|---|---|
| low | game | show |
| mate | shell | gate |
| bend | boy | lame |
| toy | mend | tell |

The list arranged according to beginning sounds:

| | | | | | |
|---|---|---|---|---|---|
| low | made | bend | toy | shell | game |
| lame | mend | boy | tell | show | gate |

The list arranged according to word families:

| | | | | | |
|---|---|---|---|---|---|
| low | mate | bend | toy | game | shell |
| show | gate | mend | boy | lame | tell |

### 181. Beginning Blends and Digraphs Booklets

A series of booklets, one for each beginning blend and digraph, can be made. The student cuts out pictures of objects beginning with the specified digraph or blend, pastes them in the booklet, and labels them. A booklet for *sh* and *ch* will be especially helpful for students who confuse these two blends.

### 182. Blends and Digraphs Shoebag

Label each pocket in a clear shoebag with a blend or digraph. The task for the student is to sort and correctly place pictures of objects or actual small objects in the pocket labeled with the object's beginning blend. Of course, this device will work just as well for single consonants.

### 183. Blends and Digraphs Path

Draw a path in sections. Print a blend or a digraph on each section. To get from one place to another, the student has to say a word that begins with each of the blends or digraphs printed on the path.

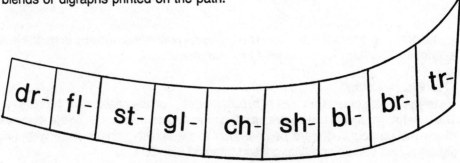

## 184. Talking Dominoes

A dominoes game in which the tiles have words or phrases instead of a number of dots makes an interesting word drill activity. We call the game "talking dominoes" because, in order to get credit for the match, the student has to say the word or phrase out loud while placing it where it belongs. You can make a number of different sets of dominoes to meet special needs. For example, one set could contain selected words from the Dolch list. A set of dominoes could be made to correspond with the vocabulary from any children's book. A given student could have a set made up to contain the words or phrases with which he or she was having trouble.

The rules for talking dominoes are basically like those of any regular dominoes game. Or, try these rules. Make a starter card for the center with a word or phrase along each of the four edges. Every other domino will have a word or phrase on two edges. The dominoes are shuffled and placed face down on the table. The first player draws a domino and attempts to place it by the starter card. If there isn't a match, or if there is but the student can't say the word or phrase correctly, another domino is taken. The player continues to draw dominoes until he or she is able to play one. Then the next player takes a turn. Play continues until the pool is exhausted, and no more dominoes held by the players can be played. The person who plays all the dominoes first is the winner. Or, if no one can play all, the person with the smallest number left wins.

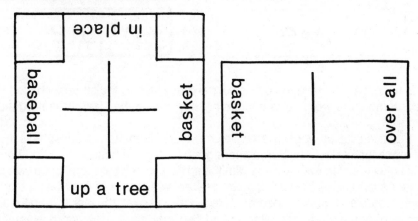

## 185. Digraph or Blend Race

This is a good relay race game for a rainy day. First, decide how many teams you will have. Use from two to four, the exact number to be determined by the availability of board space and your tolerance for chaos. Label a space for each team with a beginning blend or digraph. Locate each team behind a starting line 10′ or more from the board. At the starting signal, the first person on each team runs to the board and writes a word beginning with the team's digraph or blend, runs back to the line, and then sits down. A player who writes a word that is not correct can either stay up there and keep trying or can return to the end of the line and take another turn. Then the next player from each team does the same, and so on. The first team to have all real words on the board and every player seated is the winner.

### 186. Matching Word Parts

Cut oaktag into 2″ × ½″ sections. Print one word on each section. Space the word on each little card so that the card can be cut between the initial consonant or blend and the remaining phonogram, with all cards having corresponding parts that are the same size. Below are examples of two cards:

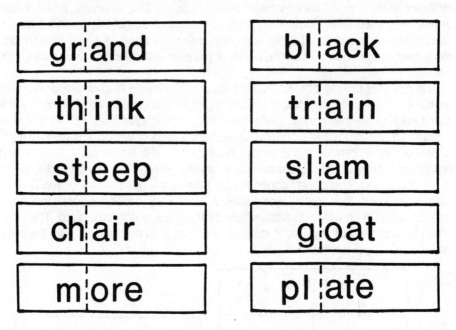

It is necessary to have the cards cut uniformly so that the students have to *read* to reassemble the word parts and cannot depend on the size of the card pieces for cues.

Place ten cut-up words in an envelope. The student has to reassemble the pieces to make ten real words. Some phonograms will go with more than one consonant. This may result in two students with the same components coming up with different lists. As long as all the words made are real words, this is fine. If a student makes eight words and has four incompatible pieces left over, the task is then to rearrange some of the already completed words so that each initial word element in the envelope is paired with a phonogram to make a word.

This activity can be done with single consonants in both initial and final positions, as well as digraphs and consonant blends.

### 187. Sound Picture Collections

For a student who is having difficulty with a particular sound, a collection of pictures of objects beginning with that sound may be helpful. Each picture should be labeled, with the symbols for the particular sound underlined. These pictures can be arranged in little scrapbooks or filed in envelopes. Arrangements with pairs of spellings often confused can be made to point out the differences to the student. For example:

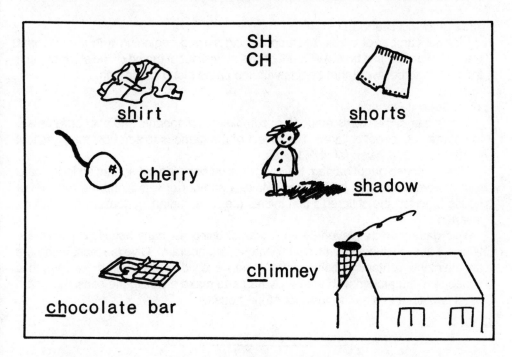

A more difficult collection of pictures would include the symbols being studied in different positions in a word. For example, using the *sh* and *ch* digraphs as in the sample above, the following pictures might be used.

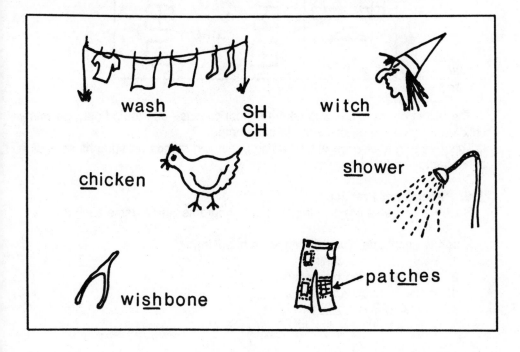

### 185. Drawing Blends

Place a number of cards, each containing a word beginning with a consonant blend or digraph, in a box. A student draws a card out of the box. The student must then say another word that begins with the same blend or digraph.

### 189. School Census

In this game, the words made from combining consonants and phonograms are the names of school children. The object of the game is to see how many school children live in a given family's house.

Make a house out of oaktag. Have a place on one side cut so that an index card with a word family can be inserted. Make a number of slits along the roof of the house in which the children's first initials (i.e., the beginning consonants) can be inserted.

This game can be played by pupil teams, using as many houses as there are teams. Label each house with a family name (phonogram). Give the team members an envelope containing consonants. When a child is discovered (i.e., when a consonant is matched with the family name to make a word), the consonant card used is placed in a slot in the roof of the house.

The object of the game is to take a school census—i.e., to find out how many children (known words) there are in each home.

This game may also be played using beginning blends or digraphs or ending consonants and blends.

### 190. Phonogram Practice

Have the students practice important phonograms with a game such as this:

Listen to each clue. The missing word has *it* in it.
  1. You _____ in a chair.
  2. A shirt that's too big doesn't _____.
  3. Inside a peach you'll find a _____.
  4. The lamp isn't _____.
  5. The pitch was too low to _____.

These missing words have *eam* in them.
1. Sew a straight _____.
2. The _____ in my coffee was sour.
3. We've got _____ heat.
4. Stay on the winning _____.
5. Don't hit your head on that low _____.

## 191. Making Words

Draw five squares on the chalkboard. In the left-hand corner of each is a consonant. Beside each consonant is a list of phonograms. The students are asked to form the words and pronounce them.

This activity has survived intact from the earliest edition of this book. Why five squares? Nobody seems to know. So, if using six suits you better, go ahead. It's the word building that's important.

```
┌─────────────┐           ┌─────────────┐
│ w   all     │           │ b   at      │
│     ay      │           │     all     │
│     ell     │           │     ell     │
│             │           │     it      │
└─────────────┘           └─────────────┘

          ┌─────────────┐
          │ s   ail     │
          │     ell     │
          │     ay      │
          │     ame     │
          └─────────────┘

┌─────────────┐           ┌─────────────┐
│ h   at      │           │ c   all     │
│     ay      │           │     ame     │
│     all     │           │     at      │
│     ow      │           │     ake     │
└─────────────┘           └─────────────┘
```

## 192. Word Building Race

Give each player an envelope containing sets of consonants and of phonograms (word families). For example, the contents of an envelope could be:

2 each: b, c, d, f, g, h, j, k, l, m, n, p, r, s, t, w
4 each: -ate, -ill, -ell, -ake, -ar, -ail, -it, -en

At the signal, "Go," each player begins to assemble as many real words as possible. Nonsense words don't count. The first player to assemble correctly all the words in the envelope, with no cards left over, is the winner. If nobody uses all the cards, the student with the highest number of correct words wins.

### 193. Word Squares

Make a word square grid (similar to a Bingo card) on a ditto, or place it on the board. Put one letter in each box and leave the center box open. Be sure to choose the letters carefully so that real words will be possible. Here is a sample:

| M | A | D | D | E |
|---|---|---|---|---|
| P | R | O | N | A |
| E | O |   | T | R |
| T | D | R | W | D |
| S | E | A | E | E |

The purpose of the game is to find as many real words as possible by moving one square at a time, either up or down, or left or right. Score one point for each word. After all the possible words have been found, a vowel of the player's choice can be put in the center. Score two bonus points for each word made using the center vowel. The student with the most points wins.

### 194. Lost Children

This game may seem a little bit corny, but young children find it fun. Appoint one of the students to act as "police captain." The others are working police officers. Tell the police captain that you are "Mrs. Ill" (or Mr. Ack, or whatever word family you wish to practice.) Before the game starts, place word cards, a number of which contain words of the family being studied, around the room. Explain that you have lost your children while shopping. The police captain then directs the officers to look for all the children of the "Ill family" (or whatever family name you picked). Places to look:

- On the streets (chalkboard ledges, rows of desks)
- In the parks (window sills)
- Bureau of Missing Persons (word card box)

The police officer (student) who finds the most lost children (words belonging to the right family) may be honored with a promotion, or whatever reward is appropriate.

## 195.  Finding Families

Divide the students into four or five teams. the captain of each team holds a large card with a family ending printed on it. Each team has a different family. Along the chalkboard ledge there are word cards facing the board. There must be at least as many word cards for each family as there are students on the team. At a given signal, the captains hold up the family names and the other students hunt through the word cards to find one that belongs to their family. The team that wins is the first to have each team member showing a card with a word that belongs to the team's family.

## 196.  Word Hospital

List on a large card (oaktag will do nicely) phonograms (word families) on which the students need practice. Each of these letter combinations can appear a number of times in the list, but a combination should not appear twice in succession. At the bottom of the chart, paste or staple an envelope containing many small cards, each with a consonant letter on it.

Call the phonograms "sick word families," and the consonant cards "medicine." The student uses the medicine and tries to see how many good words can be made from the sick families. (This can be reversed, with the families on the cards and the consonants on the chart.) This activity can also be done with blends, digraphs, or ending consonants and blends.

## 197.  Word Family Charts

Make charts to illustrate vowel sounds or word families. The pictures can be cut out of magazines or can be hand drawn. Underline the word parts being taught. For example:

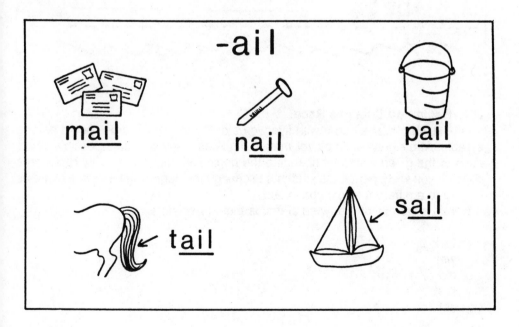

### 198. Riddles

On the chalkboard, write the name of one word family such as *ame*. One person says, "I am thinking of a word that belongs to the *ame* family. Can you guess what it is?" The student whose turn it is to respond either writes a consonant on the board or chooses from those placed along the chalkboard ledge a letter card to indicate the guess. For example, the student selects an *l* and says, "Is the word 'lame'?" The teacher (or student) may then write the word *lame* on the board, saying "No, it is not 'lame'." Another student suggests another word in like manner, and it too is listed if it is not the word the leader had in mind. This procedure continues until the right word is found.

### 199. Consonant Substitution

Make worksheets for practice in consonant substitution. Divide the page into sections. In each section draw two or more pictures that illustrate rhyming words. Supply one of the words. The task for the student is to label the other pictures.

These pages should be mounted for durability and made self-correcting for lapboard use.

Here is a sample:

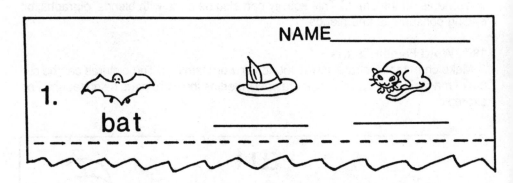

### 200. Beginning Changes Race

Give each player a paper with five words at the top. The words should be one syllable. At a signal, each player tries to make as many words as possible under each of the given words by changing the beginning consonant. Only real words count. If you wish, permit the students to change the beginning letter to a blend as well as to a different single consonant.

Here's a sample of the types of words that are suitable.

tack
well
dip
rest
set

## 201. Letter Tic-Tac-Toe

Each player in the game begins with a tic-tac-toe square on a piece of paper. One person (the teacher or a student) serves as the caller for this game. The caller names nine letters, one at a time. Each player writes the letter just called in one of the squares on his or her paper. The object of the game is to form as many real words, across and down, as possible. Score only left to right or up to down. If you think your students can handle it, add diagonal, but be sure to count left to right only. The lower left to the upper right corner can count if you wish.

Here's a sample game.

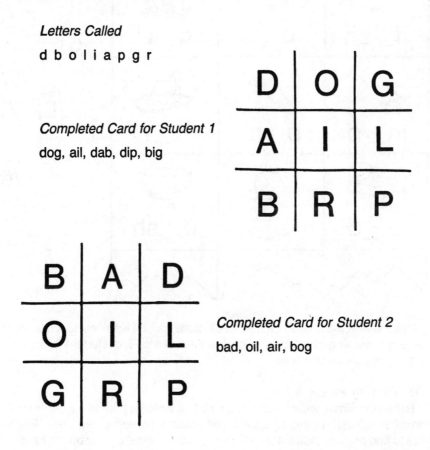

*Letters Called*

d b o l i a p g r

*Completed Card for Student 1*

dog, ail, dab, dip, big

*Completed Card for Student 2*

bad, oil, air, bog

Letter tic-tac-toe can also be played independently by one student. Prepare the materials for each game and store them in an envelope. For each game you will need nine little letter cards and some blank tic-tac-toe squares. In preparing the cards, be sure that you select letters that do make words. Include a sufficient number of vowels!

A student can play against time or simply enjoy arranging the letters to get as many words as possible. After the words are formed, you can have the student use each word in a sentence if you wish.

### 202. Missing Phonograms

Divide a 9″ × 12″ sheet of oaktag into twelve blocks, each 3″ × 3″. Each block should have a picture the name of which contains a sound on which the student is working. Label the pictures, omitting the key letters. A card for practice on short vowel phonograms, for example, might look something like this:

Make slits in the oaktag so that small cards can be inserted. Cut little cards to fit. Write the missing phonograms on the little cards. The student has to place the phonogram cards correctly.

### 203. Finding Partners

To half the class, pass out cards on each of which is printed a word family. Give to the other half of the class cards with consonants, blends, or digraphs. Each student tries to find another student with whom to make a word by combining cards. When a word has been made, the two students involved say, "We made _____ with our cards." This continues until all the students have been paired or those left over can't match up to make any real words.

### 204. Rhyming Cards

Print a list of seven or more words on a large card. Give the student an envelope containing a large number of small cards, each with a word on it. The student places each of the small cards next to its rhyming word on the large card or places it back in the envelope to indicate that it does not rhyme with anything on the large card. This activity is good for small groups or student teams.

### 205. Rhymes on a List

In a list of thirty or forty words, the student underlines those that rhyme with a given word. These may be done at the chalkboard or on a worksheet. Answer keys should be provided for student self-correction if worksheets are used.

### 206. Finding the Rhymes

Put a list of words on the chalkboard or on a chart. Pronounce all the words on the board, pointing to each as it is said. Then say a word that rhymes with one of the words on the board. The student has to point to the word that rhymes with the word said.

### 207. Card-Calling Game

Take small index cards (3″ × 5″) and on each one print a one-syllable word. Be sure to use a variety of different vowel sounds and include words that rhyme. Shuffle the cards and give four to each player. The remainder of the deck is left face down on the table. The first player reads one word from the four cards. If another player holds a card containing a rhyming word, the card must be given to the player calling it. The next player then gets a chance to read aloud any of his or her words. If a player calls for a word and fails to get a rhyming card from any of the other players, he or she draws from the pack on the table. If there still is no rhyme, or if the student cannot read the word chosen, the student must discard the word called by placing it and the one just drawn at the bottom of the pack in the center. The player with the most cards in hand when the center pack is exhausted wins.

### 208. Long and Short Vowel Pictures

Give the student a worksheet containing labeled pictures of objects. The student has to identify the vowel sound in the name of each object as "long" or "short." For example:

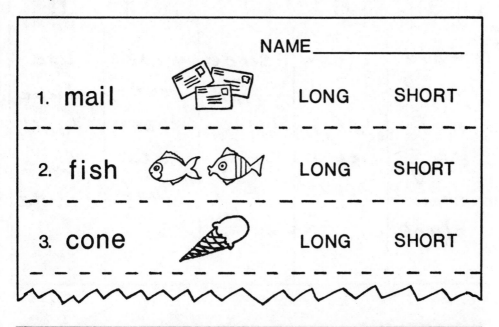

### 209. Matching Vowel Sounds

Make a worksheet with five pictures across the top, each illustrating a word with a different vowel sound. Number the pictures from 1 to 5. Then list words, each containing one of the pictured sounds. The task for the student is to indicate for each word which of the picture names contains the same vowel sound as that word.

### 210. Long Vowel Homes

This is a game that can be played by any number of students. Each student needs a paper with five houses, each house labeled with a vowel. The list of words can be presented on a chart or on the chalkboard. If only one or two students are playing, the list can be on a regular size piece of paper.

The object of the game is to read each word and to write it under the correct home of its long vowel sound. The first person to place all the words correctly is the winner. If no one has a perfect page, the one with the most correct words wins.

Here's one list that you can use for this activity.

| clean | raid | beach | fuse | strike |
|-------|------|-------|--------|--------|
| tale | slide | seat | bright | chain |
| leak | tube | toes | strange | plane |
| broke | tooth | find | roast | mule |
| use | made | toast | teeth | loaf |

A correctly completed student paper might look something like this.

Name  Lisa

| a | e | i | o | u |
|-------|-------|-------|-------|------|
| tale | clean | slide | broke | use |
| raid | leak | find | toes | tube |
| made | beach | bright | toast | tooth |
| strange | seat | strike | roast | fuse |
| chain | teeth | | loaf | mule |
| plane | | | | |

### 211. Long and Short Vowels

Give the student a list of words in which every vowel is to be marked to indicate whether it is "long," "short," or "silent." (This exercise is not especially interesting or useful and should not be overused.) A partially completed sample follows:

s ŭ n              m e
t ē ă m            c a n e
m ā k é            n e t
r ă t              m e a t
m ū l é            s i p

### 212. Missing Vowels

Prepare a worksheet containing words missing their vowels. The task is to make as many different real words as possible by using different vowels in the consonant framework provided. Include some with spaces for vowel digraphs. For example:

c_p                cap
cup                coop
cop                coup

### 213. Missing Vowel Pictures

Prepare a worksheet with labeled pictures of objects. Omit the vowels in each word. The student has to complete each word. Here is a sample page for short-vowel phonograms and one for long-vowel phonograms.

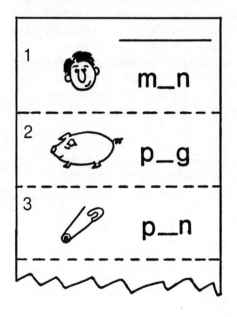

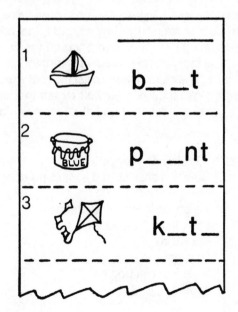

### 214. Vowel Change Race

Give each player a paper with five words at the top. The words should be one syllable with a short vowel. At a signal, each player tries to make as many words as possible under each of the given words by changing the vowel. Only real words count.

Here's a sample. Of course, you should pick words that will be meaningful to your students.

bag        pet        hit        top        bun

### 215. Rolling Letter Blocks

Make approximately twenty small (about 1″) wooden blocks. Print a letter on each side of each block with a permanent marker. Vowels should be high-frequency letters. A large plastic freezer dish with cover can be both a storage container for the blocks and a shaker for playing with them. The student shakes and dumps out the blocks and then uses them to make as many words as possible in three minutes. The student uses only the letters facing up and does not turn any of the blocks over. Scrabble tiles can be used if block-making is not your thing. (Note that the Scrabble tiles have the letters only on one side and have to be turned face up after shaking.) The distribution of letters in a standard Scrabble set is a good guide for marking the blocks.

### 216. Word-Part Wheels

Word-part wheels are a good way to give students practice in assembling words from word parts.

To make a word-part wheel, cut two circles, one smaller than the other. Fasten them securely together in the center, using a brass paper fastener. Around the edge of the outside (larger) circle, print final consonants, digraphs, or blends. Print the beginning part of a word once on the inner circle.

The task for the student is to turn the wheel and see how many real words can be made. The student should list the real words on a prepared student response sheet, which can then be checked by another student or by using an answer key.

Label each word-part wheel for easy identification and storage.

### 217. Double-O Words

Double-o words fill in the missing spaces in this activity. For example:

Write an *oo* word on each line.
   something to read _____
   not warm _____
   fix a hot meal _____
   what the wet dog did _____
   midday _____

## 218. More Double-O Words

Here is another exercise with *oo* words.
Write each word under the picture whose name has the same sound of *oo*.

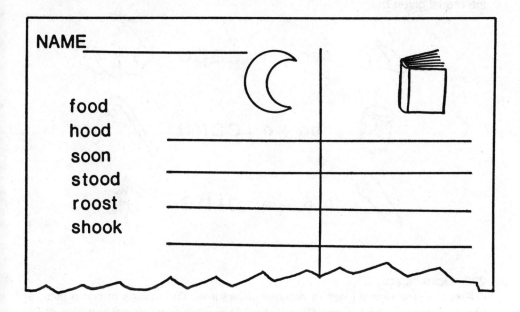

NAME_____

food
hood
soon
stood
roost
shook

## 219. Medial Vowels in Context

When a student has been introduced to different vowel sounds, provide a supportive context in which to practice them. Easy multiple-choice exercises that help the student focus on the medial vowel can be given. For example:

1. The cat sat on the living room _____. (rig, rag, rug)
2. The pig is in the pig _____. (pen, pan, pin)
3. Betty fell and hurt her _____. (log, lug, leg)
4. "Woof woof," barked the little brown _____. (dig, dog, dug)
5. Hang up your coat on the _____. (peg, pug, pig)

## 220. More Medial Vowels in Context

More practice of medial vowels in context should give the student sentences in which the task is to choose from words that include both medial vowel and initial and final consonant differences. For example:

1. The bear was asleep in the _____. (bat, log, leg)
2. The old man lived in a _____. (hut, hat, pet)
3. Snow White slept in the last _____. (bid, bed, pod)
4. The pig liked to dig in the _____. (mad, nib, mud)
5. Fry the fish in a _____. (pod, bag, pan)

### 221. "Magic E" Pictures

To show the effect of the final *e* in changing the pronunciation and meaning of a word, use illustrations. Have the students create additional examples according to the model given below.

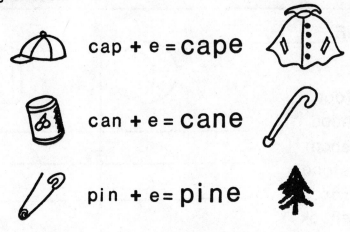

cap + e = cape

can + e = cane

pin + e = pine

### 222. More "Magic E"

Prepare a worksheet with a number of pictures. The names of some pictures should contain a short vowel. Others should have the same vowel and final *e*. The student has to circle the word that goes with the picture. For example:

NAME _____

hat    hate         can    cane

mop    mope         pans    panes

### 223. "Magic E" Cards

Flash cards to illustrate the "magic *e*" principle can be made from small pieces of oaktag or unruled 3″ × 5″ index cards. On one side of the card write a word without the final *e*. On the back of the card write the *e*. The letters should be placed so that the card can be folded to bring the *e* to the end of the word. Pairs of students can practice the words as needed.

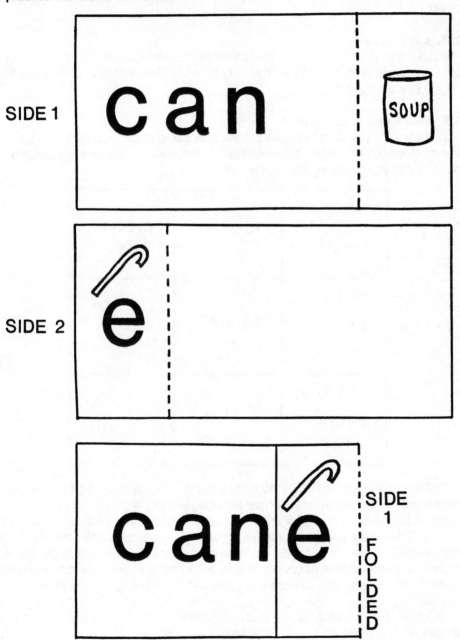

### 224. Silent letters

A practice worksheet for identifying silent letters can be made using labeled pictures, some for words which do start with a silent letter and some for words which begin with the same letter but in which that letter is not silent. The student's task is to mark off the silent letters.

This is a difficult task. Silent letters are among the last sound-symbol relationships taught.

### 225. Lazy Letters

In the words in which the first letter is silent (e.g., *write, gnome, knife*) the *w, g,* or *k* can be referred to as the "lazy w," the "lazy g," or the "lazy k," because they are "too lazy to say anything."

### 226. Word Attack Squares

This game is based on the popular television game show, "Hollywood Squares." Make a grid such as the one below. Of course, the skills you use for each box should be the ones the pupils in your group need.

| compound word | long i | prefix un- |
|---|---|---|
| short u | -ed and -ing | gl- |
| long e | suffix -er, -or | -ough |

Assign one student "celebrity" to each square. There are two contestants. The first contestant picks a square. The person assigned to that square has to answer a question based on that category. The contestant must agree or disagree with the answer. If he or she is correct, then an X (or an O) is placed in the square for that contestant. The first contestant to get three in a row (as in tic-tac-toe) is the winner. Before the game begins, of course, you have to prepare questions for each listed category. For example, a question on compound words might go like this:

Which of the following words is a compound word? Pick it and use it in a sentence.         counter         fireplace         pillow

# WORD STRUCTURE

This section on basic word structure includes activities dealing with inflected verb endings, singular and plural nouns, comparative and superlative forms of adjectives, compound words, and contractions.

These activities can be designed for beginning or remedial readers by using simple basic vocabulary. If more difficult words are selected, most of these activities are equally applicable to advanced reading skills work. Activities for vocabulary development through work with roots and affixes will be found in Section Four.

Objectives for this section are:

**BR-4.** Given a base word and possible word endings, the learner combines the base word with endings to make new words.

**BR-5.** After reading a sentence containing a verb missing its ending, the learner adds the correct ending.

**BR-6.** Given visually a singular (or plural) noun, the learner indicates its plural (or singular) form.

**BR-7.** Given visually a noun in context, the learner indicates the correct (singular or plural) form of the noun.

**BR-8.** Given visually an adjective in context, the learner indicates the correct form of the adjective for that context.

**BR-9.** Given a compound word (or two parts of a compound word), the learner indicates its component parts (or joins them to form the compound word).

**BR-10.** Given a contraction (or two words that can be contracted), the learner indicates the two words from which the contraction was made (or contracts the two words).

## 227. Word Structure Wheel

Use a circular piece of oaktag. Around the circumference print words (nouns, adjectives, and verbs). Using a brass paper fastener, attach five clocklike hands to the center of the circle. On each hand print a word ending—*er, est, ed, s,* or *ing.*

Point to a word. The task for the student is to move one of the pointers to the word to make a new word out of a base plus an ending. The student then says the word he or she has in mind. Note that certain final consonants require doubling, and some final *e*'s must be dropped, when an ending is added, if the new word is to be spelled correctly. Do this exercise on an oral level and don't worry about that here. In other words, if a student adds *ing* to *mop* and says "mopping," fine. And if he or she adds *ing* to *mope* and says "moping," that's fine too. But if *ing* is added to *mope* and the student says "mopping," that's not so good.

## 228. More Word Structure Wheel

Add context to Activity 227. Point to a word and give an incomplete sentence. The student then has to select the pointer that correctly completes the word according to context. For example, point to the word *fast.* Say, "This horse is _____ than that one." The student should then select the pointer with *er* to make the sentence correct.

### 229. Word Countdown

Here's a game that two players can play. Provide a paper with a rocket drawn on it and eleven lines on either side. Number the lines from ten to one. The last line is labeled "blast off."

On a card, write a number of word parts. Parts that could be the first syllable of the word are on the left. Parts that could be the second syllable of the word are on the right. The first player tries to make a word by combining two syllables. He or she writes the word on line ten. Then the other player makes a word. A syllable may be used more than once, but a player may not repeat a word already listed in the countdown. The object of the game is to get to blast off.

```
10                    10
 9                     9
 8                     8
 7                     7
 6                     6
 5                     5
 4                     4
 3                     3
 2                     2
 1                     1
      BLAST OFF
```

Here are some possible word parts to use. You should prepare the cards for your students using words that they are working on.

| hand | sal | tur | den | bout |
|------|------|------|------|------|
| aw | sim | cir | fast | part |
| in | be | num | ny | set |
| ba | rab | lem | cide | by |
| up | de | up | bit | side |
| a | fun | on | cause | ful |
| break | gar | cle | ad | ing |
| teach | pur | tle | er | |

## 230. Word-Ending Rotating Wheel

The rotating wheel designed for practice in consonant substitution can be used for giving practice in word endings. Construct the wheel as described in Activity 175. Write base words around the inner circle and endings around the outer one.

Dictate a sentence with one of the base words on the inner wheel. The task for the student is to match the word with the ending that makes it correct in the given context.

## 231. Word-Ending Drill

Put three columns of words on a chart or the chalkboard. For example:

| | | |
|---|---|---|
| walk | walked | walk |
| jumps | jump | jump |
| water | water | watered |
| wait | waiting | wait |

The task for the student is to locate the word that is different, say it, and indicate the part (ending) that makes the word different.

## 232. Authors with Endings

Use a deck of sixty cards. Make four cards for each of fifteen root or stem words to be practiced. Place a different key word at the top of each card. Here are examples of the four cards for the stem word *jump*.

| *jump* | *jumps* | *jumped* | *jumping* |
|---|---|---|---|
| jumps | jumped | jumping | jump |
| jumped | jumping | jump | jumps |
| jumping | jump | jumps | jumped |

Here are examples of four cards for the stem word *grow*.

| *grow* | *grows* | *grown* | *growing* |
|---|---|---|---|
| grows | grown | growing | grow |
| grown | growing | grow | grows |
| growing | grow | grows | grown |

Make four cards in this manner for each of the remaining words.

Directions for play: Deal six cards to a player. The players will sort their cards, placing any that have the same root word together. Any player who has four cards with the same root word may make them into a "book" (i.e., a complete set) and lay that book down. The player to the left of the dealer calls for any one of the three words listed below the key word on any card in his or her hand. If another player holds the card containing the called word as a key word, he or she must give the card to the player who called for it. A player continues to call words as long as a card is drawn from another player. A player who fails to get a card must draw from the pack. That ends the turn. The object of the game is to complete as many books as possible. The game may be terminated after a specified time limit and the player with the most books is declared the winner. If all the cards in the pack have been drawn before the game is over, the move goes to the next player on the left without drawing from the pack. This brings the game quickly to a close.

### 233. Word Endings

Print a list of words on the chalkboard. Leave considerable space between the words. Ask the students which words in the list can be correctly changed by adding *s*. Then add *s* in colored chalk to each word correctly indicated. Then do the same for the ending *-er*, and so on. Eventually a word may get crowded with endings:

> walks
>   ed
>   er
>   ing

Rewrite the base by the new endings as needed:

> walks    walker
> walked   walking

### 234. Endings Envelope

Give the student a large card or worksheet containing several sentences in each of which there is an omitted word. The student also has an envelope containing an assortment of words. Each word should be represented in several forms—singular and plural for nouns, comparative and superlative for adjectives and adverbs, and the various tense and number forms for the verbs. The task for the student is to find a correct word for each blank. For example:

> My dog is _____ than Larry's.
> My dog can _____.
> The cat _____ with the ball last night.

Among the possible words will be *big, bigger, biggest; walk, walking, walks; play, playing, played, plays.*

### 235. More Ending Envelopes

Give the child an envelope with word endings in it and a large card or worksheet containing sentences each with a word without its ending. The task for the student is to select the appropriate endings for the unfinished words.

### 236. Missing Word Endings
Prepare sentences or paragraphs in which a number of word endings are omitted. The task for the student is to add endings to each word to complete it correctly. For example:

> The first thing this morning I jump_____ out of bed and look_____ out the window. The ground was cover_____ with snow and the white flake_____ were still com_____ down. I want_____ to go out sleigh rid_____ right away.

### 237. Singular and Plural Chart
On a large sheet of oaktag put pictures of single objects or pairs of groups of objects. Cut slits on the chart to hold a word card under each picture. The task for the student is to match words with pictures.

### 238. Plural to Singular
Make a worksheet containing plural nouns. The student has to write the singular form of each noun. Provide an answer key for self-checking.

### 239. Singular to Plural
Make a worksheet containing singular nouns. The task for the student is to write the plural form of each noun. An answer key makes the activity self-correcting.

### 240. Singular or Plural?
Divide a worksheet into blocks each containing an illustration of an object or objects. In each block, print both the singular and plural form of the name of the object pictured. The student has to indicate which word goes with the picture.

The simplest level of this exercise would have a picture and its noun with the regular singular and plural forms. More difficult levels would include nouns with irregular plural forms and some choices spelled incorrectly.

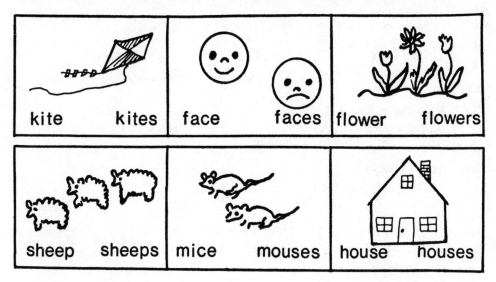

| kite    kites | face    faces | flower    flowers |
| sheep    sheeps | mice    mouses | house    houses |

### 241. Comparative Adjectives

Give the student a worksheet divided into sections. In each section place three pictures representing the three comparative forms of an adjective. Label one picture. The student has to label the other two. For example:

### 242. More Comparative Adjectives

As an alternative to Activity 241, divide the paper into blocks and write the three forms of an adjective in each block. The task for the student is to illustrate each adjective.

NAME_____

1.

fat          fatter          fattest

### 243. Endings in Context

Prepare a worksheet with sentences as follows. The task for the student is to select the correct word for the context.

               big
This tree is bigger than the house.
               biggest


          tall
Larry is taller than his brother Ron.
          tallest

tall
Sandy is the taller of them all.
tallest

thin
Sally is the thinner of the two.
thinnest

fat
Susan is a very fatter girl.
fattest

## 244. Still More Comparative Adjectives

Prepare a worksheet with questions requiring the student to make comparisons in size or intensity. The task for the student is to select the picture that correctly answers the question. For example:

NAME_____

1. Which is fullest?

- - - - - - - - - - - - - - - - - - - -

2. Which is gladdest?

- - - - - - - - - - - - - - - - - - - -

## 245. Adjectives in Context

Have the student complete sentences by inserting the correct form of the missing adjectives.

1. Jerry was the _____ boy on the block.
   small
2. Susan is much _____ than her little sister.
   tall
3. Of the two, my horse jumps _____.
   high

### 246. Compound Words from Phrases

Make worksheets on which the student has to write the compound word suggested by a phrase. The easiest level of this task will have phrases that contain both halves of the compound word, and the student simply has to find the halves and write them as one word. For example:

a stack of hay      =   haystack
yard around a barn  =
a spoon for tea     =

In the more difficult examples, the words making up the compound word may not appear in the definition. For example:

glow from a satellite  =  moonlight (or moonglow)

### 247. Compound Pictures

Make a worksheet on which the student has to write the compound word suggested by two pictures. For example:

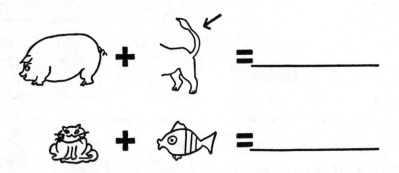

### 248. Compound Word Puzzles

Make a series of cards, each containing a compound word. Cut the cards in half, each with a distinctively jagged line.

Place twenty of the word card pieces in an envelope. The student should assemble them as quickly as possible. If the activity is done by a pupil team, one can assemble the words and the other can keep time and check off each word made and read correctly. Then, the positions can be reversed.

A more difficult version of this activity uses cards that are cut on a straight line, so that the only clues for correct assembly are provided by the words themselves.

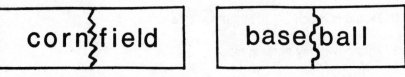

### 249. Making Contractions

Give the students sentences to read in each of which two underlined words can be contracted. The student has to write the contraction for each of the underlined words. For example:

She will come home today.        _____
I did not see the comet last night.        _____
They are having a great party.        _____

These worksheets should be made self-correcting.

### 250. Making More Contractions

Make a worksheet giving the students lists of words that can be contracted and space to write each contraction. These worksheets should have answer keys to make them self-correcting.

### 251. Contractions in Context

Write a short selection in which there could be many contractions. Omit the contractions on the worksheet and have the student write in the missing ones. For example:

It _____ a very nice day. _____ started to go on a picnic, but we _____ get as far as the car before it started to rain. We _____ keep dry no matter what we did.

"_____ go home," said Bill.

"No, _____ going to stay right here under the tree until the rain stops and _____ drier out there," said Nancy.

"Well, _____ going to stay right here under the tree until the rain stops and _____ drier out there," said Nancy.

"Well, _____ going home even if _____ staying here," Bill answered back.

"Go ahead! _____ a long walk. _____ got the car keys."

You can make the task easier by listing the words from which the missing contractions should be made. The task would be even easier if you listed the missing contractions themselves.

### 252. Undoing Contractions

Give the students sentences to read in each of which there is a contraction. The student has to write the words from which each contraction was made. For example:

I just couldn't do it.        _____
Don't sleep on the subway.        _____
Aren't you being too noisy?        _____

These worksheets should be made self-correcting.

## 253. Contraction Tic-Tac-Toe

Make a tic-tac-toe grid with a contraction in each box. The game is played just like regular tic-tac-toe, but before a player may place an X or an O in a box, he or she must read the contraction out loud, say the two words from which it was made, and use the contraction in a sentence.

| | | |
|---|---|---|
| they've | won't | she's |
| you'll | didn't | he'd |
| can't | you're | don't |

## 254. Find Your Way

Mazes are a fun format for practicing certain skills. Here's one for practicing contractions. To get through the maze correctly, the student has to go from one word to another in the order that the words make up the listed contractions. Of course, a mistake adds up to a wrong turn. You can design mazes like this for a number of different skills.

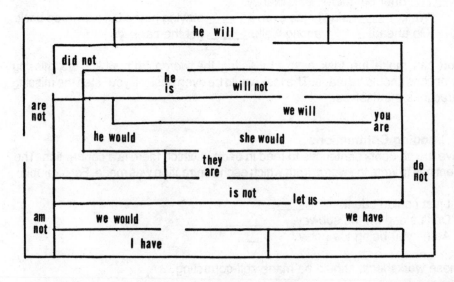

### 255. More Undoing Contractions

Make a worksheet giving the students lists of contractions and space next to each to write the words from which the contractions were made. Be sure to provide an answer key to make the worksheet self-correcting.


## EASY THINGS TO READ

There are many sources of easy things for students to read. One source is the students themselves. They can dictate and later write their own material. The graded word list beginning on page 156 is arranged to facilitate your own writing of easy-to-read selections. Numerous published materials are listed in Section Five of *Reading Aids,* beginning on page 257.

The suggestions presented here by no means exhaust the possibilities. However, they are a start. Some comprehension exercises are provided in this section. In addition, a number of the comprehension activities described in Section Four, Advanced Reading Skills, can be prepared using easier materials.


## Objectives for Easy Things to Read

The overall objective for the following activities is:

**BR-11.** Given an appropriate (in content and level) selection to read, the learner will read it and demonstrate comprehension of the selection as directed.

In this section of *Reading Aids,* there are numerous activities for the following specific objectives:

**BR-12.** After reading a direction, the learner will perform the specified task as directed.

**BR-13.** Given several pictures and a phrase or sentence to read, the learner will indicate which picture best matches what has been read.


### 256. Word List for Easy-to-Read Things

The following graded word list is arranged by parts of speech to facilitate writing easy-to-read things. The words on the list were collected from a number of sources and reflect the controlled vocabularies now in use in many beginning reading materials.

At first glance, a few of the words on the list may appear to be located incorrectly. Look again. Each of the words can be used as the part of speech listed. For example, *go* is most often a verb, but it can be a noun too: "Have a go at it!"

## Graded Word List

| Level | Nouns | Pronouns | Adjectives | Verbs | Adverbs | Connectives |
|---|---|---|---|---|---|---|
| **Pre-primer** | can<br>go<br>will | all<br>he<br>his<br>I<br>it<br>me<br>one<br>she<br>that<br>them<br>they<br>we<br>what<br>which<br>you | a<br>all<br>big<br>his<br>little<br>my<br>one<br>that<br>the<br>what<br>which | are<br>can<br>do<br>go<br>have<br>is<br>see<br>was<br>went<br>will | all<br>not<br>out<br>there<br>up | about<br>and<br>at<br>for<br>in<br>of<br>on<br>to<br>up<br>with |
| **Low first grade** | back<br>boy<br>call<br>day<br>down<br>help<br>house<br>make<br>man<br>mean<br>play<br>saw<br>say<br>take<br>time<br>two<br>water<br>well | any<br>him<br>its<br>many<br>this<br>us<br>who | an<br>any<br>better<br>good<br>her<br>just<br>long<br>many<br>mean<br>no<br>old<br>over<br>some<br>this<br>two<br>your | back<br>be<br>call<br>came<br>come<br>could<br>did<br>get<br>give<br>had<br>help<br>house<br>let's<br>(v. + pron.)<br>like<br>long<br>looked<br>made<br>make<br>man<br>mean<br>must<br>play<br>please<br>put<br>ran<br>running<br>said<br>saw<br>say<br>take<br>tell<br>thank<br>time<br>wanted<br>water<br>well<br>were<br>would | again<br>away<br>back<br>better<br>here<br>how<br>just<br>now<br>over<br>so<br>then<br>too<br>well<br>when<br>where<br>why<br>(inter.) | as<br>but<br>by<br>down<br>from<br>into<br>like<br>over<br>so<br>then<br>when<br>where |

| Level | Nouns | Pronouns | Adjectives | Verbs | Adverbs | Connectives |
|---|---|---|---|---|---|---|
| **High first grade** | above, bear, bed, bird, black, blue, book, brown, car, catch, chair, children, cover, cut, dog, door, eye, fast, feel, find, fine, first, four, friends, girl, gray, guess, half, hand, head, hope, keep, know, last, laugh, letter, love, matter, meet, might, milk, more, morning, mother, near, night, nothing, oh (interj.), open, pay, present, rabbit, school, sleep, still, thing(s), three, tree, try, use, vat, walk, way, white, wish, work, year, yes (interj.), young | another, both, other, such | another, best, black, blue, both, brown, even, fast, fine, first, four, gray, half, hard, last, live, more, most, mother, Mr., near, new, open, other, same, still, such, sure, their, three, very, white, young | asked, bear, bed, been, black, blue, book, brown, catch, chair, close, cover, cut, does, dog, eat, even, eye, fast, feel, find, fine, found, gave, got, guess, hand, has, head, hear, heard, hope, keep, know, last, laugh, letter, live, love, matter, meet, might, milk, mother, named, open, pay, present, read, school, seem, send, sleep, still, stopped, think, took, tree, tried, try, use, work, write | alone, along, before, best, close, even, far, fast, first, gray, last, more, most, much, never, off, once, soon, still, sure, under, until, very, walk, wish, without | above, after, against, before, between, if, near, or, under, without |

| Level | Nouns | | | Pronouns | Adjectives | Verbs | | Adverbs | Connectives |
|---|---|---|---|---|---|---|---|---|---|
| Low second grade | animal | great | room | each | afraid | ate | miss | ago | around |
| | baby | green | round | our | ago | baby | need | almost | because |
| | bad | high | second | those | bad | ball | paper | always | either |
| | ball | hold | set | | clean | began | part | around | than |
| | basket | home | show | | cold | being | pass | bad | till |
| | being | hundred | sing | | each | believe | people | each | upon |
| | birthday | land | six | | either | boat | place | early | yet |
| | boat | lay | something | | enough | bring | point | enough | |
| | buy | light | stand | | evening | buy | pull | fair | |
| | care | line | street | | every | care | reach | high | |
| | change | mind | summer | | fair | carry | reason | late | |
| | city | miss | table | | fall | change | remember | only | |
| | cold | month | talk | | few | clean | rest | today | |
| | country | need | ten | | glad | done | right | tougher | |
| | dinner | paper | till | | great | egg | roll | yet | |
| | egg | part | today | | green | end | room | | |
| | end | pass | town | | happy | evening | sat | | |
| | enough | people | train | | high | fall | second | | |
| | evening | place | turn | | late | farm | set | | |
| | fair | point | wait | | light | father | show | | |
| | fall | pull | week | | only | fire | sing | | |
| | farm | reach | whole | | our | going | stand | | |
| | father | reason | word | | right | green | started | | |
| | few | rest | yellow | | round | hold | summer | | |
| | fire | right | | | second | kept | table | | |
| | going | roll | | | several | land | talk | | |
| | | | | | short | lay | till | | |
| | | | | | six | learn | train | | |
| | | | | | ten | light | turn | | |
| | | | | | those | line | wait | | |
| | | | | | true | mind | | | |
| | | | | | whole | | | | |
| | | | | | yellow | | | | |

| Level | Nouns | | | Pronouns | Adjectives | | Verbs | | | Adverbs | Connectives |
|---|---|---|---|---|---|---|---|---|---|---|---|
| High | anything | field | piece | these | beautiful | strong | arm | garden | sit | already | behind |
| second | arm | fill | pig | | bright | these | bag | gone | snow | also | through |
| grade | bag | fish | poor | | busy | third | bit | ground | speak | ever | while |
| | barn | five | quiet | | coming | warm | blow | grow | stay | often | |
| | behind | floor | rain | | company | watch | board | held | stone | sometimes | |
| | bell | flower | ride | | cry | wood | box | hide | suppose | tomorrow | |
| | bit | fly | ring | | dark | | bread | hill | surprise | | |
| | blow | fun | road | | different | | cap | hit | thought | | |
| | board | game | shake | | fell | | coat | hole | told | | |
| | box | garden | shoe | | five | | coming | jumped | top | | |
| | bread | grass | side | | floor | | cost | knew | warm | | |
| | brother | ground | sister | | flower | | course | leave | watch | | |
| | cap | hill | snow | | fly | | cry | left | while | | |
| | child | hide | song | | full | | dance | leg | win | | |
| | coat | hit | stay | | game | | doll | lost | wind | | |
| | company | hole | stone | | grass | | don't | move | winter | | |
| | cost | horse | story | | hot | | draw | noise | | | |
| | course | kind | sun | | hungry | | dress | number | | | |
| | cry | kitty | surprise | | kind | | drink | picture | | | |
| | dance | leave | third | | large | | duck | piece | | | |
| | dark | left | thought | | left | | except | quiet | | | |
| | doll | leg | tomorrow | | lost | | face | rain | | | |
| | draw | lost | top | | minute | | feed | ready | | | |
| | dress | lot | watch | | Mrs. | | fell | ride | | | |
| | drink | men | wind | | poor | | field | ring | | | |
| | duck | minute | window | | pretty | | fill | seen | | | |
| | ear | money | winter | | quiet | | fish | sell | | | |
| | everything | move | woman | | ready | | floor | shake | | | |
| | face | noise | wood | | side | | flower | shall | | | |
| | feed | number | yard | | small | | fly | shoe | | | |
| | feet | party | | | | | | should | | | |
| | fell | picture | | | | | | side | | | |

| Level | Nouns | | | Pronouns | Adjectives | Verbs | | Adverbs | Connectives |
|---|---|---|---|---|---|---|---|---|---|
| **Low third grade** | address | fix | sea | mine | air | address | leg | afternoon | across |
| | afternoon | foot | seven | myself | clear | air | mail | east | except |
| | air | front | ship | whose | cross | beg | mark | else | instead |
| | body | hair | sign | yourself | dead | begin | mine | low | past |
| | break | hat | silk | | deep | break | nest | next | though |
| | build | heart | sound | | eight | brought | note | past | whether |
| | cake | lady | south | | else | build | ought | quite | |
| | card | lead | spring | | family | cake | page | rather | |
| | case | leg | step | | front | can't | plant | south | |
| | cause | mail | stick | | heavy | card | print | though | |
| | Christmas | mark | store | | low | case | save | west | |
| | class | mile | suit | | next | cause | ship | yesterday | |
| | color | mine | sweet | | nice | class | sick | | |
| | copy | music | thousand | | quick | clear | sign | | |
| | cross | next | touch | | real | color | sold | | |
| | dead | note | visit | | seven | copy | sound | | |
| | deep | page | wall | | sick | cross | spring | | |
| | die | past | war | | silk | didn't | step | | |
| | drive | plant | wash | | sold | die | store | | |
| | cast | print | weather | | spring | dig | suit | | |
| | eight | quick | west | | sweet | drive | teach | | |
| | family | real | window | | thousand | dropped | touch | | |
| | felt | river | wonder | | wide | except | visit | | |
| | finish | robin | wrong | | wrong | felt | wall | | |
| | fit | Santa Claus | yesterday | | | finish | war | | |
| | | | | | | fit | wash | | |
| | | | | | | fix | wear | | |
| | | | | | | foot | weather | | |
| | | | | | | forgot | wonder | | |
| | | | | | | front | wrong | | |
| | | | | | | goes | wrote | | |
| | | | | | | lead | | | |

| Level | Nouns | | | | Pronouns | Adjectives | |
|---|---|---|---|---|---|---|---|
| **High third grade** | act | farmer | middle | shoot | anybody | able | least |
| | amount | fight | mistake | shot | everybody | alike | nine |
| | apple | fold | mix | sir | nobody | alive | paid |
| | bank | food | mountain | size | whom | all right | possible |
| | beat | fruit | news | skin | | angry | rich |
| | bill | glass | nine | slip | | awful | sad |
| | bother | gold | nobody | smoke | | bottom | safe |
| | bottom | grade | north | son | | broken | Saturday |
| | bridge | handle | nose | spoil | | business | slow |
| | brush | hang | office | stamp | | certain | soft |
| | burn | horn | order | star | | church | sorry |
| | business | hour | paint | state | | cloth | steel |
| | button | hunt | pencil | station | | cool | strange |
| | candy | hurry | person | steel | | decided | straight |
| | cent | hurt | pick | stitch | | dry | struck |
| | chicken | idea | plan | study | | fat | Sunday |
| | church | inside | pound | Sunday | | free | swimming |
| | climb | iron | practice | supper | | funny | tonight |
| | cloth | I'm | price | swim | | glass | understood |
| | clothes | it's | push | teeth | | gold | wet |
| | college | kick | rich | throw | | horn | written |
| | cook | kill | rock | tie | | interesting | |
| | cool | knock | rubber | tire | | | |
| | corn | least | rule | tonight | | | |
| | count | lie | safe | toy | | | |
| | cow | life | sail | trade | | | |
| | cup | lift | sale | trip | | | |
| | doctor | likes | Saturday | trouble | | | |
| | dollar | measure | seat | wagon | | | |
| | dry | meet | seed | wet | | | |
| | excuse | | sheep | wrap | | | |
| | fat | | shine | | | | |

| Level | Verbs | | | | Adverbs | Connectives |
|---|---|---|---|---|---|---|
| High third grade | absent | fed | lose | slow | ahead | although |
| | act | fight | measure | smoke | apart | among |
| | add | finger | meet | spend | asleep | apart |
| | amount | fold | mix | spoil | certain | during |
| | bank | follow | nose | stamp | hardly | inside |
| | beat | forget | order | star | inside | nor |
| | belong | free | paid | state | north | since |
| | bill | glass | paint | station | really | |
| | born | grade | pencil | steel | sad | |
| | bother | grew | pick | stitch | since | |
| | bottom | handle | plan | struck | sorry | |
| | bridge | hang | pound | study | | |
| | brought | happened | pour | swim | | |
| | brush | haven't | practice | swimming | | |
| | burn | horn | price | take | | |
| | button | hunt | push | threw | | |
| | candy | hurry | received | throw | | |
| | caught | hurt | rock | tie | | |
| | choose | I'm | rule | tire | | |
| | climb | interesting | sail | toy | | |
| | cook | iron | seat | trade | | |
| | cool | it's | seed | trip | | |
| | corn | kick | sew | trouble | | |
| | count | kill | shine | understood | | |
| | cup | knock | shoot | weigh | | |
| | decided | least | shot | wet | | |
| | doctor | lie | shut | won't | | |
| | doesn't | lift | size | wouldn't | | |
| | dry | likes | skin | wrap | | |
| | excuse | listen | slip | written | | |

| Level | Nouns | Pronouns | Adjectives | Verbs | Adverbs | Connectives |
|---|---|---|---|---|---|---|
| **Above third grade** | cousin<br>February<br>goodbye<br>Halloween<br>January<br>October<br>squirrel<br>stationery<br>Thanksgiving<br>writing | | February<br>January<br>October<br>teacher's<br>Thanksgiving. | getting<br>suppose<br>writing | sometimes | |

Reprinted, with permission, from Cohen, S. Alan, *Teach Them All to Read: Theory, Methods, and Materials for Teaching the Disadvantaged.* New York: Random House, 1969.

### 257. Playing Postal Service

Have the students write short letters or notes and send them to each other addressed by name and perhaps the location of the receiver's desk. One student can be designated to run the classroom postal service for the day and can deliver the letters. A student who wishes to do so can read his or her letter to the class.

### 258. Playing Author

Some students like to dictate or write stories for others to read. This should be encouraged but not forced. Students can illustrate their work and make a cover for it. The cover should be like a commercial book jacket—i.e., it should have all the necessary information on it and be attractive as well.

### 259. Consonant Configurations

To demonstrate to the students the importance and usefulness of the consonants, make up sentences that have all their consonants, but omit the vowels. See if the students can read these sentences correctly. For an easy version of this task, include picture clues. For a more difficult task, use only the text. Here are some sample sentences:

NAME_____

G_ j_mp _n th_ l_k_!

Th_ b_g br_wn h_rs_
j_mp_d _v_r th_ f_nc_.

Th_ thr__ l_ttl_ k_tt_ns
l_st th__r m_tt_ns.

## 260. Phrase Cards

The use of phrase cards can accustom the students to avoid word-by-word reading. Short easy phrases, such as *all day, up the wall, I ran,* should be used at first. When these present no difficulty and can be read instantly at sight, longer and more complicated phrases should be introduced. A number of little phrase cards may be put together to construct a story.

Each student can keep a personal envelope of phrases made from words in his or her word bank.

## 261. Reading Phrases

Place phrase cards along the chalkboard ledge. Read one aloud and call upon two students to run to the board and select the phrase card that was read. The first student to get to the correct card keeps it. This is a rainy day and Friday afternoon activity.

## 262. Matching Phrases

Prepare duplicate sets of phrase cards (9″ × 12″ pieces of oaktag cut in half lengthwise will do nicely). Give each student a card with a phrase written on it. Place the duplicate cards around the chalkboard ledge. The student finds the phrase on the ledge that matches his or her phrase card and stands in front of the place where that phrase appears. When all the students have found their matching phrases, each reads the card aloud.

## 263. Emphasizing Phrases

Practice in reading by phrases rather than word by word can be facilitated by marking the appropriate groups of words in some way. This will give the student additional cues as to which words go together. The goal, of course, is for the student to become a fluent enough reader so that these cues are no longer necessary.

Here are three different ways to mark off the words to be read in phrase units.

| | | |
|---|---|---|
| The sly fox | ran quickly | into the woods. |
| The sly fox / | ran quickly / | into the woods. |
| The sly fox | ran quickly | into the woods. |

## 264. Easy Scrambled Sentences

Write jumbled sentences on cards or on the board. A student has to reassemble the sentences and write them correctly. Pick the sentences carefully so they are at an appropriate level for the student who will try to read them. Here are some relatively easy ones:

1. The the into road ran chicken silly.
2. kitten gray up tree the ran A.
3. Baby down from seat her slid.
4. I swimming don't in water cold like to go.
5. over walls Horses jump can stone.

### 265. The Big Book

Make the cover of a big book from bristol board. Use lighter weight oaktag or construction paper for the pages. Hold them together with chicken rings, loose-leaf rings, or string. On the left side of each set of facing pages, paste two pictures one above the other. On the right side cut slits so that two small strips of oaktag can be inserted opposite the pictures. On strips of oaktag, cut to fit in the slits on the right-hand pages, write sentences corresponding to the picture on all the left-hand pages.

Give the student the sentences and the book. The task is to place each sentence in its correct place. This is an excellent activity for use by pupil teams.

The sentence slips can be stored in an envelope pasted inside the front cover of the book.

| The horse is jumping. | The boy is wet. |
| The horse is wet. | The boy is a horse. |

## 266. Sentences to Read

Encourage the students to make comments on books they have read, the news of the day, activities they enjoy, or to compose original mini-stories. Print these student-created sentences on cards for each "author" to read. The cards may be stored in an envelope or illustrated and made into a book.

## 267. Sentence Mix-Ups

Students can get practice understanding the correct placement of words in sentences by unscrambling sentences presented in mixed-up order.

Here's a game for two or three students. Place a card with the following mixed-up sentences on a table where all the players can see it.

1. bird did you the fly see
2. needed many to nails Noah his ark build
3. many work hands make light
4. clowns circus made laugh five us
5. horse white over the jumped fence the
6. night cold this going be is very to a
7. flag big that did she sew really
8. my throw sweater to down me
9. don't the dish floor the on drop
10. the pony little wouldn't stay the in field

At a signal, the players try to write each sentence correctly on a piece of paper. The first one to finish all the sentences correctly is the winner. If no one has them all right, the one with the highest number wins. Some of the sentences can be unscrambled in more than one way. Any version that makes sense is acceptable.

## 268. Making Sentences

Prepare small cards with phrases on them. File each card in one of three envelopes—subject, verb, object. Here are some possible phrases for the cards:

| Subject | Object | Verb |
|---------|--------|------|
| the horse | his partner | knocked out |
| a boxer | her friend | climbed over |
| four roses | the radio | began to spread |
| a mountain | a friend | appeared to be |
| a puppy | a penny | ran off with |
| the carrots | the floor | boiled over |
| a dentist | the television set | started to work on |
| six cats | the kitchen floor | danced around |
| a gremlin | his sister | almost disappointed |
| the car | two victims | ran over |

The first student selects a card from each of the three envelopes, makes a sentence from the phrases, and reads it out loud. Each student does this in turn. Note that subject and object phrases can often be interchanged. The resulting sentences will be quite entertaining.

Students will enjoy making their own cards to file in the envelopes.

### 269. Vowel-Less Messages

Try writing sentences in which all the vowels have been omitted. See how quickly the students can read them. Let students write letters to each other in this fashion. For example:

D--r J-hn,
M--t m- -ft-r sch--l t-d-y,
s- w- c-n pl-y f--tb-ll -n th- p-rk.

P-t-r

M-ry:
-t's y--r t-rn t- p-ss th- m-lk
-nd c--k--s. D-n't f-rg-t th-
n-pk-ns.

Ms. Gr--n

### 270. Bulletin Board

Place very short bulletins, each containing a picture and one or two words or phrases about the picture, on a bulletin board. Change daily.

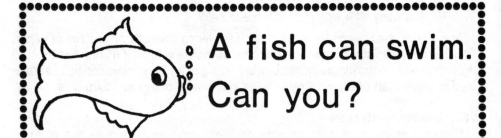

A fish can swim. Can you?

### 271. The News Corner

Set aside a space on a bulletin board to be used as a news corner. Encourage the students to consult it frequently. Bulletins should be posted periodically during the day. The news corner may be used for announcements (e.g., "We are going on a trip to the zoo next Monday," or "Bring your milk money tomorrow") or for news pertaining to the students (e.g., "Scarlett has a new baby sister," or "Today is Kim's birthday").

### 272. Cast of Characters Wall Chart

Make a large wall chart with pictures of all the characters in a story being used in the classroom. Label each of the pictures so that the students will come to recognize the names at sight.

These charts should be made on oaktag for durability. A chart not in use can then be stored until the next time a student or group of students will be working on the corresponding story.

## 273. Experience Charts

Whenever the opportunity arises, students can be encouraged to dictate a group story to be displayed on an experience chart. These stories can later be bound into a class book if desired.

The experience chart story is an excellent tool for getting young children to acquire some basic sight vocabulary. One effective technique involves identifying each child's contribution by means of his or her name and using quotation marks. For example:

---

### We Went to the Zoo Today

Johnny said, "I think the hippo is very big and ugly."
Susan said, "I cried when the elephant took my peanuts."
Tammy said, "The zoo smells funny."
Roger said, "Why do giraffes have such long necks?"
Alan said, "Monkeys are just like people."
Dick said, "I like the zoo."
Jane said, "I like the zoo too."

---

## 274. Special Vocabulary Book

If a student is interested in a special kind of story, such as animal stories, adventure stories, or ghost stories, try having the student collect words and phrases that are essential in reading that particular kind of material. These words may be listed in a special personal dictionary and illustrated if desired.

## 275. Riddles

Have the children find or make up riddles to read aloud. The others try to guess the answer to the riddles. These riddles can range from the simple and direct "What am I?" types to the absolutely ridiculous, depending on the taste and sense of humor of the student. An excellent easy-to-read source of the latter is Bennett Cerf's *Book of Riddles,* a Random House Beginner Book.

Some sample riddles:

I am small. My fur is dark gray. I have a long bushy tail. I live in a tree and eat nuts. I can give your finger a nasty bite if you get too close. What am I? (a squirrel)

Why did the silly child throw the clock out the window? (to see time fly)

What is the difference between an elephant and a blueberry? (an elephant is gray)
What time is it when an elephant sits down to rest on a fence? (time to get a new fence)

### 276. Picking a Book by Hand

Children should be encouraged to select the books they want to read. Most students are able to pick books of suitable difficulty level, although some may need more guidance than others. Here is a device that has been used for years for getting the right book to the right child. Instruct the student as follows:

1. Pick a book you want to read.
2. Open it to a page near the middle.
3. Read it to yourself.
4. If you get to a word you don't know, put a finger on it.
5. If you get to another word you don't know, put a finger on that too.
6. If you use up all the fingers and the thumb on one hand, the book might be too hard.
7. Open to a new page. Try again. If it's still too hard, maybe you want to get another book.
8. If it's just right, enjoy it!

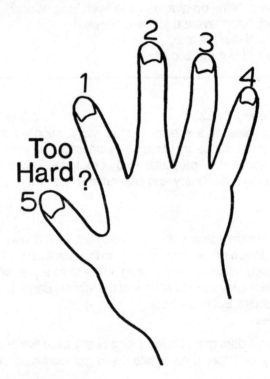

### 277. Personal Story Book

Have the student dictate or write a story, which should then be typed using a typewriter with large type. The student then reads his or her own story. Such material may be collected, illustrated, and bound into a book.

Words from each story should be entered in the student's own Word Bank. For a description of how to use the Word Bank, see page 108.

## 278. Jingle Booklet

The student writes his or her own jingle booklet to illustrate word families. For example:

| | |
|---|---|
| I play | I'll bake |
| All day | A cake |
| In the hay. | To take |
| All day | To the lake |
| I play. | When I wake. |

Your students will probably be able to do a much more interesting job on jingles than we did.

## 279. Hunting for the Action

A small group of students, all of whom have read the same story, work together on this activity. One student acts out silently a part of the story. The others look for the exact lines in the story that tell the part being dramatized. The first one who finds it may read it aloud if he or she wishes.

## 280. Guessing Pictures

Give each student a phrase card and the directions to draw a picture that corresponds to what the card says. When a student finishes illustrating the card, the picture should be held up for the others to see. The other students have to guess what the phrase card said. If no one can guess correctly, the student then reads the phrase card to the class. Here are some examples of the type of phrases you could put on the cards:

| | |
|---|---|
| Three big cats. | A rabbit and a hat. |
| A big green tree | Clouds in a sky. |
| A small red house. | A horse and wagon. |
| A car on a road. | Four balloons on strings. |
| A cat and a mouse. | A doll on the table. |

The activity should be timed. Permit no more than five minutes or so for a student to illustrate a phrase. In this way, a student will be able to illustrate more than one phrase. You will also avoid a situation in which the more painstaking students appear to be preparing their sketches for exhibition in the local museum.

## 281. Answering with Phrases

Short phrases from a story read in class may be placed along the chalkboard ledge. Ask a question and have a student select the phrase card that answers the question. For example, in answer to the question "Where did.the naughty little dog hide?" the child would select the card that said *under the bed.*

### 282. Prepositional Phrases

To give practice in reading and understanding prepositional phrases, try an exercise that has a picture and then a description of what's going on. The student has to pick the correct one of two prepositional phrases to complete the description. For example:

NAME _____

The turtle is

under the bird.
on top of the bird.

He has a smile

on his face.
above his face.

The doll is

into the table.
on the table.

The fish is

on the hook.
below the hook.

### 283. Tag

Here is another rainy day game. Write the directions for this game on the chalkboard. Don't discuss them. The students have to read the directions and play the game.

1. Everybody stand.
2. Move all furniture to the sides of the room.
3. Walk to the empty space and make a circle.
4. Hold hands.
5. The student tapped by the teacher is "It."
6. "It" runs around the outside of the circle.
7. "It" taps someone else.
8. The person tapped tries to catch "It" before "It" reaches the hole in the circle.
9. If "It" runs around and reaches the hole in the circle safely, then the person tapped becomes "It."

You can, of course, create personal variations of this activity that do not require furniture moving. The important thing to remember is that the purpose of it all is to have the students read the directions and follow them.

## 284. Following Directions in Color
Give the student a picture with short and precise directions to read and to follow.
For example:

NAME_____

Color the girl's dress red.　　Color the grass green.
Make her hair black.　　Draw a line from the boy to the duck.
Put an X on the little duck.　　Circle the rabbit.
Color the sky blue.

## 285. Following Directions
Simple exercises for following directions can be made using words and pictures.
These worksheets should be prepared to be self-correcting, either with acetate
overlays or with the answers on the back for lapboard use. A sample worksheet:

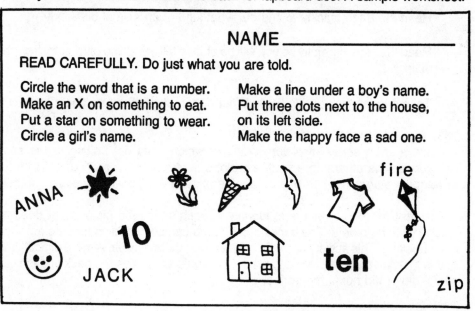

NAME_____

READ CAREFULLY. Do just what you are told.

Circle the word that is a number.　　Make a line under a boy's name.
Make an X on something to eat.　　Put three dots next to the house,
Put a star on something to wear.　　on its left side.
Circle a girl's name.　　Make the happy face a sad one.

ANNA

fire

10

JACK

ten

zip

### 286.  Did You Follow?

Another kind of following directions exercise gives the directions and then a sample of these directions carried out. The task for the student is to indicate whether or not the directions were accurately followed. For example:

NAME_____

Put a circle around the cone.
Draw a box around the turtle.

Is this right?     YES    NO

On the above worksheet, the directions for the first item were not carried out correctly. The cone has a box around it, not a circle. The turtle is underlined instead of boxed. Students seem to enjoy checking up on the accuracy with which others have followed directions.

### 287.  Reading for a Purpose

Even beginning readers can and should be encouraged to read differently for different purposes. For example:

Read the page quickly to find out what kind of an animal bit Sandy.

**or**

Read the story carefully so you will be able to tell me all the different things that Julie did.

**or**

Take a quick look at this book. What do you think it will be about?

### 288.  Categorizing Pictures

Place a short series of pictures, one of which does not belong in the same category as the others, in a small envelope. Make a number (20 or so) of these envelopes. Magazines are a good source of pictures. Comic strips are another.

The task for the student is to identify in each series the picture that does not belong with the others. The backs of the cards can be coded so that the activity is self-checking. This activity can vary from easy to quite difficult. A more difficult level of this task, for students who can read well, would explain on the back of each card why it did or did not fit the series.

### 289. Pictures to Sentences

Make a worksheet that has for each item a picture of an object, at the left of the page, and at the right of the picture three sentences using words of similar appearance. The task for the student is to pick the sentence that goes with each picture.

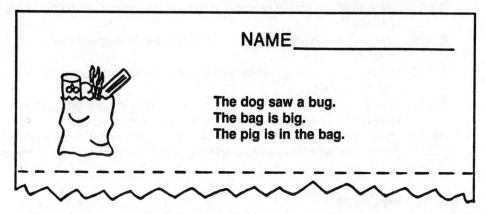

NAME_____

The dog saw a bug.
The bag is big.
The pig is in the bag.

### 290. Answering Questions

Give the students phrase cards based on a story they have read. On the board write a question that can be answered by one of the phrase cards. The student with the phrase card that answers the question holds it up and reads both the question and the answer aloud. The answer should be written on the board before going on to the next question. For example:

Where did the rabbit run? (into the garden)
Where were the brown leaves? (in the yard)
Where was the little dog? (under the tree)

### 291. Draw the Answer

Divide a worksheet or large paper into sections. Write a question at the top of each section. The student has to illustrate an acceptable answeer to each question.

### 292. Find the Question

Divide the worksheet as in Activity 291. You provide the illustrations and the student has to come up with the questions.

# REMEDIATION OF SPECIFIC DIFFICULTIES

The activities in this section are designed to aid the learner in overcoming certain reading difficulties that commonly occur. Practice on some of these activities may help prevent the beginning reader from developing the problems these exercises were designed to correct.

Most of the exercises were suggested with the hard-to-teach reader in mind. The activities for developing skills in use of context to aid word recognition and comprehension are extremely important for all readers.

Teachers of learning disabled students may find a number of these exercises to be useful devices. However, in the case of a severely disabled reader, none of these activities are intended to be a substitute for a structured program designed to assist students in need of clinical help.*

**BR-14.** Given easily reversed or inverted letters, the learner will identify each correctly.

**BR-15.** Given easily reversed or confused words, the learner will identify each correctly.

**BR-16.** Given a reading task, the learner will work from left to right and from top to bottom on the page.

**BR-17.** Given material (appropriate in content and level) to read, the learner will read (orally or silently) without omitting words or phrases.

**BR-18.** Given material (appropriate in content and level) to read, the learner will be able to read silently without pointing to the words, if he or she chooses to do so.

### 293. Tracing Letters

Have the learner trace a word with which he or she has been having difficulty. Write the word in fairly large letters. The student should trace each letter in order while saying its sound (not its name). The student should make the sound last as long as it takes to trace the letter, thus coming out even with both sound and tracing. Encourage rapid and smooth blending of sounds.

### 294. Transparent Letters

Print the letter *b* on a regular index card and the letter *d* on a clear acetate sheet the same size. Place the acetate on top of the card. Have the student compare the *b* and the *d* and note the difference. The same types of comparisons can be made for other visually similar letters such as *p* and *q*.

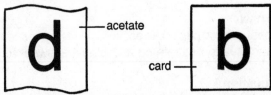

*For well-structured approaches to use with severely disabled readers, try *Remedial Techniques in the Basic School Subjects,* by Grace Fernald, McGraw-Hill, 1942 or *Remedial Training for Children with Specific Disabilities in Reading, Spelling, and Penmanship,* by Anna Gillingham and B. Stillman, Sackett and Williams, 1940.

## 295. Problem Letter Pictures

Use pictures that illustrate words beginning with difficult letters such as *b, p,* and *d.* Locate the picture alongside the round part of the letter. For example, put a picture of a boat next to the lower part of the *b* and to the right. Try a picture of a pig next to the upper part of the letter *p.* Try a duck or a dog next to the lower left part of the letter *d.* In each case, the picture accents the direction of the rounded part of the letter.

## 296. Letter Riddles

For students still having trouble with the names of commonly confused letters, refer back to the letter stories in Activity 53. Then try riddles such as the following.

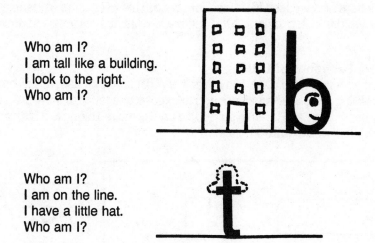

Who am I?
I am tall like a building.
I look to the right.
Who am I?

Who am I?
I am on the line.
I have a little hat.
Who am I?

## 297. Confused Letters in Sentence

Write sentences containing words with letters often confused to give practice in noting letter differences.

The boat was full of ducks.
Put Paddy down quickly.
Eddy took a bit of a dip in the middle of the pond.

### 298. Tricky Letters

Sometimes a student will have to rely on a trick to help in remembering the difference between letters commonly confused. Help the student to develop whatever device works.

For example, consider a child who confuses *b* and *d* but is able to spell the word *bed* right every time, "b-e-d." Have that child write the word so it "looks like a bed"—making sure the loops face in, and the posts are at the ends. This is a sure way to remember the difference between *b* and *d*; all that the student has to do is write *bed* to look like a bed.

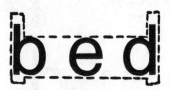

Another way to remember which one is the small *b* and which one is the *d* is to note that the small *b* is just like the capital *B* without the top loop.

### 299. Sequence of Letters

Hold up a word card covered with a marker. Move the marker slowly to the right so that the letters are exposed in proper sequence. This will aid the student in moving along the word from left to right. (One can't read what has not yet been uncovered.)

### 300. More Sequence of Letters

Hold up a printed word card. Slide over it another card that has a small opening in it. The opening should be small enough to expose one letter of the word at a time. When all the letters have been exposed, the card is moved along to a larger opening that shows the whole word at once.

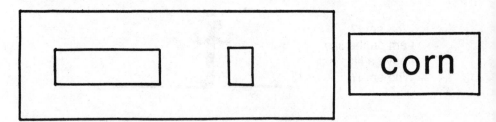

### 301. Distinguishing Features of Letters and Words

In teaching letters, show variation in length, number, and location of ascending and descending lines. Encourage the student to find individual characteristics within a word in its physical appearance to aid in distinguishing it from other words of similar appearance.

## 302. p, b, d, q Dominoes

A variation of dominoes can be used as a visual discrimination exercise for students with p, b, d, q reversal and inversion problems. Make a special set of dominoes, each containing two of the problem letters. Make a starter card containing all four of the letters. Four students play. The first student draws a domino from the pool and tries to match it to the starter card letter directly facing himself or herself. If no match can be made, the student keeps the domino and draws another, and another, until the letter can be matched exactly. Then the next student goes. Each student can build only on the column directly facing him or her. The first student to get rid of all the dominoes in hand is the winner. If no one uses up all the dominoes in hand, then the one with the fewest remaining when the pool is gone is the winner.

## 303. Left-Right

Give the student a large piece of drawing paper with the left half and the right half labeled. Provide scissors and a pile of old magazines. The task for the student is to find things facing to the left and to paste them on the side of the paper labeled *left*. Things facing right are pasted on the half of the paper labeled *right*. A partially completed page is shown below.

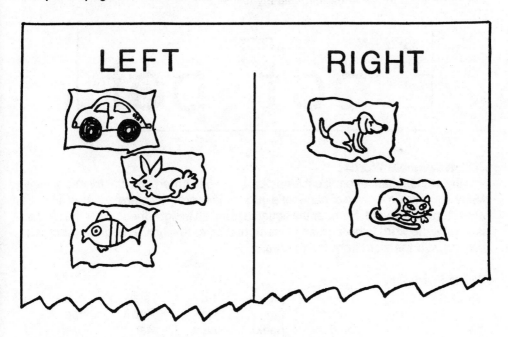

## 304. Transparent Words

Print a word on a regular index card, and on a piece of clear acetate print a word with which it is commonly confused. Place the acetate on top of the card. Have the student note where the two words differ.

### 305. More Transparent Words

On transparent paper or acetate print a word which is causing trouble. Have the student find the word by placing the acetate over words in a known sentence until he or she comes to the word that exactly coincides with the one on the transparent paper. For example, if the student confuses the words *boy* and *big,* write the word *big* on acetate. Have the student locate the word *big* in several sentences, the first few of which do not contain the word *boy.*

The house is big.
My cat is big.
The big dog is brown.
The boy is big.
THe boy has a big cat.
The big boy has a big dog.

### 306. Stop and Go

Frequently reversed words should be printed with the first letter in green and the last in red. Tell the student to obey the lights. Start on green and stop on red. Print the same word in black ink immediately following.

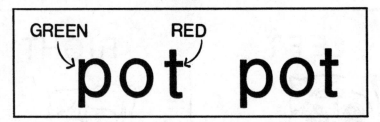

### 307. Reversible Words

If the student can recognize the numbers 1 to 5 in order, you can try this activity. Make squares on a piece of paper or a large index card—as many squares as there are letters in the word. Number the squares from left to right. the task for the student is to write the word to be learned in order, one letter to a box. This gives practice in dealing with the word from left to right.

**Words Frequently Reversed**

| | | | | | | |
|---|---|---|---|---|---|---|
| am | lap | no | pal | rat | star | ton |
| bad | ma | north | pat | raw | tap | top |
| dab | nap | now | peek | saw | tar | war |
| deer | net | on | pot | spot | team | was |

**Words Partially Reversed**

| | | | | | | |
|---|---|---|---|---|---|---|
| even | from | felt | spilt | stop | tried | trial |
| never | form | left | split | spot | tired | trail |

## 308. Tracing Words

Select a word with which the child is having difficulty. Write the word in cursive or manuscript letters on half of an 8½" × 11" sheet of paper. Pronounce the word for the child and have it repeated several times to make sure the child is saying it correctly. Then the child traces the word with a finger while saying it out loud, syllable by syllable. The child then writes the word without copy, once again saying it syllable by syllable. The syllables should be said as they are written. The word is traced until it can be written twice correctly without consulting the original. The word then should be presented to the child in printed (typed) form and subsequently be used in context. Note that what the child says while tracing and writing is each *syllable* of the word, not the letter names or individual letter sounds.

If this technique seems useful to you, you should read Grace Fernald's *Remedial Techniques in the Basic School Subjects* (New York: McGraw Hill, 1943).

## 309. Picture Cards with Tracing

For students who have great difficulty in mastering certain sight words, try picture cards with tracing. Each card should have an unambiguous picture correctly labeled in large letters. The teacher (or a student helper) says the word. Then the learner says the word and at the same time traces the word with his or her finger. He or she should trace and say the word as many times as needed in order to learn it.

## 310. Word Cards for Tracing

In preparing word cards for learners to trace, write the word in soft crayon. Use smooth card stock. The crayon provides a textured word that the student can feel with his or her fingers. Ink marker is not nearly as effective. It doesn't provide raised letters. And some permanent ink markers may soak through the paper, making a blurred mirror image on the other side. Students with difficulties don't need this added source of confusion. So, stick to crayons.

## 311. Glitter Words

A much more expensive way than crayon to create textured words for tracing is to use glue and glitter. First print the word on a card. Then go over the letters with Elmer's Glue. Before the glue dries, sprinkle glitter, small beads, or colored sand on the card. When the glue dries, the excess glitter will shake off, leaving the word.

This procedure is time-consuming, expensive, and extremely messy. It should be saved for extra special occasions and carefully selected words.

## 312. Confusion Drill

Special exercises can be prepared for drill on sounds and symbols that are frequently confused. Cut out and mount on oaktag pictures whose names begin with similar sounds. Store all the pictures in a big brown envelope. Have two smaller envelopes, each labeled with the appropriate letter(s). The task for the student is to sort the pictures according to the specified symbols.

For example, one set can be designed for the *sh* and *ch* digraphs in both initial and final position. Include pictures of things such as these:

chair, witch, cherry, watch, chain, chicken
shower, shell, ship, fish, dish, wish(bone)

A set for practice on *b* and *d* could include these:

ball, crib, balloon, crab
dish, dog, doll, pod

Don't include *bed* or *bird* because they have both sounds.

### 313. Using Context

When a student encounters a word he or she cannot read, encourage the reading of the rest of the sentence before coming back again to the unknown word. This teaches the student to anticipate meaning and to use the context while reading.

The teacher may ask questions or make comments that will help lead a student to what the troublesome word is. For example, if the word happened to be *sandwich,* in the sentence "Dagwood didn't know what kind of sandwich to make for lunch," you might ask the student to tell you what people eat for lunch. When the student says "food," you can counter with "That's right, but what kind of food do people often eat for lunch? The word we're looking for begins with *s,* like *sun* and *sample.*"

Extensive drill on context clues may help eliminate many substitutions. The child should be taught to see that the word he or she has substituted for the correct one does not have much meaning in relation to the sense of the words correctly recognized. Example:

*Correct sentence:*  The bear went to sleep in a hollow log.
*As read:*  The bear went to sleep in a hollow dog.

The child can be led to see that in this sentence "a hollow log" makes sense, whereas "a hollow dog" does not.

### 314. Sounds in Context

Give the troubled reader help in using a *combination* of beginning sounds and contexts to figure out an unknown word. For example, if the word giving trouble is *lake,* give the student the clue that it begins like *lamp* and it's something you can swim in.

### 315. Confused Words

Difficulty in distinguishing between certain similar words, such as *band* and *hand,* may be overcome by constructing sentences, nonsense or otherwise, which contain the confused words. Here are several sentences with commonly confused words.

A *band* leader's *hand* must be very quick.
The sun *shines* on the *shore.*
The little *children* took care of the baby *chickens.*

In *winter* the *weather* is cold.
The *kitten* drank milk in the *kitchen*.

After reading the sentences, there may be discussion of word differences.

### 316. Context for Similar Words
Different types of completion sentences can be given that employ words of similar appearance.

Boy and girls live in _____.
_____ live in barns.
*houses heather horses*

A _____ is the home of a bird.
Clean children are _____.
*near nest neat*

The leader gave the _____ for them to _____.
*sign sing*

A _____ is bigger than a _____.
*horse house*

### 317. More Context Clues
Give incomplete sentences that demonstrate the use of context as an aid to picking the right word. For example:

R_____ fell from the clouds.
*run rain rat roll*

### 318. Still More Context Clues
Teach the student to look beyond a troublesome word to see if the following context may give some help. For example:

Ron lived at the top of a *high* hill.

The student who didn't get the word *high* at first glance might get it after reading *hill*.

### 319. Multiple Choices
Give drill on commonly confused words and phrases through multiple-choice exercises. For example:

When did Peggy to go school?
  in water
  in winter
  in wanted

### 320. Reversible Words—Irreversible Context

For giving practice on pairs of words frequently reversed or confused, use sentences in which the context clearly permits only one of the choices to be correct. Here are some examples:

*was - saw*
The apple _____ on the table.
The cat _____ the mouse.
_____ Jane a good girl?
Can you _____ the wood?
Rick _____ not a bad boy.

*on - no*
The dog was _____ the floor.
_____ boys went to the park today.
_____ top of her hat was a flower.
Did you say off or _____?
Did you say yes or _____?

Be careful to avoid ambiguous sentences in which either word could be correct. Save *those* sentences for the next activity.

### 321. Reversible Words—Reversible Context

As a contrast to the exercise above, in which only one of the reversible words can fit and make sense, the following exercise gives sentences in which either of the words could make sense. The student then matches the sentence with its picture. For example:

Willie was a pig.

Willie saw a pig.

"On ice!" said the flight attendant.

"No ice!" said the flight attendant.

### 322. Omissions

Try this for students who tend to omit one or more words as they read a sentence.

On the chalkboard (or on paper) write a sentence that the student has just read incorrectly. Write it exactly as the student has read it. Then write it as it should have been read. Have the student compare the two sentences word for word. This will help point out to the student that each word has a definite meaning and is of importance to the sentence.

> The father lion ate his cubs.
> The father lion ate before his cubs.

### 323. Missing Words

Prepare a set of word cards, each card with a word of a sentence. Give each child in a small group of learners one of the cards. Have the students line up in order so that the sentence makes sense. Then tell a student to sit down, thus removing a word from the sentence. Then have the sentence read again with the word missing. The students should note that the sentence has changed in meaning or lacks meaning entirely when all the words are not there.

### 324. Building Sentences

Give each student a word card as in Activity 323. The child who thinks he or she has the first word should stand at the beginning of the line. Each student in turn should take a place so that the sentence makes sense. This will call attention to the importance and correct location of each word in the sentence.

### 325. Noisy "Silent" Reading

Beginning readers and readers with severe problems often do their "silent" reading out loud—just a little bit quieter than their oral reading. Don't make a big deal about it. One way to discourage a child from reading "silently" but noisily is to suggest a finger on the lips while reading. This helps a child become conscious of the problem.

### 326. Lip Reading

If you feel that you must discourage a persistent lip reader, you might suggest a stick of gum to chew. My personal preference has always been Double Bubble. However, with other people's children, a sugarless variety is a more prudent choice. The rhythm of vigorous chewing will make it virtually impossible for the student to mouth the words while reading.

If allowing students to chew gum in class isn't your style, a pencil held between the teeth while reading will also achieve the desired results.

### 327. Pointing

Like lip reading, pointing to the words is a common occurrence among young beginning readers and students with serious reading problems. Don't make a big deal of it. Most students will stop using a finger to mark the place when the need is no longer there. If you wish, you can give the student a marker to help keep the place line by line and discourage finger pointing.

### 328. Remedy for the Materials Loser

Do you have students who never seem to be able to put things away in the right place? In a one-to-one clinical situation, this may not appear to be a terribly big problem. In an individualized learning environment which is used by many students, however, accurate refiling of materials is a must.

To cure the chronic loser of materials, try this. Give the student a long oaktag strip (4″ × 18″ or so) with his or her name on it in nice large letters. Each time the student removes a card from a kit, or a workbook from a shelf, the marker must be left in its place. The student can retrieve the marker when the material is put back in the correct place. Having the marker with the student's name helps the student to find the place quickly.

Markers can be color and/or symbol coded by class. The size suggested above is large enough to protrude visibly from even the largest kits or workbooks. If all students are using the marker system, the teacher or another student can quickly locate a needed item even if it is in use.

# Advanced Reading Skills

Section Four of *Reading Aids Through the Grades,* Advanced Reading Skills, is divided into four major categories of activities:
- Vocabulary Development
- Things to Read and Comprehension Skills
- Reference Skills
- Survival Reading

A number of the activities in this section lend themselves to reading in the content areas. Keep this in mind as you choose the materials from which to construct a given exercise. The particular items you use can be designed to fit the precise needs of the students who will use them.

Many of the comprehension activities can, if prepared using easy vocabulary, be used for poor readers. These activities should be kept in mind when you are using material from Section Three.

Survival Reading is a category new to the Fourth Edition of *Reading Aids*. While Reference Skills is a section devoted primarily to school-related behaviors, Survival Reading takes reading out of the classroom and into the real world.

## VOCABULARY DEVELOPMENT

The activities in this section are designed to increase the learner's ability to associate words with their meanings. There are essentially two steps (performed virtually simultaneously and silently by the proficient reader) to reading a word. The first step translates the visual symbols into sounds; the second step links those sounds to meaning. The activities in this section are primarily concerned with that second step—from spoken word to meaning. If the student is having difficulty with the first step—decoding visual symbols and matching them with sounds—the exercises in Section Three on basic grapheme-phoneme relationships should be considered.

The Noall-Cohen Test of Word Analysis Skills (Activity 333) is an individually administered rapid assessment of a learner's ability to decode words. Try it with older students if you are not sure of their word attack skills competence.

The overall behavioral objective of the activities in this section is as follows:

**AR-1.** Given a word visually (alone or in context), the learner correctly reads the word (i.e., knows what it means).

Specific objectives for the various activities in this section include these:

**AR-2.** Given a word visually, the learner identifies its synonym or a definition of the word.

**AR-3.** Given a word visually, the learner identifies its antonym.

**AR-4.** Given a number of words visually, the learner classifies them according to specified criteria.

**AR-5.** Given two homonyms visually, the learner identifies the correct one for a given context.

**AR-6.** Given word parts (prefixes, suffixes, and roots), the learner combines them to make words and identifies the meanings of these words.

### 329. Read Your Way to a Bigger Vocabulary

Perhaps the best way for a person to increase his or her reading vocabulary is to read more. Wide reading in a variety of books has been demonstrated to be at least as effective in increasing measurable vocabulary as specific vocabulary building exercises. Therefore, you needn't feel that you are neglecting vocabulary skill development when you let the learner "just" read.

### 330. Dictionary Readiness

Encourage each student to make and maintain a personal dictionary. When a new word is encountered and learned, it should be entered with its meaning in the student's dictionary. When eight or ten words accumulate on a page, they may be rewritten in alphabetical order. Loose-leaf pages in a cover give greater flexibility than does a bound composition book.

This activity provides good readiness for dictionary work because it approximates the format of a published dictionary on a small personal scale that the student can handle.

## 331. Word Meaning Bank

An alternative format to the personal dictionary described above is the word meaning bank. Each word in the bank is kept with its meaning on a 3″ × 5″ index card. The word bank has some advantages over the notebook form of dictionary in that each word is on a separate card offering maximum flexibility for word study activities. Cards can be divided into "known words" and "words being worked on" or classified in other ways such as by meaning or part of speech. They can be easily returned to alphabetical order and new words can be added without recopying of pages. However, using a personal dictionary notebook is behaviorally closer to using a real dictionary than is the card file system.

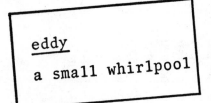

eddy

a small whirlpool

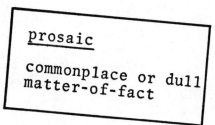

prosaic

commonplace or dull matter-of-fact

## 332. Category Dictionary

A student can make personal word collections by category. For example:

Words for horses—whinny, quarter horse, stallion, mare, colt, filly, bay, hoof, withers, gallop, canter, trot, saddle, bridle, harness, thoroughbred, hunter, dressage, martingale

Words about the neighborhood—turf, block, corner, curb, street, avenue, no trespassing, gang, police officer, traffic

School words—chalkboard, teacher, assignment, report card, vacation, schedule, cafeteria, recess, history, math, detention, principal, coach

## 333. Noall-Cohen Test of Word Analysis

The Noall-Cohen Test of Word Analysis is helpful in determining whether or not an older reader has adequately mastered and internalized the work attack skills necessary to read fluently. Most of the words on the test are real words, selected from the most infrequently used words listed in the Thorndike and Lorge *The Teacher's Word Book of 30,000 Words.* The rarity of their apearance in print makes these words functionally nonsense words for most of the students you will be testing. This list will thus be a real test of decoding ability rather than known sight words for these students. But they are real words, and you can be sure that they accurately represent feasible sound–symbol relationships.

To administer the test, you will need two copies of it—one with all the examiner's information on it and one containing only the list of words. Give the word list to the student. Record the responses on your copy, which then can become part of the student's record.

This test is suitable for students in grades 4–12. For younger children a format more like the phonics exercises in Section Three of this book is better.

# Noall-Cohen Test of Word Analysis*

*Instructions to Examiner:* Ask the student to read lists in order. Write in substitutions and errors. Place a check by each word on which the examinee hesitates. After list is read at Levels 2, 4, 5 ask the following questions when appropriate: (*a*) What would the word be without the ending? (*b*) What are the prefixes, roots, and suffixes in List 5? (*c*) What does each affix mean? On the summary chart at the bottom of the page, tally the errors.

**Level 1**

1. cos
2. pyx
3. kip
4. fez
5. labs
6. stept
7. draff
8. crux
9. blent
10. veld

**Level 2**

1. gadding
2. dace
3. thrid
4. flitch
5. glebes
6. schist
7. mulct
8. plebs
9. helving
10. kipper

**Level 3**

1. ca
2. braise
3. shrieve
4. ceil
5. loess
6. swart
7. squall
8. hawse
9. erst
10. shirr

**Level 4**

1. phlox
2. spew
3. gneiss
4. bedgown
5. anthrax
6. boileau
7. fecund
8. brassiest
9. tiping
10. burnoose
11. coign
12. tout

**Level 5**

1. deduction
2. prospective
3. retainer
4. suffice
5. efferent
6. applicable
7. diffidence
8. bilobed
9. omniscient
10. appendectomy

## Summary of Results

_____Short vowels on all words

_____Blends on 3–9.

_____Final vowel on number 1.

_____Silent g/ on 3,11.

_____Mispronunciations on all.

_____Consonant blends on words 5 to 10.

_____Inflected endings on 1,5,9,10.

_____Two-vowel combinations on 2–5.

_____o/ on 1, 4.

_____Common prefixes.

_____Taking off endings on 1, 5, 8–10.

_____a/followed by r/l/w/ on 6–8.

_____Diphthongs 2,6,11,12.

_____Assimilated prefixes on 4–7, 10.

_____Vowel plus letter r/ on 6, 9, 10.

_____Taking off endings on 8,9.

_____Common roots on 1–7.

_____Syllable errors on 3–10.

*The Noall-Cohen Test of Word Analysis was developed by Dr. Mabel Noall and Dr. S. Alan Cohen.

### 334. Completing Word Categories

Give the student a worksheet each line of which contains two or three words that go together in some way. The task for the student is to add words to the category.

| | | | | |
|---|---|---|---|---|
| 1. horse | cow | ___ | ___ | ___ |
| 2. planet | moon | ___ | ___ | ___ |
| 3. rose | petunia | ___ | ___ | ___ |
| 4. book | magazine | ___ | ___ | ___ |
| 5. mansion | cottage | ___ | ___ | ___ |

This activity can be very easy or very difficult, depending on the level of sophistication you demand. For example, you could accept any animals for number one *or* farm animals only. Decide on the ground rules *before* you play.

### 335. Classification Race

This can be a game for two or more players or an activity for one student. The purpose is to place words from a list with others of the same classification. Present a card with a list of words, two or more words per category. For a group game, the words can be placed on the chalkboard. Here's an example of the way the words should be listed.

1. chicken, duck, goose
2. pencil, crayon, brush
3. juice, soda, coffee
4. calf, colt, piglet
5. star, comet, moon
6. setter, spaniel, terrier

From fifteen to twenty categories should be listed. A second card (or list on the chalkboard) presents an additional item for each category. For example, the second card for the above categories might read *hound, tea, pen, turkey, sun, lamb.*

The object of the game is to list the words on the second card in the correct order by category. In other words, *turkey* would be listed with category 1 to accompany *chicken, duck,* and *goose.*

### 336. Alternative Classification Race

This is a somewhat more difficult version of the previous activity. The words in the numbered category are listed on a card or on the chalkboard as before. In this game, however, the student is not supplied with an additional word to put in each category. The object of the game is to supply as many more words for each category as possible in a limited time. The student with the largest number of correctly placed words is the winner.

### 337. Things Needed

Here's a classification game that can be played by any number of students. The object of the game is to list under a question the items that would be needed in order to perform the action described. The easiest version of the game provides a number of possible reponses (perhaps on one large sheet of paper or the chalkboard) that the students can arrange under each item. A more difficult version requires the students to supply their own choices for each. The highest number of correct responses in a given number of time wins.

Here are some sample questions:

1   What would you need to cook and serve an egg?
2.  What would you need to play baseball?
3.  What would you need to keep a pet rabbit?
4.  What would you need to plan a surprise birthday party?
5.  What would you need to go away for the weekend?
6.  What would you need to go roller skating?

### 338. Persons, Places, Things

Make a worksheet with three columns, one for *People* or *animals,* one for *Places,* and one for *Things.* Give the students a list of common and proper nouns. Have them list each noun in the appropriate column. Try to include a few words that could go in more than one column. Here is a list:

Charlotte, dime, puzzle, California, bread, Chicago, brother, cocker spaniel, hound, frog, quarters, campfire

Note that *Charlotte* could be both a person and a place. *Frog* could be both an animal and a thing. *Quarters* could be put in the column for places as well as for things.

### 339. Noncrossword Puzzles

For a vocabulary review, try "noncrossword" puzzles. Supply the definition, the first letter, and the number of spaces for the letters of each word. For example:

1. to take hold of
2. to blow up with air
3. neither good nor bad
4. where two roads cross
5. having courage

(Key: grasp, inflate, mediocre, intersection, bold)

The success of this activity depends, of course, on careful selection of appropriate words. Many students enjoy constructing puzzles of this type for their own use and for their friends.

## 340. Real Crossword Puzzles

Crossword puzzles are an excellent source of vocabulary development material. Some people are good at constructing good puzzles. Most of us are not so good at it. Commercial sources of puzzles are a boon.

Try giving the crossword puzzle out of your local newspaper to your students who read well. To make it suitable in level, complete the more difficult words before you distribute it. (You can even wait until the answers are published to be sure!) Then give the puzzle, which now has a limited number of words to complete, to your students.

Crossword puzzles are an excellent activity for pupil teams.

## 341. Two-Way Words

This is a good activity for student teams. Each partner chooses a word for the other. The words should have the same number of letters. The words are written as follows:

```
C_____E        
A_____L        
S_____T        
T_____S    G_____R
L_____A    A_____E
E_____C    N_____D
                         D_____N
                         E_____A
                         R_____G
```

Each student tries to fill in the lines with words that begin and end with the given letters. There are two ways to score this game. The student finishing the list first with real words can be the winner. Or, if you wish to encourage long words, you can score one point for each letter filled in in a correct word. The person with the highest number of points would then win.

## 342. Synonyms

Prepare a worksheet in which there are rows of four or five words each. In each row the student has to circle the synonym of the first word. For example:

| courteous | coarse | polite | regal | cruel |
| beneath | above | under | foreign | close |
| simple | easy | sample | difficult | Simon |
| rugged | ready | tiled | rigged | rough |

### 343. More Synonyms

Number a column of words. Parallel to this column place a second column of words that have the same or almost the same meanings as the words in the first column. The words in the second column should not be numbered and their order should be different from the order of the words in the first column. The student has to match the words in the first column with their correct synonyms in the second column. For example:

| | | |
|---|---|---|
| 1. enemy | ( | ) easy |
| 2. morning | ( | ) sleepy |
| 3. simple | ( | ) difficult |
| 4. tired | ( | ) dawn |
| 5. hard | ( | ) foe |
| 6. jarred | ( | ) rattled |
| 7. victory | ( | ) refused |
| 8. boxed | ( | ) huge |
| 9. enormous | ( | ) triumph |
| 10. declined | ( | ) crated |

### 344. Synonym Supply

Prepare a set of cards (10 or more, depending on how many students are playing), each one containing a word. Each player picks a card and tries to write as many synonyms for the word on the card as possible. The player or team with the highest number of words after a given time wins. Here are some suggestions for words on the cards:

| | | | |
|---|---|---|---|
| said | went | ran | sent |
| laughed | little | nice | big |
| bad | move | make | want |

### 345. Overworked or Vague Words

Give the student a passage to read in which there are a number of "overworked" or imprecise words that are underlined. List words that can substitute for these over-worked words. The task for the student is to pick a word from the list to replace each of the underlined words. For example:

Captain, the good old watchdog, sat in the old house chewing a stale crust of bread and an old bone. With his nice old master now dead and gone, Captain was alone in the empty farmhouse. But Captain never gave up watching the old house.

| | |
|---|---|
| *faithful* | *abandoned* |
| *guarding* | *elderly* |
| *kind* | *ramshackle* |

### 346. Finding Better Words

Give the student a paragraph to read in which there are a number of dull or overused words. Using a thesaurus or a dictionary, the student has to select and indicate at least two acceptable alternatives to each underlined word. For example, using the same paragraph as in Activity 345, the student might come up with alternatives such as:

good: trustworthy, faithful, loyal, dependable
old: ramshackle, broken-down, dilapidated
nice: gentle, kindly, pleasant
old: elderly, aged
empty: abandoned, desolate, deserted
watching: protecting, guarding

### 347. Choice of Words

Prepare a worksheet with twenty rows. Each row should contain words one or more of which answer a dictated question. The teacher or a student leader reads aloud a question, statement, or direction. The other students circle the appropriate words on their worksheet. For example. _____:

*Script*
1. Circle words to describe a cold day.
2. Pick the softest.

*Worksheet*

| | | | | |
|---|---|---|---|---|
| 1. frosty | snowy | warm | tepid | nippy |
| 2. boulder | pillow | wood | iron | carpet |

As an alternative to having the questions dictated, put them on another sheet for each student to read independently.

### 348. Story Words

Print on the chalkboard or on a worksheet lists of words, some of which are appropriate to a theme or specified type of story. The task for the student is to indicate which of the words would go with a particular theme or story. For example:

*Circle the words that would best be used in a fairy tale.*

| | | |
|---|---|---|
| magic | corral | lasso |
| giant | dwarf | cowboy |
| ranch | asteroid | comet |
| dragon | light-year | interplanetary |
| rocket ship | gnomes | laser |
| pasture | crater | retro-rocket |
| gantry | capsule | ogre |
| maiden | frog | nose cone |

You can make some worksheets do double duty by picking your words carefully. For example, the directions for the above list could also have been to identify the words you could use in writing about space travel or raising cattle.

You can put these exercises on 5″ × 8″ index cards. A series of them can be made up and filed in kit form. The correct answers can be placed on the back of each card.

### 349. How Do You Do It?

Prepare a worksheet with four columns and a list of action words. The task for the student is to place each word in the proper category column according to how it is done (with the eyes, the hands, the mouth, or the feet). A dictionary may be used. Here is a sample list of difficult words:

canter, scan, scrutinize, perambulate, visualize, wend, vocalize, point, gesticulate, pontificate

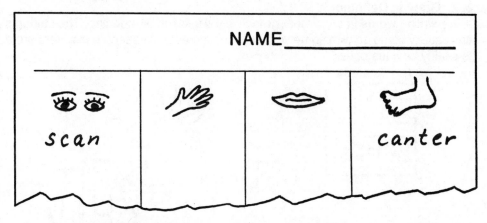

Here's a sample list of very easy words:

trot, walk, yell, grab, kiss, look, read, blink, handle, hold

Note that it's possible for a given word (e.g., read) to fit in more than one column.

### 350. Happiness is _____

Ever since Charlie Brown declared that "Happiness is a warm puppy," teachers have been letting kids do "happiness" and other abstract noun books which, of course, can be illustrated. Try:

Delight is _____.
A friend is _____.
Love is _____.
Nervousness is _____.
Sharing is _____.
Anger is _____.

Encourage unusual and clever responses.

### 351. Simile Race

This game can be played by two or more students. Prepare cards (index cards will do) with an unfinished sentence on each. One card is drawn. Using the beginning on the card, the players try to make as many different complete sentences as possible. The person with the most sentences at the end of a time limit (five minutes or so) is the winner of that round.

Here are some possible starters for the sentences.

1. He was as funny as. . .
2. It was as quiet as. . .
3. She was as tall as. . .
4. They were as weird as. . .
5. It was as rough as . . .

### 352. Graphic Definitions

Try writing words in a way that graphically depicts their meaning. The students can usually come up with some very interesting creative presentations. Here are a few fairly obvious ones.

## 353. Understanding Idioms

Certain words and expressions don't always mean what they seem to. Working with idiomatic expressions can be fun. Try preparing sentences with expressions that can have other than literal meaning. Ask multiple choice questions about the meaning of the expressions in the given context. Mix items that contain idiomatic expressions with items using the same or similar expressions that can be interpreted literally. Here are some examples:

I got home late and my mother went up the wall.
  My mother
      a. likes to climb.
      b. took off her shoes.
      c. was very upset.

We screamed when we saw the mouse go up the wall.
  The words "up the wall" tell
      a. that the mouse was angry.
      b. where the mouse went.
      c. what time it was.

William was beside himself with joy.
  William
      a. had a twin brother who sat next to him.
      b. was unable to tell what to do next.
      c. was very happy about something.

Wendy put her picnic lunch down beside her.
  You can be sure that
      a. Wendy was very happy
      b. Wendy had brought her food with her.
      c. two mice ate Wendy's picnic lunch.

## 354. Idiomatic Pictures

Provide pictures of idiomatic expressions and three possible choices for the meaning. The task for the student is to select the expression suggested by the picture. Here are some examples:

She looked in the mirror.
She was beside herself.
She had a twin sister.

He was very blue.
He spilled some grape jam.
His face matched his shirt.

### 355. Literal and Other Meanings

Sometimes an expression can mean more than one thing. Here's a list of expressions that can sometimes have a special meaning. Sometimes these expressions can be interpreted literally. The task for the student is to select the two possible meanings for each expression.

Read each sentence in column A. Then write the two letters of the items in column B that tell what the sentence could mean.

**A**

Justin spilled the beans.

Suzy spent the afternoon up a tree.

Cross that bridge when you come to it.

What a crab he is!

Sally broke her word.

**B**

a. She was upset.
b. Don't worry before it's necessary.
c. That's a large bit of seafood.
d. She knocked the letters off the game board.
e. He spilled the vegetable on the floor.
f. He told on someone.
g. Go across the river on the bridge.
h. She sat in her treehouse.
i. He's in a very bad mood.
j. She didn't do what she said she would do.

### 356. Idioms Delight

Here's an entertaining game to play while learning to interpret idiomatic expressions. Each person in the game takes a blank piece of paper and tries to illustrate an idiomatic expresssion. Give each player about three minutes to create the illustration. Then have each player in turn hold up his or her picture for the others to see. The others try to write the expression suggested. When everyone's picture has been displayed, the person with the largest number of correct interpretations is the winner. Here are some expressions that lend themselves to easy illustrations:

spill the beans
to be beside oneself
break your word
get cold feet
throw the book at him or her

### 357. Literal Meanings

See how many sentences a student can write containing an expression that would be humorous if interpreted literally. Here are some examples:

He was the apple of her eye.
She kept tripping over her tongue.
You shouldn't break your word.
Please lend me your ears.
Her eyes lit up when she saw it.

The sentences can be illustrated with the literal interpretation if you wish. Then the student should write another sentence that expresses the idiomatic meaning of the sentence. Here are possible sentences to accompany the five above.

He was her absolute favorite.
She couldn't say the words straight.
Do it if you say you're going to.
Listen to me.
She was very pleased to see it.

## 358. Sensory Imagery

Make a worksheet containing a passage to read, next to each part of which are symbols (eye, ear, nose, mouth, and hand) for the five senses. Have the students read the passage and indicate which of the senses are being evoked. Of course, this works especially well for poetry.

This activity is very good for group discussion and oral reading of the passage.

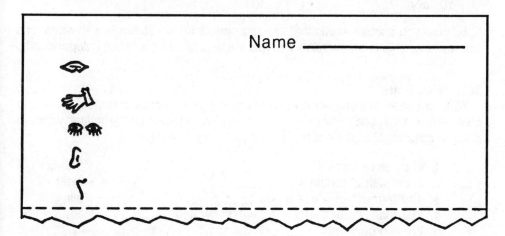

Name _____

## 359. Vocabulary Football

Follow the directions for Sight Word Football, Activity 145 in Section Three. In this version of the game, the task is to define each word drawn as well as pronounce it correctly. The point after goal can be obtained by using the word correctly in a sentence.

Of course, the game as described in the earlier section works for more advanced readers too. Simply use a difficult list of words.

## 360. Antonyms

Prepare a worksheet in which there are rows of four or five words each. In each row the student has to circle the antonym of the first word. For example:

| polite | kind | rude | police | cruel |
| above | about | on | below | around |
| near | far | neat | reach | listen |

### 361. More Antonyms

Number a column of words. Parallel to this column place a second column of words that are the opposites of the words in the first column. The opposites are not numbered and their order does not correspond to the order of the words in the first column. The student has to match the words in the first column with their correct antonyms in the second column. For example:

| | | | |
|---|---|---|---|
| 1. | enemy | ( | ) light |
| 2. | dark | ( | ) evening |
| 3. | pretty | ( | ) difficult |
| 4. | easy | ( | ) friend |
| 5. | morning | ( | ) ugly |
| 6. | rugged | ( | ) tethered |
| 7. | exciting | ( | ) sank |
| 8. | untied | ( | ) smooth |
| 9. | floated | ( | ) boring |
| 10. | ally | ( | ) foe |

Be sure you choose words that are appropriate for the students with whom you are working. This is an exercise that many students can construct independently.

### 362. Word Pairs

Write a series of sentences each using a pair of words commonly found in combination. Omit one of these words from each sentence. List the omitted words in another column. The student has to complete each sentence.

| | |
|---|---|
| 1. Mary wore black shoes and _____. | stockings |
| 2. I sew with a needle and _____. | saucer |
| 3. The farmer has a horse and _____. | chair |
| 4. The mail carrier trudged through snow and _____. | sleet |
| 5. We like butter and _____ on our toast. | jelly |
| 6. We could not find the paper or _____. | |
| 7. The cup and _____ are on the table. | pencil |
| 8. Push the _____ to the table. | wagon |
| 9. The count on the batter was two balls and no _____. | cream |
| 10. Would you like strawberries and _____? | thread |
| | strikes |

### 363. Synonym or Antonym Mazes

Instead of using a set of two columns for having students match words with their synonyms or antonyms, this maze format can be a pleasant change. It looks a bit more interesting on the page, although the behavior being practiced is the same as in the ordinary exercise. Don't overdo it or the novelty will wear off. Of course, this format can be used any time you have a matching exercise involving two columns of items.

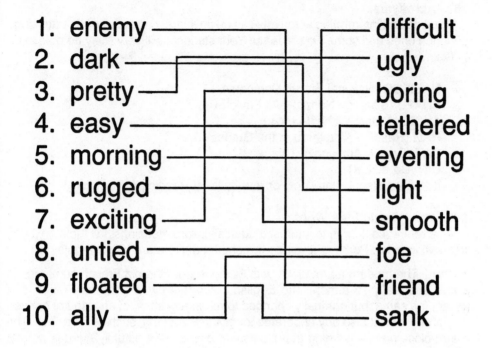

1. enemy — difficult
2. dark — ugly
3. pretty — boring
4. easy — tethered
5. morning — evening
6. rugged — light
7. exciting — smooth
8. untied — foe
9. floated — friend
10. ally — sank

### 364. Arriving Words

An exercise that could be accompanied by the one that follows is to list words that are arriving on the scene of current usage (or old words with new meanings). One of the interesting things about these two exercises is that the words listed as "arriving" one year might well be on the "departing" list another. Some new words, of course, endure. Sources of new words are fads, clothing, hobbies, politics, technology, and other current events or trends. We are not going to provide any examples here, because by the time you read this book they may well be out of date!

### 365. Departing Words

An exercise that some students may find fun is to list and perhaps illustrate words which appear to be in danger of disappearance from common usage, or words which have recently disappeared. The teacher can be an excellent source of words which have dissapeared just prior to the lifetime of the students. Many of these words describe clothing, objects, or passing fads that are no longer current. For example: hula hoop, bermuda shorts, rock 'n roll, schmoo, knickers.

### 366. From Brand Name to Generic Term

Some brand names become so associated with the product they label that the name tends to become a generic term for any similar item regardless of who manufactures it. For example: Kleenex, Xerox, Scotch Tape, Magic Marker, Band-Aid, Formica, TV Dinner. Can you and your students think of others?

## 367. Acronyms

Creating and interpreting acronyms can be an interesting activity. Here are some common ones and some we made up. Your students will very likely be able to do better.

> NABISCO (National Biscuit Company)
> SNAFU (Situation Normal—All Fouled Up)
> AWOL (Absent Without Leave)
> RAG (Reading Aids through the Grades)
> CAT (Canine Antagonist Thing)
> DIN (Do It Now)
> IRA (Irish Republican Army or International Reading Association)

## 368. Story Behind the Word

As a reference source to interest students in word meanings, tell the story of an interesting word. Perhaps it will be remembered. Here are two examples:

ALARM   The modern alarm clock gets its name from the old French summons to battle, *Alarme!* ("To arms!") The English *alarm,* borrowed from the French, first meant the same, but gradually changed to mean a warning of any kind of danger, and finally meant also any apparatus for giving a warning, such as a fire bell. The alarm clock rings a warning that it's time to get up—but actually there is no real cause for "alarm" in it. (Unless, of course it's a school day and you ignore the warning!)

REHEARSE   When you begin to rehearse your next play or a speech you have to give, you probably won't be thinking about the old French word *herce,* meaning a "harrow." Long ago, a *herce* or harrow was a triangular frame of wood with wooden teeth to break up the clods and level the ground in the farmer's fields. "To harrow" was *hercier,* and "to harrow over again" was *rehercier.* This was adopted in the English language as "rehearse." So, to "rehearse" means to "harrow over again." When you rehearse, you smooth out your speech or play until there are no rough spots in it.

## 369. Word Origin and Change

Give the student a brief selection to read, and a dictionary with good etymologies. A special dictionary of word origins is also an excellent—and entertaining—thing to have available. Underline certain words in the selection. The student has to complete a worksheet asking for the *meaning in context* of each underlined word, *its origin,* and *its present usage.* Finally, the student could translate the given selection into more current or colloquial usage.

An example is given below. We don't guarantee that what this particular "student" came up with is the best possible interpretation of the evidence concerning *lists.* In any case it's more than could be expected of your average student. It's the result of fascinating researches—in a good "college" dictionary, in the *Shorter Oxford English Dictionary,* and in *World Book 1974.* The last word has yet to be spoken. Usage isn't all that changes; so does knowledge about past usage. Hopefully your good student will come up with something meaningful and reasonably accurate as an interpretation of what the sources reveal. It's up to you to point to good sources and be ready to help the interested student to read them.

*Wit* they not that I am king of this land? *An* were I not, we would do battle in this *lists!*

| Word | Meaning in Context | Origin | How It Got To Present Meaning |
|------|------|------|------|
| wit | know | Anglo-Saxon | Cleverness, sense. A person who *knows* many things we think of as being clever. Also, if he *knows* a lot, he has good sense. |
| an | if | Anglo-Saxon | Not used any more. *An* meaning *a* or *one* is not the same word. |
| lists | field for combat | Anglo-Saxon and French | Knights of the Middle Ages held tournaments in which they charged at each other on horseback, holding the reins in one hand and wielding a long, heavy lance with the other. Each tried to knock the other off. The areas they fought in were sometimes bounded by tall fences and sometimes they were divided into narrow lanes separated by railings (so that the horses wouldn't collide as the knights rode swiftly toward and then past each other). These fence and rail barriers were called *lists,* and so were the areas they enclosed, because a *list* in those days meant a *strip* of something, or a *border.* The names of the men who were to fight *in the lists* (in the enclosed areas) may have been displayed *on the lists* (on the barriers). *List* now usually means a catalog of names or words arranged in a row or column, like a *strip.* |

*Translation:* Don't they *know* that I am king of this land? *If* I weren't, we would meet on the *field of battle.*

### 370. Homonyms in Context

The study of homonyms can be useful. Give the student homonyms and a dictionary. The task is to use each word correctly in an interesting sentence. Some suggested words:

aloud, allowed; bare, bear; boar, bore; borough, burrow; bough, bow; bridal, bridle; cell, sell; break, brake; course, coarse; peace, piece; rein, rain, reign; their, there; site, sight; lesson, lessen; fair, fare

### 371. Almost Homonyms in Context

Certain pairs of words, although not homonyms, are very close in pronunciation or spelling and are frequently confused. Like homonyms, these "almost homonyms" should be practiced in correct context. Give such words as these:

alleys, allies; except, accept; recipe, receipt; quiet, quite; tried, tired; whether, weather

The student should use each in an interesting sentence, consulting the dictionary if necessary.

### 372. Homonym Riddles

Homonym riddles are an entertaining way to pass the time and to call the attention of your students to homonyms. Give a definition that requires in response a pair of homonyms. Here are some examples. (Note that we were having so much fun that we just couldn't stop.)

1. fur of a rabbit    (hare hair)
2. listen in place    (hear here)
3. reasonable price    (fair fare)
4. untied piece of string    (not knot)
5. unadorned jet    (plain plane)
6. equine with sore throat    (hoarse horse)
7. evening for man in armor    (knight night)
8. peel a fruit    (pare pear)
9. peel two pieces of fruit    (pare pair)
10. for a couple    (to two)
11. naked grizzly    (bare bear)
12. consumed more than seven    (ate eight)
13. an Alaskan dwarf    (Nome gnome)
14. whips vegetables    (beats beets)
15. rented less than anyone else    (leased least)
16. squeezes jewelry    (wrings rings)
17. listened to the cows    (heard herd)
18. a levy on fasteners    (tacks tax)
19. afternoon refreshment on the golf course    (tee tea)

## 373. Multi-Meaning Words in Context

To give practice in using context to determine the exact meaning of multi-meaning words, make a worksheet with sentences, each of which demonstrates one use of the multi-meaning word. The student has to write the meaning of the word as it is used next to each sentence. If you provide a list of meanings, this exercise can be done as a matching task rather than completion items. The student can, if you wish, be permitted to use the dictionary. Here are some examples:

1. She has a *run* in her pantyhose. _____
2. The oil wells have *run* dry. _____
3. In time of panic, there may be a *run* on the bank. _____
4. *Run* along now, and don't bother me. _____
5. Hank Aaron hit his 715th home *run* in 1974. _____
6. My old broken-down car won't *run*. _____
7. Can you *run* a movie projector? _____
8. The melting ice cream began to *run* down my arm. _____
9. Jeans will *run* if you wash them in hot water. _____
10. I left my dog in his *run* in the yard. _____

The unabridged dictionary is a good source of words and meanings for this exercise. Of course, most words will not have as many possible meanings as the word in the above example.

## 374. Multi-Meaning Words—Dictionary

Present multi-meaning words in groups of sentences. Give the student a dictionary. The student has to look the word up and indicate which of the dictionary meanings of that word each sentence exemplifies. Here are some sentences for the word *strike*.

1. Did Reggie Jackson *strike* out?
2. Don't you dare *strike* that child.
3. That's an extremely *striking* outfit.
4. The workers went out on *strike*.
5. I hope the fish will *strike* the bait.

## 375. Write the Right Word

Give the student a series of sentences each of which contains a common error in word usage. The task for the student is to correct the wrong word. For example:

1. The whether was rainy and cool.
2. I wanted to except the lovely gift.
3. I got the paper at the stationary store.
4. I can't tell weather or not it will fly.
5. "Days of Our Lives" is my favorite TV cereal.

### 376. Write the Right Word in the Right Place
Prepare sentences that omit two commonly confused words. The student has to put each word in its correct place. For example:

1. The doctor _____ to magazines for the waiting room and _____ pills for the patients.   (prescribes, subscribes)
2. _____ or not we go to the beach depends on how nice the _____ is.   (weather, whether)
3. The increase in transit _____ isn't _____ to people on fixed incomes.   (fair, fare)
4. My favorite TV _____ advertises a crunchy breakfast _____.   (cereal, serial)
5. _____ for her best friend's suggestions, she wouldn't _____ any advice.   (accept, except)

### 377. Homographs
Make a worksheet with sentences containing homographs with different pronunciations. The student should figure out from context the correct pronunciation of each homograph and mark the accented syllable of each. For example:

1. Our teacher objects to certain objects in the classroom.
2. Do not refuse to put the refuse in the trash cans.
3. The law does not permit a young child to get a learner's permit.
4. Do not convict the convict before the trial.
5. Even if it looks like a reject, don't reject it until you try.
6. Are you content with the content of your composition?

### 378. More Homographs
Able students may enjoy writing sentences using homographs. This is a good activity to encourage dictionary use. Some suggestions for homographs:

| | | | |
|---|---|---|---|
| wind | excuse | content | row |
| lead | live | close | conduct |
| rebel | project | refuse | annex |
| read | permit | object | subject |
| reject | perfect | produce | address |

### 379. Meanings to Homographs
Give the students a list of meanings of a multi-meaning word. The task is to guess the homograph to go with the meanings. For example:

| | |
|---|---|
| hit, stop work, appeal to | *strike* |
| kennel, stocking flaw, steak, hurry | *run* |
| tavern, prevent, stripe, song part | *bar* |
| money, places to live, fractions | *quarters* |

## 380. Common Prefixes and Suffixes

Knowledge of common prefixes, suffixes, and roots can be an aid in figuring out the meaning of words. The following list can be placed on a chart and made available. It should not be memorized, but referred to as needed.

| Prefix | Meaning | Example |
|--------|---------|---------|
| a-, ab- | from, away | abnormal |
| ad- | to | adjacent |
| be- | by | beside |
| com- | with | combine |
| de- | from | depart |
| dis- | apart, not | disbelief |
| en- | in | engulf |
| ex-, e- | out | evict, expunge |
| in- | into | insert |
| in- | not | insignificant |
| pre- | before | predict |
| pro- | in front of | proceed |
| re- | back, again | rebound |
| sub- | under | submarine |
| un- | not | unfortunate |

The following chart, which should be used for reference, contains common English suffixes.

| Suffix | Meaning | Example |
|--------|---------|---------|
| -able | that can be | admirable |
| -ance | state of | abundance |
| -ant | that does | defendant |
| -en | like, made of | wooden |
| -er | that does | teacher |
| -ful | fulness | hopeful |
| -hood | state of | childhood |
| -ible | that can be | irresistible |
| -ion | act of | decision |
| -ish | pertaining to, like | greenish |
| -ism | system of | socialism |
| -less | without | careless |
| -ly | like | princely |
| -ment | act of | development |
| -ness | state of | badness |
| -ory | pertaining to | supervisory |
| -ous | full of | porous |
| -ty | state of | brevity |
| -y | pertaining to | rainy |

## 381. Vocabulary Builder

Here is an effective technique for enlarging vocabulary. Give a multiple choice test on the words you want the students to master. As soon as the pretest is completed, give them a page with each of the words used in the meaningful context of a sentence or two. After the students have had a chance to read the sentences and ponder them a bit, let them try the test again. By this time they'll probably get them all right.

This technique is more useful than making a list of words and looking them up, one by one, in the dictionary. As evidence of the effectiveness of the approach, here are five words at your level for you. Of course, when constructing exercises for the students, you will pick words that you want them to know.

*Sample Vocabulary Pre- and Post-Test*

On the line at the right, write the correct letter for the meaning of the word.

|  | PRE | POST |
|---|---|---|

1. bartizan _____ _____
   a. craftsman
   b. lingerie manufacturer
   c. parapet or lookout
   d. small breed of deer
2. mugient _____ _____
   a. bellow or moo
   b. produce a new species
   c. musical interlude
   d. become quiet
3. lycanthropy _____ _____
   a. illicit donation to charity
   b. study of fungi
   c. light therapy for diseased plants
   d. delusion of wolfhood
4. fard _____ _____
   a  paint used on the face
   b. river crossing (var.)
   c. singer of ballads
   d. gastric distress
5. graben _____ _____
   a. species of predatory bird
   b. selfish individual
   c. depression in the earth
   d. coarse gravel

1. The knight stood in the tower's topmost bartizan, overlooking the fields from which the enemy would come.

2. They named their dog Mugient, because he bellowed and mooed just like a cow.

3. The girl didn't know she was sick. She bared her teeth and howled and really believed she was a wolf. Her psychiatrist called it lycanthropy.

4. The clown was a master of the art of fard. His painted face endured long beyond his years of clowning.

5. After the earthquake, a depression remained between the two faults. No one wanted to rebuild on this graben.

If you don't have time to construct your own exercises of this type, a series of booklets based on basic vocabulary grades 2–8 is available from Random House. The program is called *Practicing Vocabulary*.

## 382. Prefixes

Present, as a model, a pair of sentences one of which employs a prefix, such as the prefix *un*. These sentences should be carefully constructed to ensure that the context demonstrates the meaning of the prefix. For example:

The farmer tied the horse to a tree.
The farmer untied the horse and rode away.

The helper loaded the wagon with fruit.
The helper unloaded the wagon and put the fruit away.

Then have a series of sentences in which the student must supply the prefix where needed. For example:

She hitched her horse to the post.
She _____ hitched her horse and galloped home.

The teacher tied the boy's shoelaces.
The little boy _____ tied his shoelaces and kicked off his shoes.

These exercises could be done at the board. After one model is presented, worksheets could be done independently.

### 383. Prefixes Make Opposites

Make a worksheet containing words. The task for the student is to add a prefix to each word so that it means the opposite of the given word. Here are some sample words:

| | | | | |
|---|---|---|---|---|
| opportune | hitch | fortune | literate | attractive |
| legible | regular | kindly | normal | appear |

### 384. Worksheet for Suffixes

Prepare worksheets with suffixes and words listed. The task for the student is to combine the suffixes and the words to make as many new words as possible.

### 385. More Suffixes

List some suffixes. The task for the student is to make as many words as possible containing the suffixes. Examples you might want to use:

| | | | |
|---|---|---|---|
| -ious | -ial | -ous | -ence |
| -ive | -tion | -al | -ance |

### 386. -er and -or Suffixes

The suffix -er or -or added to the base of a verb signifies "one who" does whatever that verb expresses. Have the student write the noun that matches each of the following:

one who sails _____            one who directs _____
one who rides _____            one who plays _____
one who hunts _____            one who farms _____
one who leads _____            one who teaches _____
one who follows _____            one who keeps _____

### 387. Number of Syllables

Students who need practice in structural analysis may be given a list of words that are to be arranged in columns according to the number of syllables in each of the words. For example:

gem, freight, body, turtle, cruise, through,
thorough, chasm, duel, beauty, beautiful, diamond,
sympathetic, irregular, dental, enterprise, ago

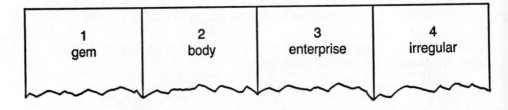

| 1 | 2 | 3 | 4 |
|---|---|---|---|
| gem | body | enterprise | irregular |

For some students this activity might be more interesting if all the words dealt with a specific topic or theme. For example, here is a list of words on space.

astronaut, retro-rocket, supersonic, light, moon, gantry, capsule, weightless, environment, interplanetary, cosmonaut, skylab, module, lunar, reentry, meteor, comet, asteroid

| 1 moon | 2 gantry | 3 astronaut | 4 supersonic | more interplanetary |
|---|---|---|---|---|

## 388. Hunt a Word

To prepare "Hunt a Word" sheets, rule a paper into a large number of blocks—for example, eight rows often—or use graph paper. Write the words that you want students to find, one letter to a block. Words may be written up, down, and diagonally. If you really want to make the puzzle difficult, the words may also be written backwards. Then fill in all the rest of the blocks with random letters. The task for the student is to find all the words as directed.

| V | T | L | C | T | X | S | R | E | B |
|---|---|---|---|---|---|---|---|---|---|
| N | R | R | A | B | B | I | T | A | N |
| A | Y | R | T | S | A | N | D | D | S |
| G | O | R | F | J | K | H | G | L | F |
| B | R | U | S | L | E | E | P | B | E |
| A | K | N | B | T | T | O | B | J | Z |
| K | I | T | V | C | O | R | E | D | P |
| A | B | I | L | L | Y | A | D | H | K |

Can you find these words?

| pool | nag | cat | to | rabbit | peel |
|---|---|---|---|---|---|
| ore | tan | bit | bed | sleep | bill |
| Billy | core | be | at | day | loop |
| he | sand | bake | Kit | and | an |

Many students enjoy preparing their own word search puzzles. Provide a list of words and the paper and let them go to it.

### 389. Word Building

Print a word on the chalkboard (or worksheet) in column form (i.e., the first letter on the first line, the second letter underneath the first on the second line, and so forth). Opposite the first column, the same word is printed going in the other direction (beginning with the bottom line). For example, the word *care* would look like this:

```
c _____ e
a _____ r
r _____ a
e _____ c
```

The student has to think of words beginning and ending with the letters that are opposite each other and write them in. In the example above, the first word could be *cake.* Any word that begins and ends with the given letters on a line may be accepted, or special rules such as three- or four-letter words only may be established.

The winner would be the first one to finish or, in the event of no finishers, the one with the most words in a specified time period.

### 390. Little Words in Big Words

Give the student a word. The task is to find as many little words in that word as possible. Each given word can be at the top of a box ruled on the page. The student can write the words found under the given word. The given words need not be compound words, although, of course, a compound word will always have at least two smaller words in it.

> # cornhusking

| | | | | |
|---|---|---|---|---|
| corn | husk | skin | in | husking |
| or | us | kin | | king |

### 391. Compound Words from Difficult Phrases

Make worksheets on which the student has to write the compound word suggested by a phrase. The easiest versions of this activity will have phrases that contain both halves of the compound word, so that the student simply has to find the two halves and write them as one word. The more difficult phrases will require the student to make a change in one or both of the word parts before writing the compound word.

Here are some easy ones:

| | | |
|---|---|---|
| time after the noon hour | = | afternoon |
| pen to hold pigs | = | pigpen |
| room with bed | = | bedroom |

Here are the same words with different clues:

| | | |
|---|---|---|
| time after midday | = | afternoon |
| an enclosure for pigs | = | pigpen |
| a room for sleeping | = | bedroom |

### 392. Describe-a-Word Puzzle

Prepare puzzles each spelling out the name of an animate or inanimate object. For each letter in the name, the student has to think of an adjective that *could* describe the given word. For example:

| | | | | |
|---|---|---|---|---|
| S | strong | | S | silky |
| O | outstanding | | P | pert |
| L | loyal | | A | argumentative |
| D | daring | | N | nice |
| I | interesting | | I | irritable |
| E | energetic | | E | entertaining |
| R | rebellious | | L | lively |

Note that it is not necessary to have all the descriptions be consistent with each other—e.g., it's okay to use both "rebellious" and "loyal" for *soldier*.

### 393. Scrambled Words

Print on the chalkboard or on a worksheet a list of words in scrambled form. Next to each scrambled word place a clue, such as the definition or classification of the word. The student has to reassemble the word and write it, spelled correctly, on the line. For example:

1. thneaderun_____
   This word means "below."
2. hcerecs_____
   Here is another word for "howl."
3. hptanmo_____
   Somewhat like a ghost.

### 394. Anagram Words

Give the student a multi-syllable word and a time limit. The task is to see how many words of three or more letters can be made out of the given word. If the given word contains an *s*, you may or may not permit simple plural words to count. Just decide the rule in advance. Here is a start on the word *phantoms:*

*Phantoms*

| | | | |
|---|---|---|---|
| moan | pants | tops | spat |
| ants | pant | ham | math |
| pan | atom | moths | mash |
| man | top | mop | sham |
| than | stop | span | shot |

There are many more  Can you find them?

## THINGS TO READ AND COMPREHENSION SKILLS

Most of the activities in this section can range in difficulty from very easy to extremely difficult, depending on the choice of content.

By the time a student has mastered word attack skills, a major source of material for his or her reading should be real books. In addition, short selections from a variety of sources can be used to develop comprehension skills using the formats described on the following pages. Articles from newspapers and magazines can be excerpted and adapted for classroom use, and you can develop comprehension exercises for them. For most of us, this is easier than creating original selections completely from scratch.

Objectives in comprehension skills include:

**AR-7.** Given a selection to read, the learner will read it and identify the main idea (or best title).

**AR-8.** Given a selection to read, the learner will read it and answer questions about details in the selection.

**AR-9.** Given a selection to read, the learner will read it and answer questions that require inference beyond what is directly stated in the selection.

**AR-10.** Given a selection and questions about it, the learner will refer back to the selection to verify answers to the questions.

**AR-11.** Given a selection to read, the learner will read it and match elements of cause and effect.

**AR-12.** Given a selection to read, the learner will read it and identify the correct sequence of events from the selection.

**AR-13.** After reading a selection or book, the learner will be able to discuss what he or she has read with peers or a teacher.

**AR-14.** Given a selection to read, the learner will read it and identify which parts are fact and which are opinion.

**AR-15.** After reading a selection, the learner wil outline it.

**AR-16.** Given appropriate level selections to read, the learner will read them and increase his or her reading rate.

**AR-17.** Given a selection, the learner will read it orally with appropriate expression.

### 395. Multiple-Choice Questions

After reading a short selection, the student may be asked to select the answer to a question about the selection. Multiple-choice items tend to be easier than completion items on the same selection.

When preparing multiple-choice items, there are a few things you should keep in mind:

- Avoid the tendency to have the correct answer longer than the others. Choices should be about the same in length.
- Be sure that the choices are grammatically consistent with the item stem.
- Make sure that there is only one "best" or correct answer.
- Don't give away the answer by a badly written item.
- Don't give away the answer to an item in the previous item or one immediately following.
- If you want to include an occasional funny or "way out" choice to keep interest high, that's fine. Most of the choices, however, should be believable.

### 396. Cloze Reading Passages

Cloze reading passages are becoming an increasingly popular form of testing reading comprehension. Preparation of a cloze passage is very simple. All you have to do is delete certain words. For example, every tenth or every seventh or every fifth word might be omitted. You shouldn't delete proper nouns or words in the first sentence of the passage. The task for the student is to complete the passage with words that make sense. Easier versions of cloze reading provide the words from which the student can select to fill in the blanks. A more difficult task is for the student to come up with original items to complete the selection.

Here is a sample of a cloze reading passage from a current practice workbook:

## It Went to His Head

In 1934, Bobby Cruickshank was fighting hard for the
_____ in the United States Open Golf Tournament. He
1
was _____ well until he came to the eleventh hole. This
2
_____ had a creek cutting right across the fairway.
3
Cruickshank _____ his ball and watched it head right
4
for the _____ . He wanted to cry until he saw the ball
5
_____ hit a rock in the creek and bounce onto
6
_____ green.
7
Cruikshank shouted with joy and tossed his club _____
8
into the air. This wasn't such a smart move, _____ the
9
club came down right on his head. He _____ so dizzy that
10
he couldn't play well the rest _____ the round. Instead of
11
winning, he ended up in _____ place.
12

| |
|---|
| doing |
| of |
| high |
| hole |
| was |
| the |
| third |
| lead |
| water |
| luckily |
| drove |
| because |

## 397. Reading Power Tests Using Cloze

A number of reading competency tests use a modified version of the cloze format. Key words are deleted, and four or five choices are provided for each missing word. Most of the choices should be syntactically consistent with the missing word, but only one should complete the passage so that it really makes sense. In this way the student's comprehension of what he or she is reading is being tested.

Here is a sample from a currently used program:

# People Under Glass?

In Winooski, Vermont, people have thought of a way to deal with

_____ New England winters. They plan to build a dome
1

over their entire town. The _____ bubble-shaped dome
2

would save energy and spare the townspeople from the harsh effects

of winter weather.

However, not everyone in the town thinks that a dome would be

such a good idea. Some _____ that living under a
3

bubble would give them a closed in feeling. Others fear a possible

disaster such as a plane _____ . And one woman was
4

heard to ask, "Who's going to clean it?"

| | | |
|---|---|---|
| 1. | warm | mild |
| | pleasant | cold |
| 2. | small | giant |
| | square | brick |
| 3. | hope | plan |
| | wish | worry |
| 4. | flight | trip |
| | meal | crash |

Reprinted by permission of Scholastic Inc. from *Reading Cloze Selections*, copyright © 1980 by Scholastic Inc.

## 398. Machine-Scored Response Sheets

The correct completion of answer sheets that are to be machine scored can make the difference between scoring well and failing many a test. No matter how well a student reads, if he or she does not present the answers in a way that can be read by the computer, the score will not be accurate.

It's important to give your students practice in using the special answer sheets that are used for so many tests these days. Design worksheets in the same format. Some important points to remember:

1. Be sure that the number of the item you are answering corresponds exactly to the number on the answer sheet.
2. Don't mark more than one answer for each item. Even if one of the marks is right, it won't count if more than one item is marked.
3. Be careful not to skip a line. Students have been known to leave one out and then to have every response that follows be wrong because it is in the wrong place.
4. Fill in the little circle carefully and neatly. Use the writing tool the directions tell you. (A number 2 pencil and a ball-point pen are not interchangeable.)

### 399. Writing the Facts

After reading a short selection, the student can be asked to write the answers to questions about the selection. These questions can refer to directly stated facts, or require the learner to make inferences. This type of exercise, in which the student has to recall the answer and produce it, is usually more difficult than a multiple-choice format in which the student simply has to recognize the correct answer where it appears.

### 400. Anagrams

Give the student a short selection to read, some questions on that selection, and an envelope of anagrams (cardboard letters). The student answers the questions by making words from the letters in the envelope.

This exercise should be used sparingly. It is simply another way of getting students to answer questions about a selection. It will benefit the rapid careless reader by making him or her slow down and ponder potential responses. It is not a good activity for the slow painstaking reader, who might spend all day pushing the anagrams around to get them just so.

### 401. Reading to Note Details

Give the student a paragraph containing many specific details. After reading it, the student lists as directed details to answer certain questions. For example:

> The clown stood in front of the people. His face was painted red, white, and blue. He had big black circles painted around his eyes. The tip of his nose was like a big ball. He wore a funny white suit with round green dots on it. The big wooden buttons on his suit looked just like wheels.

> What were the colors on the clown's face? _____
> List all the things in the story that are round: _____

### 402. Who, Where, When, What, How, and Why?

Give the student a sentence to read. Then ask a specific question about the sentence. These questions can ask who, what, where, when, how or why? For example:

1. Tom studies so he can pass the test.
   Why does Tom study? _____
2. Susan took the book home.
   Who took the book? _____
3. Every morning we eat bacon and eggs.
   When do we eat? _____
4. Hanging on the old oak tree was a yellow ribbon.
   Where was the ribbon? _____
5. We go to school on the school bus.
   How do we get to school? _____

### 403. More Who? Where? When? What?

Write some sentences on the chalkboard or on a worksheet. Tell the students that parts of the sentences answer the questions "Who?" "Where?" "When?" and "What?"

In the *who, where, when,* and *what* boxes next to each sentence number, the student should write the part of that sentence that answers the question. This is a more difficult version of the previous activity.

These sentences can be taken directly from the books students are reading or they can be constructed from the reading vocabulary. Here are some sentences:

1. All night Declan did his homework at the desk.
2. Six big dogs ate our meat on the table before dinner.
3. One day our teacher got mad in school.
4. In the morning some people like to sleep in their beds.
5. Every night the children go into their houses.

Here is the finished worksheet.

|   | Who | When | Where | What |
|---|-----|------|-------|------|
| 1 | Declan | all night | at the desk | did his homework |
| 2 | six big dogs | before dinner | on the table | ate our meat |
| 3 | our teacher | one day | in school | got mad |
| 4 | some people | in the morning | in their beds | like to sleep |
| 5 | the children | every night | in their houses | go |

### 404. Picture Captions

The stimuli for this activity are pictures from magazines or other sources. The task for the student is to write a caption for each picture, using a complete sentence.

This activity can be played as a game by two or more student teams. Two points are awarded to each student whose caption adequately expresses the main idea of the picture *and* uses a complete sentence. One point is given for a good summary caption that is not a complete sentence. The team with the most points wins.

## 405. Building Sentences for Main Idea

Begin with simple two-word sentences such as "Dogs bark." Discuss the two parts of these sentences. Have the students try to picture what each sentence means. You can prepare a series of worksheets in which the task is to match each sentence with its picture. The easiest worksheet will have the two-word sentences. The more difficult worksheets will have the same pictures but more complex sentences to match them.

## 406. Identifying the Main Idea in Simple Sentences

In simple sentences such as the ones in Activity 405, the student can be asked to identify the main idea by circling or underlining. For example:

Underline the two words that tell most about the main idea. The first one is done for you.
The big black and white <u>cow chewed</u> all morning.
The TWA jumbo jet flew into the air.

## 407. Matching Titles

After reading a short selection, the student has to pick the best title from a list provided. For example:

My dog Scarlet is very smart. One day she jumped up on the table. She hit a vase of flowers, and it fell on the floor. The water went all over the place. That doesn't sound very smart. But, what she did next was very clever. She ran into the kitchen and got a big dish towel. She brought it to me so I could wipe up the water.

Pick the best title:
A Vase of Flowers
Clean Water
In the Kitchen
A Clever Dog
Dogs on the Table

This type of exercise frequently appears on standardized tests. Note that picking the best title from choices is behaviorally very different from making up a clever title of one's own. On tests, what is often required is picking a title that expresses the main idea of the passage. Be sure that your students can do this.

## 408. Choosing the Main Idea

A frequently found exercise on standardized tests and in reading skill materials is one which requires the student to read a passage and then select from choices the best statement of the main idea of that passage. You can construct these exercises yourself, by gathering short reading selections and adding your own questions. The choices given the student should include some statements that are true of the story but are not the main idea (i.e., specific details), and, if you wish, some statements that do not accurately pertain to the story.

For example, after reading the story used in Activity 407, the student could be asked to pick the main idea instead of the best title. The choices might be:

Water needs towels.
The dog did a bad thing.
Scarlet is a smart dog.
I don't like messes.

### 409. Predicting Outcomes
Here is a sample worksheet for practice in predicting outcomes.

A good writer gives you clues about what is coming next. Watch for the clues as you read. Sometimes you can tell exactly what is coming. Sometimes you can't be sure. If you understand what you are reading, you can always get *some* idea about what will happen next. Try it with this story:

I don't like to get involved. If I see trouble, I turn the other way. Late last night when I was out walking the dog, he began to growl. He tugged at the leash and very nearly pulled me over. Then I saw what had caught his attention. Three men were climbing down from the roof of a store. They were breaking into the place. I didn't want to get involved, so I dragged the dog along and ran away. Just then we heard a siren. A police car raced around the corner and slammed on the brakes. The cops didn't want to believe my story. "But officer," I said, "I was just out _____."

Not only did I get involved, but I almost ended up _____.

### 410. Fact and Opinion
A good reader reads critically and is able to distinguish fact from opinion. Inexperienced readers tend to accept at face value much of what they see in print. The student must be taught to examine carefully whatever he or she reads.

Students should be given practice in reading material and identifying what is fact and what is opinion. Give the student a selection to read. Fact can be underlined in one color and opinion in another. This is an activity in which class discussion can be valuable.

### 411. Understanding Characters in Literature
Encourage students to try to understand as real people the characters they meet in literature. To give practice in this, try presenting short descriptive paragraphs with specific questions designed to help the student focus on what the character is really like. For example:

He was an ugly old man, wrinkled and gray. He was poor and badly dressed. His coat was worn and shabby, his trousers patched and threadbare. A rusty safety pin held his suspenders in place. But his lively dark eyes lighted up his worn old face and gave it a soft warm glow. For all his poverty and potential troubles, he seemed happy and contented.

1. Can you imagine some other qualities about this old man?
2. What kind of a person do you think he is?
3. Who do you suppose are his friends?
4. How do you suppose he would act if you went up and spoke to him?

The purpose of this exercise is to get the reader thinking. Note that there are no "right" answers. One student may portray the old man as a kindly person rich in spirit if not in things. Another may comment that the old man is probably too senile to notice how poor he is. Some students may describe a number of friends the old man might have. Others may say he has no friends but the pigeons in the park. The students' previous experiences will greatly influence how they interpret a character in literature.

## 412. Verifying a Statement

After reading a selection, the student may be asked to tell whether a given statement agrees or disagrees with the selection. This type of exercise is good for getting students to refer back to a selection while answering about it. Here is a sample:

Do you think there's life on other planets? On Mars, perhaps? Mariner 9, a space probe that orbited Mars for several months in 1972, gave scientists a totally new look at the Red Planet. Before Mariner 9 relayed photos and information back to scientists on Earth, it was thought that Mars was dry and inactive. Those of us who liked to think there might be life on Mars received no support from scientists.

Mariner 9, however, gave scientists a new look at Mars. It convinced them that Mars was once a planet where water flowed, ice ages appeared and disappeared, and the phenomenon of continental drift was under way.

These signs point to the possibility that life did indeed exist on Mars at one time. The information gathered by Mariner 9 was not enough to enable scientists to calculate how long ago life might have flourished on Mars. But it provided some clues suggesting the existence of life there sometime in the past.

Little green men? Flying saucers? Probably not. Life of some variety? Why not?

Write *A* next to each statement below which *agrees* with the selection you have just read. Write *N* next to each statement which does *not* agree. Write *?* next to each statement which cannot be verified by the passage (i.e., statement which is not included).

_____ Mariner 9 orbited Mars in 1972.
_____ Mariner 9 proved that there are people like us on Mars.
_____ Mariner 9 told scientists everything they wanted to know.
_____ Some scientists suspect that there is life on Venus.
_____ Scientists now believe that Mars once had water and ice.

### 413. Cause and Effect
After reading a paragraph, the student answers questions about cause and effect. For example:

> Nicky went into Mr. Ben's barn to play. He fell asleep on the hay. While he was asleep, the door blew shut. When Nicky woke up he was all alone. The barn was cold and dark. Nicky tried to open the door, but it wouldn't open. He felt trapped.

> What made the door shut? _____
> How did Nicky feel? _____
> Why? _____

### 414. Matching Cause and Effect
Prepare worksheets designed to give the student practice in matching cause and effect. These worksheets should, of course, be self-correcting.

The student should draw a line from the cause listed in the left-hand column to the appropriate effect in the right-hand column. For example:

| Cause | Effect |
|---|---|
| icy street | start fire |
| fall down | hurt knee |
| strike match | wake up baby |
| bark loudly | car skids |

### 415. Sequence
Give the students a paragraph to read. After reading it, they answer questions about the order of happenings in the paragraph. For example:

> We waited and waited and waited. At last the animals were led into the ring. How excited we were! First came the elephants in a long gray line. Then came the camels. After that came horses. Last in the animal line were the bears. A big brown bear fell and rolled on his back. We all laughed and laughed and laughed.

> 1. Which animals were last?
> 2. Which animals were first?
> 3. What did we do before the animals came?
> 4. What did we do after the bear fell?
> 5. Which animals came just before the horses?

### 416. More Sequence
Instead of answering questions, another approach to practicing skill in detecting sequence of events is to have students rearrange mixed up statements from a previously read selection.

For example, after reading the selection about the circus animals (see Activity 415), the student might do the following:

> Number these statements in the order they happened in the story. Put 1 next to the first thing. Put 2 next to the second thing, and so on.

_____ The animals were led into the ring.
_____ We laughed.
_____ We waited.
_____ The elephants came.
_____ The bears came.
_____ The camels came.

## 417. Comic Sequence

Cut a cartoon strip from the funny papers or a comic book. Cut each frame and mount it on oaktag for durability. The task for the student is to place the frames in correct order so that they tell a story. Be careful, of course, to select a series of frames that does have an obvious order to it. The backs of the cards can be numbered in order to make the activity self-checking. Each story sequence can be stored in its own envelope.

## 418. Assembling an Outline

Give the student a selection to read and an envelope containing a cut-up outline of the selection. (Before cutting, mount the outline on oaktag for durability.) The task for the student is to assemble the outline correctly. This is easier than copying the pieces of an outline, because the student can arrange and rearrange them until they look right. This is an excellent technique for teaching outlining skills before asking the student to make an outline independently.

## 419. Completing an Outline

After a student can assemble an outline of a reading selection, the next step is to complete an outline of a selection. Provide some major headings and some of the other items. The student should be able to fill in the missing parts before you expect him or her to construct a total outline from scratch.

### 420. Modified Outline Form

Instead of the usual outline form, a modified outline form using columns of categories can be used. Here is an example using a reading selection about polar bears.

## Polar Bears

Polar bears live far, far away in the north. Their home is on the islands of the Arctic Ocean. The islands are covered with snow all the year. These islands are called the polar country.

Only animals that can stand the cold live in the far north. The polar bear is one of these animals. Polar bears have a thick coat of white fur to protect them from the cold. Even the soles of their feet are covered with thick, long hair.

The polar bears are fine swimmers. They seem to be more at home in the water than on land. Using paws as paddles, polar bears are able to swim many miles out to sea. Polar bears are very playful in the water, too.

When polar bears become hungry, they hunt for food. They prowl about on the ice during the long winter nights looking for fish, seals, or walruses. If a polar bear sees a seal, he or she creeps up and kills it with a blow of a forepaw. Polar bears use sharp claws to catch fish.

## Polar Bears

| Location | Fur | Habits | Food |
|---|---|---|---|
| In far north Where there is always snow | Very thick to keep out the cold White as snow | Fine swimmer Paws as paddles | Found on ice Fish, seals, walruses |

### 421. Another Modified Outline Form

Provide a selection to read and an unfinished diagram following the sequence of items in the selection. Here is a sample story and completed diagram. What the student writes is in italics.

Dorothy was surprised to see such a large library on the ship. Rows and rows of beautifully colored books lined the walls of the room. In the center there were a few small reading tables. Each table had a lamp with a pale yellow shade. In one corner of the room stood a large cabinet. On top of the cabinet was an electric fan. The breeze of the fan blew against the lamp on a table nearby.

Only the windows were different. They were round and high up, and the glass was very thick. They were called portholes and had to be closed in case of a storm. The glass in the portholes was set in a thick metal ring about one inch wide. The metal ring was a guard for the glass and made opening and closing easy. It was easy because of the hinge at the side.

Conversely, you may give a selection accompanied by a bare diagram. The children plot the events without the questions.

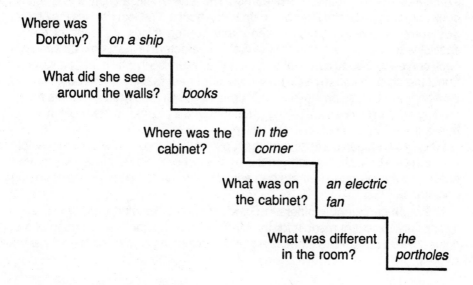

| | |
|---|---|
| Where was Dorothy? | *on a ship* |
| What did she see around the walls? | *books* |
| Where was the cabinet? | *in the corner* |
| What was on the cabinet? | *an electric fan* |
| What was different in the room? | *the portholes* |

## 422. Directed Reading Cards

Each card contains the name of a book and a chapter or section to be read, with three of four questions about it. Students must find the section of the book and read it and then respond to the questions. Key cards should be provided so that students can check themselves. If you pick your books and questions carefully, this activity may tease students into reading the entire book. Be sure to select a section that leaves the reader hanging.

## 423. Matching Books and Authors

Give each student a numbered list of books he or she has read. In another column write in mixed-up order the authors of the books. The task for the student is to match each book with its author. The student should be permitted to consult the class library to refresh the memory as needed. This serves two purposes. It makes the task reasonable, and it encourages the student to browse through books and perhaps stumble on something interesting that he or she hasn't read.

## 424. Book Reports: No

You will note that we do not include follow-up exercises for children's books, although reading real books is an activity we value highly. This was not an oversight, but a deliberate act. Students should be encouraged to choose books and read widely. However, we would like to discourage the proliferation of irrelevant follow-up activities, often called "enrichment," that are simply book reports in elaborate disguises. Building dioramas or making murals is far more time-consuming than instructive, as far as reading is concerned. We would like students to feel that the reward for reading a good book is the chance to get their hands on another one.

### 425. Book Conferences: Yes

A conference with a teacher about a book just read can be a valuable learning experience for both teacher and learner. The learner has a chance to discuss the book and what he or she liked and didn't like about it. The teacher has the chance to give some on-the-spot personalized instruction on things like parts of the book, special features, key elements of the plot or characters of that book, and so on. The book conference should be a dialogue, not an exercise in which the teacher tries to "trick" the student into revealing a less-than-perfect reading of the book. Make the experience a discussion, not a test. Of course, you will see which students are really reading and which ones are faking. Students who try to fake it need help in selecting books they would rather read than skip.

When your students are all reading books of their choice, it will be impossible for you to give every child a conference on every book. Some students will need to check in with you often. Others can easily do five or ten books without needing a conference.

The book conference folders in *Random House Reading Program, Orange* or *Yellow,* are excellent models for the kinds of activities that can be done in a book conference. You can use them as a guide in designing conferences on other books as well.

### 426. Oral Expression

Read a series of sentences or situational descriptions out loud. Have the students react to each one using the same word or phrase. The inflection and tone of voice used to respond will vary according to the statement presented. For example, try these with the word *no* as an answer.

1. Christmas vacation has just been cancelled.
2. We will get out of school an hour early this afternoon.
3. You can't go out to recess today.
4. Would you like a million dollars?
5. The president has just been shot.
6. Did you steal the money?

Try these with *ah* as a response.

1. You just got what you wanted for your birthday.
2. The doctor says, "Stick out your tongue."
3. A big nasty dog is about to jump up on you.
4. The teacher has just asked you a question you can't answer.

## 427. More Oral Expression

Read a short sentence out loud. Each time emphasize a different word and see how the meaning changes. Here is an example.

| | |
|---|---|
| George is my best friend. | (George, not Tommy.) |
| George is my best friend. | (He really is.) |
| George is my best friend. | (He's mine, not yours.) |
| George is my best friend. | (Better than all the others.) |
| George is my best friend. | (Friend, not best something else.) |

Now try it with these examples:

We had lunch in the cafeteria today.
Annie walked home without him.

## 428. Speedy Reading in Phrases

The format of the following selection was designed to assist the student in reading by phrases or thought units, rather than word by word. Instruct the reader to try to take in each group of words all at once. Virtually any material can be prepared in this format.

Some people    are so careful    that they make ready
for many things    that never happen.    They save old clothes
they will never wear    or prepare    for a rainy day    that never comes.
They are like    the White Knight    who had never learned
to stay on his horse    but who set out    upon his journey    with a mousetrap
because he *might* need    to catch a mouse.    The author tells
how Alice (in Wonderland)    met the White Knight.

"But you've got a beehive    or something like one    fastened
to the saddle,"    said Alice.
"Yes,    it's a    very good beehive,"    the knight said
in a    discontented tone,    "one of the best kind.    But not a single bee
has come near it yet.    And the other thing    is a mousetrap.
I suppose the mice    keep the bees out    or the bees    keep the mice out.
I don't know which."
"I was wondering    what the mousetrap was for,    said Alice.
"It isn't very likely    there would be any mice    on the horse's back."

"Not very likely, perhaps,"    said the knight;    "but if they *do* come,
I don't choose    to have them    running all about."
"You see,"    he went on    after a pause,    "It's as well    to be provided
for everything.    That's the reason    the horse has    all those anklets
round his feet."
"But what are they for?"    Alice asked    in a tone    of great curiosity.
"To guard against    the bites of sharks,    the knight replied.

(Lewis Carroll, *Through the Looking Glass*)

### 429. Rate of Reading

Easy-to-read material, a stopwatch or kitchen timer, and a progress plotter can be combined in an effective way to increase rate of reading. A learner can increase his or her reading speed without the aid of expensive mechanical devices or commercial courses.

The material for practicing to increase reading speed should be easy—at least a year in level below that which the reader can handle. Either divide the material into fixed amounts (*x* number of words or pages) and use a stopwatch to time how long it takes to do each section, or set a kitchen timer for a fixed time and see how far you can go. This practice should be done daily and progress plotter should be kept. The key to success is effort, practice, and visual record of progress. Don't try to do it without a progress plotter.

Note: if you are plotting number of words in a fixed time, the graph goes up as you read faster. If you are plotting time it takes to read a fixed amount, the graph goes down as you improve.

## REFERENCE SKILLS

The activities in this section are designed primarily to help students locate information for school-related tasks. The exact content you use for many of the various exercises can be taken from suitable social studies and science materials that relate to what you are doing in these subject areas. Locating information in settings other than school will be dealt with in the Survival Skills section beginning on p. 239. Objectives for Reference Skills are:

**AR-18.** Given a book, the learner will use the table of contents to locate specified information.

**AR-19.** Given a book, the learner will use the index to locate specified information.

**AR-20.** Given a topic, the learner will use the card catalog and locate information about the topic in the library.

**AR-21.** Given a topic, the learner will indicate which of several reference sources is most likely to give information on that topic.

**AR-22.** Given a list, the learner will place the items in alphabetical order.

**AR-23.** Given a dictionary, the learner will use it rapidly to answer questions and locate words.

### 430. Table of Contents

Prepare a worksheet asking questions that can be answered by referring to the table of contents of a given book. For example, here are some questions than can be answered from the table of contents in *All About Great Medical Discoveries,* by David Dietz (Random House, 1960).

1. How many chapters are there in *All About Great Medical Discoveries?*
2. If you wanted to read why doctors wash their hands often, you would turn to page _____.

3. A chapter about vitamins begins on page _____.
4. The name of one chapter mentions two kinds of animals. It begins on page _____.
5. Page 26 is the first page in a chapter called _____.
6. Page 111 is in a chapter called _____.
7. The chapter about polio begins on page _____.
8. "The Murderous Germs" is a chapter with _____ pages.

### 431. Table of Contents vs. Index

Give the student a book with both an index and a table of contents. Have the student list the differences between the two. Or, give the student a list of questions about the book. The task is to indicate where to look first—the index or the table of contents—to find the answer to each of the questions.

### 432. Using an Index

Give the student a book with an index or a worksheet that reproduces a portion of a book's index. For example:

```
Airplanes
    Advantages of air travel   112–114
    Construction of   110
    Definition   103
    Disadvantages of air travel   115
    Early experiments with   104
    How brought to earth   110–112
    How controlled in the air   108
    Jumbo jets   116–117
    Modern types   115–119
    Shipping cargo by   120–121
```

Then ask to what pages one should turn to find the answer for each of the following questions.

1. How does one steer a plane?
2. How many people can fly a 747 jumbo jet?
3. Who invented the airplane?
4. How does one land a plane?
5. Can you ship a dog by air?
6. What are some of the problems of air travel?
7. How do modern planes differ from early ones?
8. What is an airplane?

### 433. Making an Index

Give the student a list of words and phrases. The task is to arrange these words and phrases as they would be in an index. For example:

cold-blooded animals
atomic energy
air pressure
electronics
red blood cells

penicillin
white blood cells
mammals
warm-blooded animals

### 434. Identifying Index Entries

Give the student a list of questions. The task is to underline in each question the key word one would look for in an index to locate the answer to that question.

### 435. Library Visit

Be sure to arrange for your class to visit the school and/or local public library. The students should be made familiar with the physical arrangement of the room and the location of the materials they will be likely to use.

### 436. Library Floor Plan

Prepare a floor plan of the school or local library with the location of different types of materials labeled. For younger children, you can add picture codes to make the floor plan easier to read.

### 437. Book Caretaker

One remedy for a student who tends to be careless about and destructive toward books is to appoint that student to be in charge of the books for a while. Let him or her inventory the classroom library and note the condition of each book on a checklist. Any major changes in a book's condition should be recorded. A spot on the bulletin board can be used for notes of this kind. For example:

Ron's dog ate six pages of *The Cat in the Hat*.
Sunny mended the cover of *The Monster Book*.

### 438. Dewey Decimal System

If your school or local public library uses the Dewey Decimal System for classifying library books, make a reference chart for your students to aid them in retrieving the books they need.

000 - General Works
100 - Philosophy (Man and his destiny) and Psychology
200 - Religion
300 - Social Science (including education)
400 - Philology
500 - Natural Science
600 - Useful Arts
700 - Fine Arts
800 - Literature
900 - History
910 - Geography
920 - Biography
930 - Ancient History
940 - Europe
950 - Asia
960 - Africa
970 - North America
980 - South America
990 - Oceania and Polar Regions

Of course, if your library uses a different system (Library of Congress, for example), you will use that system on the chart instead of the one presented above.

### 439. Cards for Card Catalog

Prepare a chart to demonstrate the different kinds of entries in the library card catalog. Here are the sample cards to illustrate a chart for one book.

Author Card

| |
|---|
| X598.1<br>H 35                Hecht, Bessie M.<br><br><br>All about snakes; illus. by<br>Rudolf Freund. Random House 1956. |

Title Card

X598.1
H 35                    ALL ABOUT SNAKES

        Hecht, Bessie M.
            All about snakes. New York,
      Random House 1956.

Subject Card

X598.1
H 35                    REPTILES

        Hecht, Bessie M.
            All about snakes. Illus. by
      Rudolf Freund. Random House 1956.

Subject Card

X598.1
H 35                    SNAKES

        Hecht, Bessie M.
            All about snakes. illus. by
      Rudolf Freund. Random House 1956.

## 440. Classroom Catalog

The students can make their own library card catalog for the classroom library by using index cards. This should be undertaken primarily as an experience to learn how a card catalog is set up and how it functions to help readers retrieve books they want or need. Classroom card catalogs should not be employed primarily as a mechanism to police book borrowers. One of the beauties of a classroom book collection is the easy and comfortable access to those books. Classrooms should avoid setting up the same procedures that tend to make children uncomfortable in libraries.

### 441. Cataloging Exercise
Divide a work sheet into five sections to correspond to card catalog drawers.

| A-E | F-J | K-O | P-T | U-Z |
|-----|-----|-----|-----|-----|
|     |     |     |     |     |

Give the student the reference to a book. The task is to locate each entry (author, title, subject) in the appropriate place. For example: *All About Birds,* by Robert S. Lemmon, would go in A-E for title, K-O for author, A-E for subject.

### 442. Parts of a Book
As an exercise to help develop ability to identify parts of a book, give the learner this questionnaire and a book.

Title:_____

Author:_____

Publisher:_____

Copyright date:_____

Copyright owner:_____

Is there a preface or introduction?_____

What is the book's major purpose?_____

Are there illustrations?_____

If so, who did them?_____

How long is the book?_____

Is there an index?_____

Is there an appendix?_____

Are there any other special features?_____

Is the book well  printed?_____

illustrated?_____

bound?_____

### 443. Alphabetizing Drill
To promote speed in alphabetizing, a timed drill can be done using exercises with many items such as the following:

What letter comes before f? _____
What letter comes before m? _____
R comes between _____ and _____.

This type of drill can be done orally or on worksheets.

### 444. Dictionary Vocabulary Drill

Few assignments are more deadly than the old standby that requires a student to look up ten words in the dictionary and write the definition of each. Neither word knowledge nor effective dictionary use tends to be enhanced by such an exercise. An exercise constructed as follows gives practice in dictionary use and develops a student's vocabulary. Try it as an alternative to the "look up and copy" approach.

(These questions were designed to use the Random House *Dictionary of the English Language*. Be sure that the ones you make up can be answered using whatever dictionary you have in your classroom.)

---

*Directions*:

Look up each underlined word in your dictionary. Then pick the answer to each question.

1. Where would you be most likely to find a *foozle?*
   a. a zoo
   b. a supermarket
   c. a golf course
   d. a department store

2. Which of these is NOT a meaning of *hock?*
   a. to pawn
   b. white wine
   c. part of a horse
   d. tool

3. You can be quite sure that a *perspicacious* person is NOT—
   a. stupid.
   b. married.
   c. male.
   d. tall.

4. One would be most likely to enjoy a *rickey*—
   a. playing in the snow.
   b. on a hot afternoon.
   c. while sleeping.
   d. in the shower.

5. Where would you look to find a *tappet?*
   a. in its nest
   b. near a valve
   c. under the bed
   d. on your shoulder

6. What is a *sporran?*
   a. kitchen utensil
   b. seeds of a fern
   c. a fur purse for men
   d. a small fast car

## 445. Easy Alphabetical Order

The easiest level of alphabetizing exercise contains words no two of which begin with the same letter. The easiest format for this exercise is one in which each word in the list is presented on an individual index or flash card. It is easier for students to shuffle and rearrange the cards with the hands than it is to do the same exercise in the head.

## 446. More Difficult Alphabetizing

After the student can alphabetize by the first letter of a word, give practice in more difficult lists. For example:

1. make, meal, money, mill, mud
2. made, make, mat, market, mail, map, magic

## 447. Sources of Alphabetizing Exercises

To come up with really interesting and difficult lists of words to alphabetize (and to ascertain for yourself their precise correct alphabetical order) just consult a good dictionary.

For example, here is a really tough list, in order, from page 1484 of the Random House *Dictionary of the English Language:*

tilth, tight, tiger, till, tiglon, tiller, tilt, tiled, tilery, tiki

Note that the words are not long ones. You can have an alphabetizing exercise that is difficult, without making it an endurance contest. The effort should be in the alphabetizing not in the copying over of words.

## 448. Special Interest Alphabets

A student with a strong area of interest can make up his or her own alphabet using only words relating to the special interest. This is especially useful for older remedial readers who are apt to feel that "A is for apple" is beneath them. For example, a student who is crazy about horses might come up with

A is for Appaloosa
B is for bay
C is for colt or Connemara pony
D is for dappled
E is for equestrian or eventing
F is for foal
G is for gray
H is for hunter
I is for Irish Draught
J is for Jumper
K is for Kimberwick
and so on . . .

### 449. Dictionary Race

Give each player a dictionary and a list of five to ten questions or directions. The winner is the first one to get all the items correct. Here are just a few examples:

1. How many numbered definitions are there for *bear?*
2. How many correct ways are there to pronounce *tomato?*
3. What is another way to spell *theater?*
4. On what page is *mustang* defined?
5. List the antonyms given for *light.*

### 450. Dictionary Guide Words

Teach the students to use the guide words on a dictionary page as an aid to locating words more quickly. Try timed exercises such as these:

Check the column that shows if the listed word comes before, between, or after the given guide words.

Guide words: energy . . . . . . . . . epidermis

|  | Before | On That Page | After |
|---|---|---|---|
| aardvark | ___ | ___ | ___ |
| entertain | ___ | ___ | ___ |
| enervate | ___ | ___ | ___ |
| elephant | ___ | ___ | ___ |
| experience | ___ | ___ | ___ |

### 451. Historical and Geographical Information in the Dictionary

Be sure to teach your students that the dictionary is an excellent source of certain kinds of historical and geographical information. Here are some questions that can be answered by looking in the dictionary. Timed exercises such as these can help the student develop speed in using the dictionary for a variety of things.

1. In what year was Beethoven born?
2. Where is the Malabar Coast?
3. Is the gila monster a native of New England?
   If not, where is he/she from?
4. In what war did the Rough Riders serve?
   Who was their leader?
5. What present-day country includes much of the ancient region that was known as Mesopotamia?

Be sure that the questions you develop can be answered using the dictionary that the students have.

# SURVIVAL READING

The activities in this section are for the purpose of helping students develop reading skills with immediate application in the real world.

**AR-24.** Given a topic, the learner will indicate which of several sources is most likely to contain information on that topic.

**AR-25.** Given a piece of reading material, the learner will skim to locate specific information.

**AR-26.** Given a practical reference source (phone book, zip code directory), the learner will locate specific information.

**AR-27.** Given a real-life reading task (newspaper, label, menu, advertisement, job-related material), the learner will read and answer questions about it.

**AR-28.** Given a map, graph, or chart, the learner wil use it to answer specified questions.

### 452. Which Source?

Give the student a list of reference sources and some questions. The task is to pick the most likely source in which to find the answer to each question. The longer the list of sources, the more difficult the task. An even harder task would be to provide no choices at all and to require the student to supply the name of the reference book.

For example: encyclopedia, world almanac, *Farmer's Almanack,* dictionary, *Bartlett's Familiar Quotations,* telephone book, yellow pages, atlas, *Who's Who in America, Guinness Book of World Records, Official Airline Guide.*

1. Where would you find the exact words of a famous saying?
2. Where would you find the address of a store that sells major appliances, if you didn't know the name of the store?
3. When is the best time to plant tomatoes in the Northeast?
4. Where would you locate a short biography of a famous person?
5. If you wanted to get from New York to San Francisco in a hurry, where could you get information on how to get there?
6. What is the definition of the word sesquipedalian?
7. What's the largest number of pies any one person has ever eaten at one sitting?
8. How far away from the sea is the capital of Brazil?
9. How high is the highest fence that a horse or pony is known to have jumped?
10. How many flights per day are there between New York and Shannon, Ireland?

### 453. Locating the Answer

To aid in developing the technique of skimming to find specific information, provide the student with a question and short selection in which to find the answer to the question. The student is to read the question first and then skim to find the answer. He or she should plot the time it takes to respond. (Note that this is a progress graph on which the line should go down, not up.)

### 454. Reading a Building Directory

In trying to find a particular office or a friend's apartment for the first time, it makes sense to consult the building directory rather than simply wandering around.

Provide a facsimile directory (your students can supply a real one from a local office or apartment) and practice questions.

### 455. Reading the Yellow Pages

Be sure that your students know how to use the Yellow Pages of the telephone directory. They should learn how to consult the list of headings to find out how to locate a service or store that they need. Provide practice by giving them practice exercises with questions that can be answered using your local directory. Here are a few sample questions.

1. You need some horse feed. Under what heading would you look?
2. If you want a locksmith to come to open your car in which you have just locked the keys, how many different places could you call in your area?
3. Your turtle is sick. Under what heading would you look for help?
4. You want to buy some new jeans. In what stores would you have a good chance of finding them?
5. You need 500 invitations printed for a special party at the local club. Where might you call?

### 456. Phone Book Drill

Practice in location of names and phone numbers will help any learner in a useful skill. This is even more important now that directory assistance calls are no longer free.

Play a game in which the task is to locate a given name faster than anyone else. You can divide the class into teams and play it like a relay race.

Your local phone company will probably cooperate in supplying you with enough directories for classroom use.

### 457. Zip Code Directory

Give the students a list of addresses and a zip code directory. Like the phone book, the zip code book is a source of a game. See which team can complete all the addresses first.

### 458. Advertising Superlatives

Intelligent, critical reading of advertising is a useful skill. The sooner students learn not to fall for all the apparent promises, the better off they will be. Have students bring in examples of ads that appear to promise a lot while perhaps delivering little.

Develop practice exercises around a collection of advertisements. Ask questions that sharpen the skill of the students in the area of informed consumerism. Here are some sample questions as an illustration of the types you might create:

1. The ad says, "Four out of five doctors questioned recommend EZ-UR-Pain." Do you have any idea how many doctors in all recommend that tablet?
2. You can be sure if it's made by Zero-Way. What does this statement mean?
3. There's no other mouthwash like it. Does this mean it's the best? Why or why not?
4. Our product gives you more. Does this mean it's better?

## 459. Ad Strategies

In teaching students to read ads critically, be sure that they are aware of the major strategies used in writing these advertisements.

1. The "expert" approach. (For example, two out of three pharmacists interviewed reported that their customers prefer Snooze-away.)
2. The "bandwagon" approach. (Everyone else is using it. Why don't you?)
3. The "Do what the stars do" approach. (U.S. golfing champ Oscar Divot likes Clean Green Aftershave best of all.)
4. The "kind words" approach. (It's the best. No other can match it.)

Have students bring in examples of each of the strategies. See if the other students can identify each of the techniques being used.

## 460. More Ad Lingo

Students will enjoy writing their own ads to sell a service or a product. Instruct them that they must not tell untruths, but that a clever use of language to convey positive notions about what they are selling is what's required.

Have each student select three products with which he or she has had personal experience. The assignment is to design an ad for each product that would sell it to others in the class. The students can then critique each other's ads as suggested in Activities 458 and 459.

## 461. Order Forms

Give your students practice in reading and filling out order forms for merchandise that might be of interest to them. This is a useful skill that focuses attention on significant but often overlooked details. (What color? What size? How many? Any special instructions?)

Catalogs such as the Sears Roebuck Catalog or newspaper ads with order forms included are excellent sources of material for practice exercises. Make sure that the students notice carefully any restrictions in the material. (For example: Give second color choice. If supply is exhausted, order will be filled with items of comparable value.)

### 462. Classified Ads for Lost and Found

Have students practice writing and reading Lost and Found ads. You never can tell when these skills might come in handy. For practice exercises using the ads, prepare questions based on sample ads. The questions could be completion, or true/false items.

### 463. Reading a Menu

Reading and interpreting a menu is an important skill. It's an activity that you might not want to schedule right before lunch if you and any of your students are trying to diet.

Gather menus from your favorite local places and prepare questions about them.

### 464. Menu Vocabulary

Reading a menu often involves special vocabulary. Be sure the students know the meaning of words and phrases such as appetizers, entrees, à la carte, complete dinner, beverage, soup du jour, prix fixe and the like.

Restaurants of different nationalities do, of course, use different words to describe some of their dishes. A bit of familiarity with key menu words can help keeping a person from being too intimidated to order what he or she really wants. (For years we avoided certain favorites in French restaurants because we were afraid to venture a try at saying the name.)

### 465. Garment Care Labels

Correct interpretation of the information on garment care labels is a useful survival skill. It can prevent ending up with a pile of spotted laundry that resulted from putting an item that runs into a hot wash with white sheets. It can prevent that cashmere sweater from ending up looking like a garment for an infant rather than a full-sized person. Reading the care labels *before* a purchase can save you money. (Can you really afford to have that pair of white slacks dry cleaned after every wearing?)

Have the students bring in the information from some real labels and prepare exercises based on them. (We don't suggest removing labels from garments, because they are needed right where they are.)

Here are some of the kinds of questions you might ask.

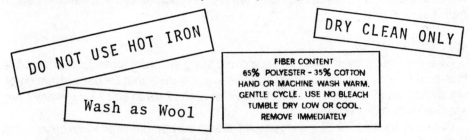

1. What would happen if this garment were washed?
2. What kind of soap should be used?
3. Are there any special restrictions on washing this item?
4. Is there more than one way to get this item clean?
5. What's the best way to get the wrinkles out?

## 466. Warning Labels

Many commonly used household products can be dangerous. It's important to read and understand the labels. Provide sample labels and questions for the students to practice this survival skill. Here are some questions you might ask:

```
HARMFUL OR FATAL IF SWALLOWED.  KEEP OUT
OF REACH OF CHILDREN.  CONTAINS PETROLEUM
DISTILLATES.  If swallowed, DO NOT induce
vomiting.  CALL A PHYSICIAN IMMEDIATELY.

COMBUSTIBLE.  Do NOT use near fire.
```

1. How or why could this product harm you?
2. What shouldn't you do with it?
3. What should you do if someone drinks (eats, touches, gets into the eyes, or whatever shouldn't be done) this product?
4. How should you store this product to make sure it is carefully used?

## 467. Words for Warning Labels

To make sure that your students can read warning labels and take appropriate action, try teaching the key words that such labels often use. Among these important vocabulary words are antidote, internal, external, poison, fatal, combustible, vapor, (in)flammable, dangerous.

## 468. Reading a Warranty

If students are going to be careful and informed consumers, they must learn how to read and interpret warranties. Provide practice. Your students can bring in samples of different warranties for things they have purchased. They should learn the difference between a limited warranty and a full one. They should note carefully any obligations the warranty places on them.

## 469. Understanding Utility Bills

Knowing what the words mean is only the first step in understanding utility bills. There are certain key questions that a consumer should be able to answer.

1. What time period is covered by this bill?
2. What are the services being billed for?
3. How much has to be paid this month?

Use copies of bills sent by the utilities in your areas to develop practice exercises.

## 470. Vocabulary for Utility Bills

The statements sent out by utility companies (phone, gas, electric) have their own special vocabulary. Knowing what these words mean is part of being an informed consumer.

Key words include message units, allowance, toll calls, directory assistance, current charges, balance, meter reading, kilowatt hours, cubic feet, budget payment, etc. Provide practice on whatever special terms the utilities in your area use.

### 471. Store Catalogs and Order Blanks

Careful use of mail order catalogs can be a great convenience to a shopper. Prepare exercises based on pages of offerings that might appeal to your students. This will give them practice in reading and correctly interpreting the material.

Here's a sample of the type of exercise that could be useful:

1. Which tennis racket comes in the smallest size?
2. If you're a beginner, which would probably be the best buy for you?
3. Do the prices given include shipping? What words in the ad tell you that?
4. How much would you have to pay for Item A if you live in Chicago? How much if you live in Los Angeles? Why would there be a difference?
5. Which racket would be best for a woman who's thinking of turning pro? Why did you pick the one you did?

### 472. Reading Road Maps

Reading road maps is a useful skill. Your local service station or automobile club used to be a ready source of maps. Since the energy shortage and inflation, these items are a little harder to come by. You might try writing to the major oil companies. Prepare task cards with specific exercises that can be done with the map. For example, you might ask questions such as:

1. How many miles is it from _____ to _____ by the shortest route?
2. What kind of a road goes directly from _____ to _____?
3. If you want to go from _____ to _____, through which towns would you go?
4. How would you get from _____ to _____ without using a toll road?
5. Where is the nearest ski area to _____? The nearest airport?

The first exercises done by the students should be with maps of familiar areas. Then the skills can be applied to maps of places they have never been. Of course, the exercises done with a road map should always close with the exercise of folding it correctly!

### 473. Local Maps

Map training can begin at home. Many communities have maps of the immediate local area. A visit to a local shopping area could be followed by construction of a map. Each student could draw a map of his or her block. Or, how about a map (floor plan) of your school, showing the classrooms, corridors, and such essentials as the cafeteria, gym, and rest rooms?

### 474. Travel Plans

Travel plans, either real or simulated, can form the basis of practice in reading timetables, bus schedules, airline guides, and the like. In addition to being fun, these activities are useful real-world behaviors.

Call your local Amtrak office for the train timetables. A friendly travel agency is a good source for old airline guides (they get new ones every two weeks), bus and ship schedules, and hotel and motel directories.

Prepare sets of problems to be solved by consulting with the various travel reference materials. For example:

1. It's cold in wintertime in New York City. You want to go to Miami, Florida, for some sun. Find the earliest nonstop flight leaving New York for Miami on Saturday morning.

What airline is it?
What time does it leave? Arrive?
Is a meal served on the flight? Free champagne?
Is there bus or limousine service from the Miami airport
    to a terminal in the city? To some hotels?
Which metropolitan airport does the flight leave from?

2. How many flights are there on a Monday between San Francisco and New York? Between Los Angeles and Atlanta? Do any flights from Los Angeles to Atlanta stop in New Orleans?

Some of these exercises can be designed to give practice in computational skills as well as reading and reference skills. For example:

3. Assuming "on time" departure and arrival, how much longer does it take to get from Chicago to Denver by train than by plane? If it takes _____ hours and _____ minutes to fly from Chicago to Denver and you leave Chicago at 10:00 A.M., what time is it when you get to Denver?

## 475. Reading Graphs

Provide practice in reading graphs that pertain to issues of concern to your students. Here's a bar graph that shows the miles per gallon achieved by six different makes of automobile.

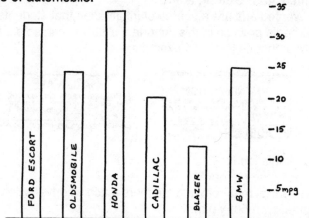

Have your students think of topics that lend themselves to having pertinent information displayed on a graph.

### 476. Pie Graphs

One of the easiest types of graph for students to construct and to interpret is the pie, or circle graph. Here's one showing how one student spent the weekly allowance. The students can help you think of other topics that could be graphed in this way.

### 477. Job-Related Vocabulary

For students who are soon to enter the world of employment, special work in the words that relate to getting jobs and fillling out employment papers should be reviewed (or taught). This is especially important for those students who are not high achievers in reading and other school tasks. Words such as application, references, availability, experience, and interview should be gone over so that students will be able to understand what the various forms are asking for.

Words that relate to a particular specialty (such as auto mechanics, cooking, etc.) should be dealt with for those students who need them.

### 478. Classified Ads: Getting a Job

The Help Wanted ads are a source of information that students should learn to deal with. To begin practice in this important skill, you can select ads and prepare questions about them. Here's an example:

1. What is this job for?
2. Is experience needed?
3. What special requirements are there (such as driver's license, high school diploma, type 50 w.p.m.)
4. How would you go about applying for this job or finding out more about it?
5. Why would (wouldn't) this be a good job for you?
6. What are the hours? The wages?

## 479. Job Applications

Give students practice in reading and filling out application forms. A local employment agency might be a good source of sample forms. If not, you can design one yourself. Here's a sample:

---

### APPLICATION FOR EMPLOYMENT
#### PRINT OR TYPE

Date_____

Social
Security No._____

Name_____
　　　Last　　　　　　　First　　　　　　　Middle

Present Address_____
　　　　　　　No. & St.　　　　　City, Town　　　State　　　Zip

Marital Status_____　　Tel. No._____

Position Desired _____

Minimum Salary _____ c) Date Available for Work_____

#### WORK HISTORY

| Have you ever: | Yes | No | If "Yes" please explain |
|---|---|---|---|
| been employed? | | | |
| applied for employment? | | | |
| had or do you now have any physical defects, limitations, or chronic ailments? | | | |
| had or do you now have any serious injury or illness? | | | |

#### EDUCATION

| School | Dates Attended | | Graduate? Degree | Major Study |
|---|---|---|---|---|
| | From | To | | |
| High School | | | | |
| Address | | | | |
| College or University | | | | |
| Address | | | | |
| Business or Technical School | | | | |
| Address | | | | |
| Other | | | | |
| Address | | | | |

---

Before having the students fill this out, ask questions about it to focus their attention on the important items. (Where would you list the names of people who know you? Under what heading would you list your recent jobs?)

### 480. More Help Wanted Ads

After the students have practiced reading and answering questions about selected ads, it's time to turn them loose on the Help Wanted section of the local paper and see if they can pick out an ad or two that could be considered. If there are not any employment situations in your community that are suitable for the students you are teaching, have them answer the questions in relation to some future goal. (There probably aren't any jobs open for skilled mechanics who are also sixth graders. Have the student pick a job that he or she might aspire to in a few years, and answer the questions as if certain interim factors such as training and experience have already occurred.)

### 481. On the Job Notices

Another source of practice exercises in real-world reading comprehension is the frequently difficult-to-decipher bulletin board notice. Provide samples from offices or other places of employment. These notices can deal with anything from absences to coffee breaks to fire drills. If your students aren't interested in job-related notices, try items that would be found on school bulletin boards.

In responding to a notice, the student should ask himself or herself the following types of questions:

1. Does this notice apply to me?
2. What is the notice about?
3. If it does apply to me, what would I do in response to the information.

### 482. Reading a Paycheck

For those who are employed, reading a paycheck is more involved than simply looking at the amount and figuring out how to spend it. Students should learn to deal with the various bits of information on the stub of the check or on the accompanying memo. For example, they should know the difference between gross and net, what the words for the various kinds of deductions are, and how to check the amount for accuracy. Provide practice with facsimile checks. Some students might volunteer their own documents for a real-life experience.

### 483. Reading a Bank Statement

Although some people just toss their bank statements into the pile on the desk, this is not a recommended procedure. Careful reading of the statement and understanding what it all means is an important contemporary survival skill.

Try using a facsimile statement and questions for practice exercises. Important words include balance, closing balance, deposit, debit, service charge, closing date, etc.

### 484. Income Tax Forms and Directions

Students who work need to know how to read and complete tax forms. This skill will be needed throughout adult life. Key terms should be taught. These include words such as deductions, dependent, exemption, filing status, joint return, compensation, etc.

You can design practice exercises using real forms and the directions provided by Internal Revenue Service. A good time to make up these exercises is at the time you prepare your own tax returns. You'll be in close touch with the types of confusions that often result from an attempt to figure out what the directions mean.

### 485. Getting a Social Security Card

Completing the application for a social security card is a useful skill for a student. Blank forms, which are readily obtainable at your local Social Security office, are short compared to a number of other bureaucratic devices. This one's a good place to begin, not only because the form is easy, but because it's one that every student will need sooner or later.

Before asking students to complete the form, ask questions about it to focus their attention on the correct way to do it. Some possible questions are:

1. Where would you find the directions for completing this form?   (on the back)
2. Which evidence of age and citizenship would you be able to provide?   (answers, from the list on the back of the form, would vary)
3. What could you use to prove your identity?   (answers would vary)
4. What could happen if you willfully give false information on this form?   (fine or prison)
5. You have to fill in the names of two other people on the form. Who are they?   (mother and father)

### 486. Newspaper Facts Vs. Opinions

A newspaper is an excellent tool to teach the difference between fact and opinion. Have each student bring in a paper. Statements of fact can be underlined in one color, and statements of opinion can be underlined in another. Time the students as they try to find ten (or more) examples of each.

You may wish to divide the class into teams, and keep track of how many examples are found within a given time. You can give double points for each statement of opinion that is found in a news story and not on an editorial page or in a column.

### 487. Newspaper Editorials

It's important for students to understand the difference between newspaper editorials and news stories. (Be sure you select well-written items in which there really *is* a difference.)

Provide examples of editorials for the students to read. Try to select topics that would be of interest. (You can encourage students to bring in editorials from the papers they get at home.) For each editorial, the student should be able to answer the following questions:

1. What topic is the editorial about?
2. Is the editorial for or against whatever its topic is?
3. What facts (if any) does the editorial use to support or justify its opinion?
4. Do you agree with the newspaper's view? Why or why not?

### 488. Newspaper Information

Give the student a copy of a metropolitan newspaper and a problem to solve, the solution to which can be found in the newspaper. Here are some suggestions for problems:

1. You want to go to the theater to see a play. Look in the paper and find one you want to see.

    What is its name? _____
    Who is starring in it? _____
    At what theater is it? _____
    How much does the least expensive seat cost? _____
    Find a restaurant near the theater where you can eat dinner. _____

2. You want to go to a drive-in movie. You know what picture is playing and where it is. You don't know what time to go or what to wear.

    The picture starts exactly 30 minutes after sunset.
    What times does the sun set? _____
    What times does it start? _____
    What will the weather be like? _____
    What should you wear? _____

### 489. More Newspaper Information

Another approach to teaching students to use the newspaper effectively is to have the students prepare questions such as those in the previous exercise. Give each student a paper and some examples of the kinds of questions that can be answered. After each student has prepared a list of questions, have the lists exchanged and see how quickly each one can answer the items prepared by a classmate.

### 490. Skimming the Newspaper

Skimming is an important skill. A newspaper is a good tool on which to practice. Give the student a page of a daily paper. It should be a page with a number of different news stories and headlines. Good choices, for example, would be page one of the *Washington Post, The New York Times,* or the *Los Angeles Times.* A poor choice would be a tabloid like the *New York Daily News* because of the limited number of topics mentioned on page one.

The task for the student is to glance over the page for one minute (or two for someone just learning to skim) and then to jot down as many different facts as he or she can remember from the page. A progress plotter of the number of items found and recalled should be kept to show improvements from day to day.

### 491. Newspaper Headlines

Give the student a clipping from the newspaper. Allow 15 or 20 seconds in which the student is to read the heading and subheadings. The student then tells what he or she has learned.

### 492. Finding the Article

Give the student a page from the newspaper. Ask him or her to find as quickly as possible an article about a specified subject. Keep track of time on a progress plotter. (Note that when plotting time, the falling graph line means quicker finding. Not all charts should go up!)

### 493. Key Heading Words

To increase the ability to skim quickly and find an article on a specified topic, have the student list in advance all the words he or she might look for in the newspaper to find an article dealing with that topic. For example, if the topic were aviation, the list might include *airline, jumbo jet, jet fuel, 747, B-52, FAA, TWA, United, crash landing,* and so on.

### 494. Technical Directions

Many students enjoy reading and following directions for constructing things and taking them apart. Try selections from automotive shop manuals, directions for assembling stereo components, and the like. Many a student who won't read much voluntarily is willing to struggle with such material.

### 495. Following Real-Life Directions

To give practice in following written directions in real situations, give written directions to students for the planning of a class activity. If each of the students follows the directions, the activity will work. In other words, the payoff for following the directions will be a real one.

For example, in planning a class party, certain students could be directed to arrange the room in a certain way. Others might be instructed to make or do something in the way of decorations or refreshments. Don't give oral directions for this one—let each student *read* what he or she is to do.

### 496. Following Directions in an Experiment

Prepare written directions for specific tasks to be carried out in a simple science experiment. For example:

*How Are Sounds Produced?*

1. Strike the edge of the school bell or another bell with a wooden hammer. Just after striking it touch your fingers lightly to the edge of the bell and note the result.
2. Pick a tightly stretched wire or string with your finger or a short stick. Make a note of the result.
3. Strike one prong of a large tuning fork with a wooden hammer and dip the prongs lightly into a bowl of water. Write a brief note giving the result.
4. Place your fingers lightly on the side of your throat. Then sing a few notes or hum a tune while your fingers are in this position. What do you discover?
5. Write two or three sentences that give your conclusion about how sounds are produced.

### 497. Make Believe

This is an excellent rainy day game. Give each student a card with written directions on it. Each student in turn has to follow the directions on the card using pantomime only—no talking out loud. The others have to guess what he or she is trying to do. Here is a sample card:

---

WASHING THE CAR

1. Rinse the entire car with the hose.
2. Fill a pail with water. Add detergent.
3. Cover surface with sudsy water.
4. Hose off the suds.
5. Dry and polish surface with a cloth.
6. Clean windows and lights.
7. Get in and drive away.

---

### 498. Recipe Directions

Simple recipes preferably requiring no cooking are usually an excellent source of following-directions exercises, if you are able to make the ingredients available. Of course, the proof of the pudding, or whatever it is, is in the eating—another example of immediate feedback.

### 499. Recipe Words

Following directions in recipes is made easier if the vocabulary (including abbreviations) is mastered. Among the important abbreviations that should be learned are:

| | | |
|---|---|---|
| tsp. | = | teaspoon |
| tbsp. | = | tablespoon |
| c. | = | cup |
| qt. | = | quart |
| pt. | = | pint |
| oz. | = | ounce or ounces |
| lb. | = | pound or pounds |
| sq. | = | square |
| gr. | = | gram |
| lit. | = | liter |
| doz. | = | dozen |
| min. | = | minute or minutes |
| hr. | = | hour or hours |
| mod. | = | moderate or moderately |

Words that have a special meaning in preparing recipes are also helpful. Examples of these are *dash* or *pinch* to refer to a tiny quantity of an ingredient, or slow, moderate, hot, to refer to oven temperaure. A good cookbook is the best reference for this sort of material. For example, Julia Childs, in her book *Mastering the Art of French Cooking,* describes a pinch as the quantity of an ingredient that can be held between the thumb and forefinger. She also points out that there are "big and little pinches."

### 500. Convenience Foods

Your students will find it useful to practice following directions for preparing and serving convenience foods. Students can bring in samples of directions from packages. Use these to prepare useful practice exercises. Here's an example from a box of frozen pizza:

---

## DIRECTIONS

**FOR CONVENTIONAL OVENS:**
Place a cookie sheet on center oven rack. Preheat oven to 425° F. REMOVE THE FLAVOR-SAVER WRAP. Place frozen pizza on PREHEATED COOKIE SHEET. Bake 14 to 16 minutes or until cheese is melted and edges are golden brown.

**FOR MICROWAVE OVENS:**
Place microwave browning grill in microwave oven; preheat browning grill at HIGH for 2½ minutes. REMOVE THE FLAVOR-SAVER WRAP. Place frozen pizza on preheated browning grill. Cook at HIGH 5 to 6 minutes or until cheese in center is melted, rotating grill ½ turn after each 2 minutes of cooking.

Read the directions for preparing frozen pizza. Then answer each question that follows.

1. Can pizza be baked on a cookie sheet?_____

2. What should you do with the wrapper if you are using a microwave oven?_____

3. Will a pizza left in a moderate oven for 10 minutes be likely to burn?_____

4. What is the time difference between a conventional oven and a microwave?_____

5. How can you tell if the pizza is done?____

---

### 501. Recipe Word Games

Here's a game to provide practice using recipe words and their abbreviations. Divide the group into teams. Each team is given a pile of cards, each of which contains a question. The first player holds up a card. A player on the other team must answer the question. If the player with the card agrees with the answer, then the person who answered gets one point. If the one with the card wants to challenge the answer, then he or she is permitted to do so. A correct challenge wins the point for the person with the card. At the end of a set time limit (or after all the cards have been played), the team with the most points wins. Here are some examples of the types of questions that should be placed on the cards.

Would a c. of milk fit in a lit. size bottle?

Which would make a small meatloaf taste better, a
  lb. of salt or a pinch?

Would a frozen pizza burn after 4 min. in a mod.
  oven?

If you pour one lit. of soda into a pt. bottle, what
  will happen?

# Published Reading Materials

The activities described in the preceding sections are only a portion of the ingredients of a good reading program. Reading instruction must consist of more than games, devices, and a bag of tricks. Because reading is, by definition, a print-mediated activity, printed materials are absolutely essential for the teaching of reading. A person learns to read by interacting with things to read. It is difficult— actually almost impossible—for a teacher personally to create sufficient materials for teaching an entire class of children for any extended period of time. Because of this, it is important that a teacher be aware of published materials and well able to select those that are appropriate for a particular student or group of students.

The essence of an effective reading program should be lots and lots of things to read—especially good children's books. The material selected to develop skills should lend itself to personalizing activities for each student. In other words, each learner should be able to work on what is personally needed at a given time, not on what his or her neighbor needs or what is next on a list.

The annotated list of instructional materials in this section is intended to give the teacher an indication of what kinds of things are now available for reading instruction. Although many different publishers and a wide variety of products are represented here, the list is by no means a comprehensive map of the field of published reading materials. Omission from the list is not necessarily an indictment of a particular program. Inclusion on the list should not necessarily be construed as an endorsement. The list includes materials that we have used in a variety of ways with different types of students. Also included are a number of recently published materials that we are currently examining. The annotations are intended to give you enough information about a given piece of material to decide whether it is something you should consider for your classroom.

In order to cover as many items as possible, we have not listed every program individually. A listing may appear under a heading such as "Books from _____" or "Games and Activities from _____." In such cases, we suggest that the catalog of the particular publisher be obtained for a complete listing of individual titles. As in the previous edition of *Reading Aids,* however, many programs are described in detail. Even so, we still suggest that the latest catalog should be consulted. Publishers do, of course, continuously update their lists of offerings. Current catalogs and visits to meetings or conferences with materials displays are the best way to keep posted on the latest materials.

We have not listed materials requiring hardware more elaborate than cassette tape recorders or filmstrip previewers. However, if you do have the funds for hardware and its accompanying software, consider each potential purchase very carefully. We strongly recommend against investing in hardware at the expense of children's books and the many interesting skills development materials now available.

For reasons that should be obvious to anyone living in today's world, we have not made any effort to include the prices of the materials listed. Now more than ever before, it's absolutely necessary to make the most of every dollar spent. As budgets shrink and prices rise, how can you obtain the materials you need? Study your students and the available resources carefully. Then ask for specific items to meet specific needs. If you articulate these needs and the exact things required to meet them, you stand a better chance of getting materials than does the teacher who constantly complains about having too little, without knowing what he or she would buy if the funds suddenly became available.

## HOW TO USE THIS LIST

This list of instructional materials contains items for skills development and sources of children's books. Some of the collections of children's literature also contain skills development material, which is described along with the books on which it is based. Sources of children's books are identified by ▮ . Skills materials are denoted by ✐ . Audio source materials are coded by 🎧 .

Beginning on page 305, you will find a complete list of all publishers whose materials are included in the annotated list. Each publisher is listed with a mailing address that, to the best of our information, was functional at the time this printing of *Reading Aids* went to press. You should be able to obtain catalogs or further information by writing to the address listed. Many publishers have local distributors in areas other than the one listed. If you live in a heavily populated area, you might try the local telephone directory to see if a given publisher has an address near you.

We welcome suggestions for additions to this list, any address changes for listed publishers, and other comments on the items listed. Please send any such information directly to the author:

Dr. Anne Marie Mueser
P. O. Box 107
Clinton Corners, N.Y. 12514

The Guide to Published Materials beginning on page 295 will give you an indication of the suitability of a given piece of material for a particular type of student. To use the chart, find the category at the top of the page that best describes the learner you have in mind (e.g., young beginning reader, older non-reader, learning disabilities, enrichment for gifted). Then look down that column for all the materials checked. If a material is marked, it *may* be suitable. You should further consider it in relation to the specific skills needs of the learner. If a material is not marked, chances are that it would not suit the learner regardless of what skills he or she needs to learn. This guide covers skills materials, and not all sources of children's trade books are listed here. Consult the catalogs of individual publishers for additional information to help you make your selections.

To design a learning environment for individualized reading instruction, identify the category or categories of students you wish to serve. Then compile a list of the materials designated as suitable for that type of learner. When ordering, remember that variety is more important than quantity. Don't buy thirty or even a dozen of any one item. Try to purchase as many different items in small quantity as possible. The most successful classrooms we have seen contain great variety, designed to ensure that there will be something to meet the needs of each learner. In deciding what to order, keep in mind the modifications you will make on the materials. Refer back to Section One for specific instructions on modifying and arranging materials.

## ABC Serendipity  (Bowmar/Noble)

*ABC Serendipity* is a collection of six colorful, humorous, and unusual alphabet books. These books are intended to enlarge and enrich the child's experience with alphabet letters. There are probably many more efficient ways to deal with the alphabet, but these books are fun. A set of Activity Cards and a Teacher's Guide are available to accompany the books.

## Action, Double Action, and Triple Action (Scholastic)

*Action* is a carefully structured reading program for secondary school students with reading and vocabulary grade levels from 2.0 to 4.0. *Action* is an 18-week teacher-directed sequence that develops basic word attack and comprehension skills through reading, writing, discussion, and role playing. The *Action* materials can be purchased as a complete unit for 10 or 20 students, including a record, multiples of three unit books, play anthologies, and illustrated short story anthologies, six posters, and a Teacher's Guide. The components are also available individually. The Action Word Attack Skills Supplement is a set of 40 duplicating masters to provide additional skills work.

*Double Action* is a program structured much like *Action*. It is designed as a second semester for students who have completed *Action,* or as a program for those students who can already handle materials with grade 3.0 readability.

*Triple Action* is a reading comprehension program for seventh to twelfth graders who read at 4.0 to 6.0.

## Action Libraries (Scholastic)

The Action Libraries were designed for secondary age students reading at grade levels 2.0 to 6.0. They may be used independently or with the *Action, Double Action,* and *Triple Action* kits.

Each of the libraries contains four copies each of five different titles, a Teaching Guide, and fifty ditto masters (ten for each book) to build skills and introduce new vocabulary. Check the latest Scholastic catalog for the libraries currently available. New collections are frequently added.

## AIMS (Continental Press Publications)

AIMS is the acronym for An Instructional Manipulative Series. These materials are designed for use in early childhood education, remedial classes, and special education. Active pupil involvement in the activities is a goal. Kits are available for pre-reading, phonics, and comprehension. You can send for a detailed brochure which describes each of the kits.

## Americans All Reading Kit (Pocket Books Educational Department)

*Americans All Reading Kit* contains more than thirty paperback titles each about a prominent American. Many different ethnic and social backgrounds are represented. The books have a range of reading levels and are aimed at grades 5 through 8. Included in the package is a motivational cassette, a wall poster, and a teacher's guide.

## Associated Press
## Newspaper Reading Skills Kit (Westinghouse Learning Corp.)

This program uses AP newspaper articles to develop reading skills and critical thinking among junior and senior high school students. The complete package includes 150 article cards, 100 project cards for followup activities, students logs, and a Teacher's Guide.

## Audio Reading Progress Labs (Educational Progress)

This cassette-based reading skills program (Levels 1–8) is an excellent support for an instructional program in a wide variety of word attack and comprehension skills. The higher levels include some work in study skills and content area reading. The teacher's manuals are cross-referenced to the major reading programs in use today.

The quality of these materials is excellent. Even the lowest levels are suitable for use with older readers who are having difficulty.

The student record booklets can be made non-consumable by using acetate sheets in loose-leaf binders. The supplementary practice pages in each teacher's manual can be duplicated (e.g., offset or dittoed) or also put in plastic. Feedback to the learner is provided as an integral part of each cassette lesson. On the practice pages, feedback can be provided by means of an acetate overlay or by duplicating the page and keying one copy. Or, if you prefer, these practice pages can be prepared for use in a lapboard.

## A-V Materials from Troll  (Troll Associates)

If you have money in your A-V materials budget, you should consult the Troll catalog. A number of programs designed to teach reading skills and vocabulary are available. High interest skill kits featuring sports and adventure topics are aimed at reluctant readers. These programs are expensive but are worth considering if you have funds available.

## Awareness Books and Read-alongs  (Davco Publishers)

These materials deal with American history in pictorial (comic book type) format. They are billed as "very high interest" for the lower reader. Reading level of the books is grades 3–4. Interest level is claimed to be intermediate grades through high school. A-V packages containing filmstrips and cassettes are available.

We seriously question the interest level of these materials and, despite the comic format which we generally find appealing, would not place these high on any list of priorities. The people chosen as subjects for these materials, while significant in the history of the United States, may not be nearly as interesting to the target audience as the publishers claim. If we were selecting famous Americans as subjects to motivate reluctant or problem readers, we would probably not include as our initial choices: John Adams, Dwight D. Eisenhower, Ulysses S. Grant, Andrew Johnson, or James Monroe, to name a few. We would love a series in this format that included some of the personalities today's kids would find relevant. Unfortunately, Davco hasn't offered this yet.

## Barnell Loft Specific Skills Series  (Barnell Loft)

The Barnell Loft Specific Skills Series provides material for each of the following skill areas:

*Using the Context*
*Following Directions*
*Locating the Answer*
*Getting the Main Idea*
*Detecting the Sequence*
*Getting the Facts*
*Drawing Conclusions*
*Working with Sounds*

Each of the above skill areas is presented in a series of booklets at different levels of difficulty, from Level A (approximately high grade 1) to Level F (approximately grade 6), and Advanced.

Because of the interest level of the reading material and the plain format, these books are excellent for older readers as well as children in the elementary grades.

The booklets in the Specific Skills Series can be cut up to make kits, although most teachers do not find this necessary. Because the selections within one book tend to be at approximately the same level, it does not matter which selections are done first. Duplicating masters for student response sheets are available.

Barnell Loft and its related company, Dexter and Westbrook, have in the past sold only to schools. If you are an educational consultant or reading person in private practice, you may have to find a school willing to place your order. The materials are worth the trouble.

### Basic Living Skills Programs  (Interpretive Education)

I.E. offers a number of high interest-low vocabulary programs for secondary students in need of basic living skills. The content of these programs is the stuff of everyday living—money handling, car insurance, apartment hunting, and application forms, to name just a few. These multi-media programs (filmstrip and cassette) probably won't do much for reading skills, but they are useful and interesting in other ways.

### Be A Better Reader  (Prentice-Hall)

These are excellent worktexts (also available in cloth-bound editions) for developing reading skills in content materials. Although these books have been around a long time, they are still a solid source of material to read. The recently revised editions have added selections relevant to minorities and current issues such as ecology and technology. Books A, B, and C can be used for the upper intermediate grades or junior high school. Books I–IV can be used in junior or senior high school.

### BEST (The Economy Co.)

BEST (*Building Essential Skills Together*) is a word analysis tutorial program that is not age specific. It has been used with young children as well as adult illiterates. The materials provide a structure to enable a person not professionally trained (e.g., paraprofessional, another student, parent) to assist a student in learning to decode.

### Books from Garrard (Garrard)

Garrard Press publishes a collection of excellent books for the classroom. Consult their latest catalog for an up-to-date listing of available titles. The lower levels are well represented; particularly good are several biographies.

### Books from Harcourt (Harcourt Brace Javanovich)

HBJ has an outstanding children's list. Get the latest catalog of the many titles available. New titles are being published each year, and the list includes many great classics that have stood the test of time. We remember fondly such childhood favorites as *The Little Red Lighthouse and the Great Gray Bridge, B Is for Betsy,* and *Many Moons.* These are still available along with numerous contemporary titles. If you're a Mary Poppins fan, Harcourt is the place to find all the books in this series.

### Books from Messner  (Julian Messner)

Messner has a solid children's list, especially nonfiction for the intermediate grades. The appearance of books from this publisher is generally plain and functional. Exciting colors or great artwork should be sought somewhere else. Nevertheless, there is much reading material of value available here and we suggest that you take a look at the catalog. We do admit to being somewhat partial to two of the titles: *The Picture Story of Jockey Steve Cauthen,* and *The Picture Story of Rod Carew.* (We wrote them.)

### Breaking the Code  (Open Court)

This is a program designed for students in grades 4 and above who haven't learned to read, write, or spell. It uses a basic, highly structured, teacher-directed phonics approach to reading instruction.

The program is aimed at the student whose failure is primarily due to poor teaching methods in the primary grades. The publisher cautions that it is not intended for students specifically diagnosed as dyslexic.

### Breakthrough  (Allyn and Bacon)

*Breakthrough* is *a series* designed for the older (grade 6 or above) remedial reader (reading levels 1–8). It contains paperback books especially designed to appeal to mature but weak readers, reading skills activities in ditto master form, and teacher's guides. The series is attractively illustrated with drawings and photographs.

Two each of the grade 1 and 2 level titles are available in Spanish for use in bilingual programs.

### Butterworth Books ■ (Grosset and Dunlap)

Grosset and Dunlap publishes a series of books about auto racing by W. E. Butterworth and others. These high-interest books are appealing to readers at the junior high school level or higher.

### The Checkered Flag Series ■ ∩ (Addison-Wesley)

The Checkered Flag Series is an exciting series of eight high-interest books with low-level vocabulary (reading levels 2.4 to 4.5). The series deals with hot rod and sports car racing, road rallies, and the like. This is a highly motivating set of materials for the junior or senior high school underachieving reader.

Checkered Flag A-V Kits with filmstrips (magnificent color photos of real cars, races, and so on) and audio cassettes are available to accompany the books. These materials are superb.

### Choose and Check  (Scott, Foresman)

*Choose and Check* is a self-checking programmed device which presents multiple-choice exercises to the primary reader. The student makes a choice, then slides a button to check the accuracy of that response. These devices are instructive as well as entertaining.

### Clarion Books for Young People ▐ (Seabury Press)

Clarion Books for Young People are high-quality trade books. For very young children, retold and illustrated classics such as *The Three Bears* and *The Three Billy Goats Gruff* are popular. Get the current catalog. A number of excellent new titles appear each year.

### Clues to Reading ✐ ∩ (Educational Progress)

*Clues to Reading* is an audio-cassette-based program aimed at the older readers in trouble. The program presents exercises on word attack and comprehension skills, all within the context of high-interest material. The audio source assists the reader with material that otherwise might be too difficult for independent work. Minority group interests are well represented in the content. The teacher's manual contains an interesting section dealing with students whose primary language variety is not Standard English (e.g., speakers of Black English or Spanish).

The student record booklets for this program are in attractive magazine format. They do not look like workbooks.

### The Codebook Series ✐ (J. B. Lippincott)

This series, which was designed for slower readers, was intended as an accompaniment to the Lippincott Basic Readers. It can be used independently as a source of skill building material to reinforce sound-spelling correspondences. The program uses a variety of games and puzzles to motivate students who are having difficulty. There are five (Levels A-E) consumable codebooks. The perforated pages facilitate modification into nonconsumable kits.

### Content Readers ✐ (Reader's Digest)

Content Readers from Reader's Digest provide materials in Science and in Social Studies. For each of these two content areas there is one book per grade level, for grades 3 through 9.

### Continental Ditto Masters ✐ (Continental Press Publications)

The Continental Press catalog lists many different books of spirit duplicating masters for readiness through grade six reading levels. Continental's masters have been around a long time. Many of them are useful. Avoid the temptation to buy one of each and subject your classroom to the "purple plague." Choose wisely and know why you are handing a particular page to a student.

We especially like the crossword puzzles and some of the material on context clues. Get the catalog for a complete listing.

### The Cornerstone Readers ✐ (Addison-Wesley)

This series of five books is designed to develop basic word attack skills, vocabulary, comprehension, and study skills. The reading level of the materials ranges from grade 1 to grade 4. These books can be used through the elementary grades, for students at or below grade level. Progress tests are provided as part of the workbook format.

**Countries and Cultures**  (Science Research Associates)
*Countries and Cultures* is a kit of reading selections about different places and people around the world. The selections are interesting and range from grade 5 to grade 9 in reading level. For each selection there is a skill card for vocabulary and comprehension.

**Crane Reading System** (Crane Publishing Co.)
If you believe the brochure for this program, you will think you have found the panacea for your beginning reading program. The program is described as a "total language approach" which is "multi-modal . . . to reach all learning styles." It claims unique vocabulary control and "unique artwork to promote maximum development of comprehension." We don't think this program is the answer to all your dreams, but there are some components that are well designed and useful. And, despite trying not to, we did like the primitive gingerbread type character who stars in the early books. We won't go as far as the ads and call it the "universal child" with whom anyone could identify, but we did find him/her/it(?) to be rather cute.

**Creature Teachers** (Economy Company)
*Creature Teachers* is an individualized learner-paced tape program for the hard-to-motivate young reader. The "teachers" on the tape are various sorts of monsters, such as a witch and a vampire.
Each of the 44 lessons deals with a specific word perception or comprehension skill. Student response books are colorful and attractive.

**Critical Reading** (Ann Arbor Publishers)
*Critical Reading* contains four (Levels A-D) self-instructional workbooks for teaching critical reading based on logical inferences. This is interesting material for intermediate grade readers or better. These self-paced workbooks are available in consumable or nonconsumable editions. The nonconsumable versions are on coated stock for use with special pens. Don't forget to order the pens if you buy the nonconsumable edition.

**Croft Comprehension Skillpacks** (Croft)
The *Croft Skillpacks* are an excellent and inexpensive source of materials for practicing comprehension skills. There are kits for primary and intermediate levels.

**Crowell Books** (Thomas Y. Crowell)
*Crowell Books for Schools and Libraries* is a large catalog that lists children's books both by level and by curriculum area. The large number of subject areas and titles is too great to be summarized adequately here. The Let's Read and Find Out Science Books for the primary grades are excellent.

**CTP Materials** (Creative Teaching Press)
CTP presents an assortment of inexpensive, interesting, although somewhat gimmicky reading games and skill packs. Each device allows for independent work. Some of the games and skill tasks seem to require a lot of cutting, pasting, and

constructing. These might be good for rainy days and Friday afternoons. One fun feature of CTP's offerings is the various Scratch 'n Sniff items—reward labels, bookmarks, and the like. A scratch releases a pleasant smell such as raspberry, grape, or root beer. We're not sure how much this all has to do with reading, but we suspect that most kids would go for a root beer bookmark.

### The Deep Sea Adventure Series ▪ (Addison-Wesley)
The Deep Sea Adventure Series contains a dozen books ranging in grade level from 1.8 to 5.0. With such titles as *Submarine Rescue, Danger Below,* and *Whale Hunt,* this is a very popular series with reluctant readers. A Teacher's Manual contains suggestions for skill development and evaluation.

### Developmental Reading Text Workbooks ✎ (Bobbs-Merrill)
The Developmental Reading Text Workbooks are a series of skills development workbooks in which there are reading selections and skills exercises. A large variety of word attack and comprehension skills are presented.

The books are illustrated in four colors and the exercises are, for the most part, self-directing. Each type of skill is clearly labeled. These workbooks can be made into nonconsumable kits. There are eight books in the series, from readiness level to grade 6.

### Dolch Puzzle Books and Games ✎ (Garrard)
Garrard publishes an excellent collection of games, flash cards, and puzzle books for teaching basic sight vocabulary and word attack skills. They are inexpensive and will save you from having to construct your own materials of this kind. Consult the current Garrard catalog for the complete list of the Dolch materials available.

### Duplicating Masters and Gameboards ✎ (Frank Schaffer Publications)
Frank Schaffer offers an interesting collection of spirit duplicating masters, games, activity cards, and activity books. These materials are inexpensive and worth a look. Get the catalog for the latest listings.

### Durrell-Murphy Phonics Practice  (Harcourt Brace Jovanovich)
This *Phonics Practice Program* provides 81 self-correcting lessons in which the student selects and writes the correct one of three words to go with a given picture. The kit includes cards on beginning and ending consonants, blends, and digraphs, and long and short vowel phonograms.

The review cards at the end of each section in this kit can be used for diagnostic and/or mastery testing. This excellent piece of material can be used independently or in the follow-up activities for the corresponding lessons in *Speech-to-Print Phonics,* also by Durrell and Murphy.

### Dutton Books ▪ (E. P. Dutton)
Dutton has a very nice children's list. A number of titles are available in paperback as well as hard cover. Highlights of the list include *Winnie the Pooh, When We Were Very Young,* and all the other A. A. Milne books. Get the Dutton catalog for a complete annotated listing of the books from Dutton and Windmill paperbacks.

## Early Learning for Reading ✏🎧                    (Educational Progress)

*Early Learning for Reading* is the reading readiness (Level A) section of *Audio Reading Progress Labs.* It provides an excellent set of cassette-based lessons on following directions, grapheme-phoneme relationships, and beginning comprehension skills. The kit also contains games and cutout upper- and lower-case letters. The Teacher's Manual is a good source of reading readiness activities.

## EARS 🎧                    (Individualized Instruction Co.)

*EARS (Early Approaches to Reading Skills)* is a twenty-lesson cassette-based program for developing auditory comprehension. The corresponding response books can be put in acetate to make them nonconsumable.

## Easy Readers 📖                    (Grosset and Dunlap)

Easy Readers are a series of children's trade books for the beginning reader. Reading levels are grades 1 and 2. A few of these titles are also available in Spanish.

## EDL Study Skills Kits ✏                    (McGraw-Hill)

EDL Study Skills Kits have long been a fine source of reference skills exercises and reading material in science and social studies. Beginning at approximately low grade 4 level, there are three kits—*Science, Social Studies,* and *Reference Skills*—at each level. Each kit contains cards with reading selections, instruction in specific skills, and comprehension checks on the reading. The corresponding student response sheet contains similar reinforcement exercises on the skill taught by each card. An orientation kit introducing students to the procedures is also available.

## Electric Company Sentence Comprehension Kit ✏🎧                    (Addison-Wesley)

This program uses characters from "The Electric Company" television series to develop skills in understanding sentence patterns found in basic reading material. The complete multimedia package is expensive. The audiovisual module and the games module can be purchased separately as well. The Teacher's Resource Book includes supplementary materials, record-keeping devices, and correlations to basal programs.

## Educational Materials ✏                    (Frank E. Richards Publishing Co.)

This publisher produces an assortment of inexpensive, supplementary reading and language arts kits aimed at the older learner with special problems. Many of the items emphasize reading skills for everyday living. The company also offers a set of rewritten classics for students who are not likely to read the material in its original form. Among the titles in this set are *Tom Sawyer, Heidi, 20,000 Leagues Under the Sea,* and *Swiss Family Robinson.* Get the complete catalog if your target audience is a remedial or special ed population.

## ETA Materials ✏                    (Educational Teaching Aids)

Materials from Educational Teaching Aids cover a wide range of content and pupil needs. There are kits and programs for basic vocabulary, phonics, vocabulary building, easy reading, and spelling. Programs are designed to be self-correcting. Send for the latest catalog to find out the complete list of programs, games, and other handy devices for a reading program.

**Extra Credit Reading** / (Random House)

This package contains two copies each of six Walter Farley books (horse stories) and six Alfred Hitchcock stories (mysteries). Each paperback has a Comprehension Card which adheres to the inside cover of the book. Questions on the cards provide a quick check on understanding. The Teacher's Guide contains a plot synopsis for each book as well as discussion questions and suggestions for using the program.

The best thing about this program is the books. We admit to having written the cards and the Teacher's Guide. Frankly, we did it to have an excuse to read *The Black Stallion* and some of our other childhood favorites again.

**Fantastic Fables** (Schloat Productions)

*Fantastic Fables* is a kit containing 30 copies of a 132-page comic book with four fables, cassettes with a dramatic reading of each story, and filmstrips to preview the reading material.

These materials were designed to motivate the reluctant reader. The comic format turns kids on, to be sure. However, these fables have not-so-hidden messages that may be a bit much.

**Fat Cats** (E. P. Dutton)

This is a series of fiction and non-fiction books for beginning readers. The emphasis is on reading rather than on instruction. The child is encouraged to select books at the right level by reading the material on the book jacket. These books are a welcome addition to a primary grades reading corner.

**First Talking Alphabet** (Scott, Foresman)

*First Talking Alphabet* is a two-part set of lessons on sound-symbol relationships. FTA Part One teaches initial, medial, and final consonants. FTA Part Two reviews the consonants taught in Part One and teaches vowel sounds. Each lesson has a record and twenty copies of a colorful nonconsumable lesson card. Duplicating masters for additional skills sheets are available for both Part One and Part Two, and are a must if the program is to be as effective as it can be.

**Flash Gordon Remedial Reading Kits** (Xerox Education Division)

Here are two high-interest kits aimed at the middle or junior high school underachiever. Each kit contains four sound filmstrips, two copies each of 16 reading cards, 24 ditto masters, 2 posters, and a Teacher's Guide. Kit 1 has a reading level of 2.5 to 3.0. Kit 2 is for 3.0 to 3.5.

The story lines and artwork in this program are based on the original Flash Gordon adventures so popular in comic form. The program is well done and should prove useful and motivating with older problem readers.

**Follett Library Books** (Follett Library Book Co.)

Follett Library Book Company is a book distributor handling books of numerous publishers in reinforced "prebound" library bindings. Books are listed in categories by curriculum area or theme, with Spache or Dale-Chall readability rating supplied for each title. In addition to the regular catalog, Follett has an excellent list by reading grade and approximate interest level of more than 2,000 titles for "slow readers."

For some time now, Follett has been flagging certain titles with a special book-mark to indicate that the content might be controversial or that some purchasers might have found it objectionable for one reason or another. The company reports that many teachers and librarians are grateful for this information. Frankly, we find such an approach to be too close to censorship for our taste. We would prefer to think that professionals are able and willing to make their own judgments based on a direct examination of the materials and a knowledge of the basic needs of the target population. It is possible to order books from Follett and request that the warning markers be omitted. That's what we would suggest.

### Ginn Word Enrichment Program   (Ginn and Co.)
This is an attractively arranged, high-quality series of workbooks for developing phonetic and structural analysis skills. The program is suitable for use in the primary grades or with older remedial students.

### Glazer Reading Involvement Program   (Perma-Bound)
*GRIP* consists of a collection of 50 Perma-Bound titles of children's literature (reading grade levels 1–4), an involvement card for each book, a Teacher's Guide, student-teacher conference sheets, and a teacher conference record.

The books in this program are excellent. The support materials are not as extensive as those in some other programs using children's literature.

### The Globe Classroom Libraries   (Globe Book Co.)
Each Globe Classroom Library (Set One, Set Two, and Set Three) is a collection of Globe's most popular soft-cover reading books. Sets One and Two are especially suited for under-achieving junior high and senior high school students. The content of these books is interesting and the reading levels begin at grade 4.

Consult the current Globe catalog for a complete listing of books aimed at the older slow learner.

### Hammond Reading Skills Series  (Hammond)
This series consists of 28 books and pads of answer sheets for each book. The skills program is designed to be a self-directing adjunct to a basal program. The program is recommended for grades 3–6, but the books are color coded rather than labeled by grade so that they can be used in a flexible manner. Each of the seven books at a level deals with a specific skill area: details, main idea, sequence, context, sound-symbol and structure, inferences, and following written directions.

### Hastings House Trade Books  (Hastings House)
Among the highlights of the Hastings House trade book list are the Ollie Books, the Adrian Nature Mysteries, and the Preserve Our Wildlife Series.

### High-Interest Books ▮ ∩ (Children's Press)

If you are teaching older, reluctant readers, get the brochure on High-Interest Books from Children's Press. This collection includes reading levels from grade 1 to grade 4, with interest levels to adult. Each book has a controlled vocabulary designed to be interesting and readable for secondary students with reading problems. The collections of books include *Pacesetters, Sports Stars,* and *Gemini Books.* The motivational tapes to accompany the books and encourage reading are called *Mates.*

### The Hilltop Series ✎ (Allyn and Bacon)

The publisher refers to this as "an individualized program for problem readers." It is designed to bring nonreaders and slow learners to the point where they can handle the materials of the regular program. There are teacher's manuals, duplicating masters, and student enrichment books for independent reading. We're not quite sure what makes this an individualized program, but it might meet the needs of certain children. It's worth a look.

### Hip Pocket Stories ▮ ✎ (Random House)

Using five nonfictional biographies (Diana Ross, Geraldo Rivera, Bill Cosby, Shirley Chisolm, and Johnny Bench), this program is designed to motivate and instruct poor readers. The readability level of the books is 2.8 and 3.3. Interest level is intermediate grades to adult. The personalities featured were well known and contemporary when the program was first published. They are somewhat less relevant now. Workbooks to accompany each biography deal with word attack skills, vocabulary, comprehension, and some study skills. A cassette narrates each story. Each kit contains 10 copies each of five books and 30 copies each of five workbooks, so that several classes could share. Although we are generally opposed to the purchase of multiple copies of such materials, these books are small and probably will be taken on permanent loan by many students.

### HITS ✎∩ (ModuLearn, Inc.)

*HITS* is a remedial reading and language program intended for reluctant readers from the upper elementary through adult and special education classes. Reading levels are grades 2 through 6. Presented in a rock radio station format, each of the four HITS-Paks includes a cassette, a criterion reference test, 20 workbooks, a student record chart, and a Teacher's Guide. Try before you buy would be our advice on anything this gimmicky. As far as we know, this company does send materials on approval.

### HITS Primary Reading System ✎∩ (ModuLearn, Inc.)

*HITS* is a reading system which uses music as an aid to teach beginning readers phonic and structural analysis, comprehension skills, and sight words. Materials include workbooks, song charts, skill sheets, songs, games, and songs on spirit masters. Children sing and read along with Donny and Marie Osmond. Frankly, this isn't the sort of program we would tend to go for at all. However, it might appeal to some of you out there.

## How and Why Wonder Books 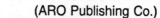 (Grosset and Dunlap)

This is an excellent series of nicely illustrated science books for the intermediate grades. Each book deals with a specific topic clearly and in depth.

Grosset and Dunlap has many other excellent trade books on science and social studies topics. Be sure to get their complete catalog. The selection of available titles is superb. In addition, for mystery fans and nostalgic teachers, they have the complete series (51 titles) of Nancy Drew books in library bindings.

## Humankind (Open Court)

*Humankind* is a series of supplementary paperbacks "designed to bridge the gap between reading as a skill and literature as a source of learning and pleasure." There are five books, A-E, which correspond to reading levels 1–5. The books include stories and poems by fine contemporary writers, and excellent illustrations. Once we got by the title of the series, we really did like the books.

## I Can Read Underwater Books (ARO Publishing Co.)

This is a series of little books beginning with no words in the first one and increasing in difficulty to 33 words in the tenth and last one. The pages are non-tear, washable paper, which probably begins to explain the title of the series.

Other books from this company (also on washable paper) are a series on holidays and the I Can Eat an Elephant set. These books are relatively inexpensive, and a bit of fun.

If you like the books from ARO, you might also like the shirts for teachers. T-shirts with slogans such as "Read books, not T-shirts," "Librarians are Novel Lovers," and "Teachers do it with Class," are available. We don't recommend these as devices for teaching reading. We don't even recommend that you try wearing one to school. However, we thought you might like to know about them.

## I Can Read Books (Harper and Row)

Harper and Row is one of the best sources of high-quality children's books. For beginning readers, try their I Can Read books. These include several collections of fiction, as well as I Can Read Science and I Can Read Social Studies sets.

## Ideal Instructional Materials (Ideal School Supply Co.)

Ideal provides a wide variety of games, spirit masters, and other supplementary materials. Many of these are colorful, inexpensive, and useful. Classroom resources such as wall charts and bulletin board displays are also available. Send for a catalog and buy wisely—avoid the purely decorative frills until you have bought the things you really need.

## Imperial A-V Materials (Imperial International)

Imperial's catalog describes a variety of audio-visual learning materials suitable for use in reading programs. Skill materials and games are also available. Take a look at Imperial's offerings if you have extra funds available for A-V materials.

**The Incredible Series** 📕                                    (Dexter and Westbrook)

The Incredible Series contains seven extremely high-interest hard-cover books and a teacher's manual. The books are easy-to-read, really exciting, true stories. They include *Titanic, The Cardiff Giant,* and *Horror Overhead* (the Hindenberg's last trip).

**Instant Readers** 📕                                      (Holt, Rinehart and Winston)

This is an excellent set of story books and cassettes beautifully narrated by Bill Martin, Jr. Instant Readers are lovely read-alongs for the beginning reader.

**Instructor Curriculum Materials** ✏                       (Instructor Publications, Inc.)

The catalog for Instructor Curriculum Materials lists a wide variety of duplicating masters, games, posters, resource handbooks and other useful devices for teachers. Many of the materials are inexpensive and worth a look.

**The Jim Forest Readers** 📕                                      (Addison-Wesley)

The Jim Forest readers, a dozen books (reading levels 1.7–3.2), have been a fixture in many a remedial reading program. They contain adventure stories about a boy and his forest ranger uncle. An inexpensive set of consumable practice books is also available. Current interest in conservation could make these old standbys quite timely.

**Joan Hanson Word Books** ✏                                      (Lerner Publications)

This set of eight, literally square (7¼" × 7¼"), little books very cleverly illustrates antonyms, synonyms, homonyms, and homographs. The books are delightfully fun as well as informative.

**The Kaleidoscope Readers** ✏                                      (Addison-Wesley)

This is a series of eight contemporary theme workbooks for secondary school students reading below grade level. Skills exercises in word attack, vocabulary, comprehension, and study methods are provided. A placement inventory is also available. Reading levels of the books ranges from grade 2 to grade 9.

**Kinder-Fun Series** ✏                                      (Ann Arbor Publishers)

Kinder-Fun Series contains two sets (Insect Series and Sports Series) each with six little paperbacks and 64 flash cards. The presentation is very clever. Picture clues are used to teach sight words. These are excellent for the young beginning reader. They are also suitable for older nonreaders.

**King Comics Reading Library** 📕✏                             (King Features Syndicate)

KFS, through its educational division, markets authentic comic books for school use. The ads usually found in comics have been deleted and replaced with ads for educational concepts and with puzzle pages to reinforce selected reading skills. Among the characters available are Popeye, Blondie, Tim Tyler, Tiger, Quincy, The Phantom and Girl Phantom, Prince Valiant, Hi and Lois, Beetle Bailey, Flash Gordon, Mandrake the Magician, and Henry.

The comics are available in two collections—the *King Comics Reading Library, I and II*—or as single titles. The library package includes a dozen copies each of eight different titles, a teacher's manual, wall charts, and a display case. It is a good way to introduce the product to a school. A cost-effective way to purchase these comics is in quantities of 100 or more per title. They are an extremely inexpensive way to motivate reluctant readers.

## Learning Systems  (Prentice-Hall Learning Systems)

Learning Systems is a collection of devices, games, ditto masters, and other classroom resources. The materials are inexpensive and useful. There are separate catalogs for primary and intermediate grade offerings.

## Learning with Laughter  (Scott Education Division)

*Learning with Laughter* contains 54 interrelated but independent kits for developing word attack skills. Each kit contains a filmstrip, audio source (either cassette or record), poster, and game or other manipulative device.

These materials were designed for young children and are intended to keep them laughing while they learn. The materials are imaginative—perhaps too much so.

## Letters and Words  (Harcourt Brace Jovanovich)

This program contains 33 individualized lesson packets of pupil and teacher activity cards for decoding lessons. There are eight packets with small-group games for reinforcement. The program is highly structured and can be used by tutors and volunteer aides with individual students.

## Listening with a Purpose  (Coronet Instructional Materials)

*Listening with a Purpose* is a cassette-based program of twelve lessons that can be useful in developing comprehension and critical reading skills. The content is suitable for intermediate grades and higher. These cassettes are entertaining as well as instructive.

## LOGOS  (Educational Products)

*LOGOS* is an individualized reading skills development kit. A cassette and chart demonstrate the ten steps for operating the program, making it completely self-directing and self-correcting. The skills areas included are phonics, word structure, syntax, and semantics.

The program is based on clearly specified behavioral objectives and includes pretest and post-tests, nonconsumable activity cards, and student record booklets in which progress is plotted.

## Magic Circle Books  (Ginn and Co.)

Magic Circle Books are a set of paperbacks for grades K-3. Although they were designed to accompany the Ginn basal readers, these titles could supplement other programs as well. A Skill Card with questions and suggested activities accompanies each book. The Teacher's Guide for each unit contains additional activities and a synopsis of each story.

### Mastering Basic Reading Skills  ✏ (Steck-Vaughn)

Here is a "back to basics" remedial program for low achievers in grades 5–9. There are four consumable books in the series, each containing high-interest stories and exercise material. The reading levels of the books range from grade 3 to grade 6. The interest level extends through junior high school.

### Match and Check  ✏ (Scott, Foresman)

*Match and Check* is an inexpensive programmed game device in which the student matches two items (e.g., a beginning consonant with a picture) and then slides a button to find out if the items are matched correctly. These devices are inexpensive, instructive, and fun to use. Check the latest catalog to see which levels are available.

### McCall-Crabbs
### Standard Test Lessons in Reading  ✏ (Teachers College Press)

With its first edition now more than a half century old, this old standby is still going strong. A new edition was published in 1979. This series of six booklets gives practice in reading short selections and answering multiple-choice items about each selection. These are good materials to give practice for standardized tests. Each selection yields a grade score which, while not always accurate, does give the student something to plot on a progress plotter. Just keep in mind that these are practice materials, not tests, and you will be able to tolerate the somewhat unreliable norms. Or, ignore the norms altogether and simply use the selections as a source of things to read. Level A can be used at about reading grade levels 2 to 3. Each level up through F gets progressively more difficult. You may design your own response sheet to conform in format to the standardized test you use.

### McCall-Harby Test Lessons in Primary Reading  ✏ (Teachers College Press)

This booklet contains 62 short stories, each of which is followed by ten true-false questions. It is suitable for students not yet able to deal with Level A of the McCall-Crabbs series. The 1980 edition contains many new stories and updated content. Ignore the directions in the teacher's manual that suggest lengthy group discussions of the responses. Perforated pages in the pupil booklets make this an especially easy book to modify for individual pupil use. Tear out the pages and prepare them for lapboards.

### MCP Phonics Program  ✏ (Modern Curriculum Press)

This program is an inexpensive set of three basic phonic workbooks—Books A, B, and C. Buy four of each title and use them in lapboards. They are an excellent source of exercises in word attack skills. Also available is a set of overhead transparencies for each level, which eliminates the need to present teacher-directed portions of the lesson material on a chalkboard.

## Miller-Brody A-V Materials  (Random House)

The Miller-Brody audiovisual materials including the Newbery Award records, cassettes, and filmstrips are now available from Random House. The catalog contains many attractive offerings. We recommend, of course, that you purchase all the books and skills materials that you need before you commit funds to high priced multi-media programs. However, if your budget includes money for A-V items, you should get the Miller-Brody catalog from Random House.

## The Morgan Bay Mysteries  (Addison-Wesley)

The Morgan Bay Mysteries are a series of eight mystery stories (reading levels 2.3 to 4.1). These suspenseful, entertaining books are a "must" for anyone who works with reluctant readers. The Teacher's Manual suggests additional activities.

## Morrow Trade Books (William Morrow)

William Morrow and Company (and the related company, Lothrop, Lee and Shepard) are an excellent source of easy-to-read books. Their list indicates the readability level of each of the titles available.

## Milton Bradley Materials  (Milton Bradley)

The Milton Bradley catalog has a wealth of materials, games, classroom displays, cards, and other devices which might prove useful. The items are far too numerous to list in detail here. Most are colorful and well constructed.

The catalog also lists Playskool puzzles and devices. Some of these directly pertain to reading, although many do not. The catalog is worth a look.

## Mini-Systems Programs for Individualized Instruction 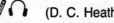 (D. C. Heath)

An individual mini-system includes a cassette lesson, teacher's guide, and a package of thirty copies of an activity sheet.

There are 100 mini-systems for beginning reading skills. The catalog specifies the objective(s) for each mini-system so that you can order wisely. Mini-systems can be used in the primary grades or with older remedial readers.

## The New Linguistic Block Series  (Scott, Foresman)

There are four sets of plastic cubes in the New Linguistic Block Series. The blocks have letters, letter clusters, pictures, and punctuation marks. Students roll the blocks and arrange them to form words and sentences.

## Open Court Lit Kits (Open Court)

These are collections of excellent children's books arranged by readability and interest level. Special interest kits (e.g., mysteries, myths, how-to books) are available. Many of the titles included in these collections are outstanding. Children's classics are well represented. Before you buy, however, make sure that this is an economical approach to acquisition of these books. You might do better assembling your own collections.

### Our Book Corner ■ (Addison-Wesley, Juvenile Division)

*Our Book Corner* is a delightful paperback library developed in England for young children. There are 72 different small books for small hands. These books are informative, inexpensive, and a welcome addition to any early primary classroom.

### Owl Books ■ (Holt, Rinehart and Winston)

The Owl books are lovely collections of books for children. In order of difficulty, the sets are: Kinder Owl Books (20 titles); Little Owl Books (40 titles); Young Owl Books (40 titles); Wise Owl Books (20 titles). These books are attractive and reasonably priced.

### Oxford Children's Books ■ (Oxford University Press)

Oxford reentered the children's book market during the fall of 1978, bringing a number of high quality titles from England as well as new editions of some old classics. Among the highlights of this excellent quality list are books magnificently illustrated by Brian Wildsmith.

### Pal Paperback Kits ■/ (Xerox Education Publications)

Pal Paperbacks are collections of paperbacks for junior and senior high school students who are reading way below grade level. Each kit contains three copies each of eighteen titles. Kit A reading levels are 1.5 to 3.5. Kit B levels are 3.5 to 5.5. Within a kit, color coding identifies the difficulty levels. Also in a kit are a full-color poster and a Teacher's Guide. These books are very nice and fill a real need. For those of you who already have some of these, check your Xerox catalog. New collections of titles have recently been added to the series.

### Panorama Reading / (Steck Vaughn)

*Panorama Reading* is a series of four 96-page worktexts aimed at the intermediate grade and junior high remedial market. Reading levels range from grade 2 to grade 4. Each book contains reading selections and exercises. Many of the selections are of high interest. The exercise material, however, attempts to teach too many skills in too little space. A page or two on a given item is hardly enough for most students in this target audience. We think it would have been better to select a few essential skills and to do them well, rather than to give superficial attention to a great number.

The format of the pages may present some difficulties to the intended audience. The pages—especially those with exercises—are badly designed, too cluttered and busy. Although the reading level of Book 1 in the series is claimed to be below 2.5, the book presents a far more formidable appearance. There is just too much type in too little space for problem readers. We think that Scholastic's *Sprint* or *Action* programs would probably be a better bet for this population.

### Paperbacks from Avon ■ (Avon Books)

The Avon publishing company is a good source of contemporary paperbacks for mature readers. Consult the current catalog, because new titles are added frequently.

## Paperbacks from Bantam ▉                       (Bantam Books)

Bantam Books is an excellent source of paperbacks with contemporary themes and appeal to the mature reader. If secondary students are your population, the latest Bantam catalog for grades 7–12 should be helpful. Books can be purchased by individual title or in special interest collections arranged by theme. The catalog provides readability levels and identifies titles that are suitable for readers functioning below grade level. Teacher's Guides are available for a number of titles.

For primary and intermediate grade students, get the Bantam Catalog for Young Readers. Skylark Books, an excellent collection, are featured. Be sure to consult a current catalog. Publishers such as Bantam are continually adding new titles.

## Patterns, Sounds, and Meaning ✏                       (Allyn and Bacon)

This is a word analysis skill program in workbooks for four levels: *Clues to Consonants; Views and Vowels; Letters and Syllables; Letters and Words.* For each skill there are introductory and reinforcement exercises and diagnostic review pages. Cassettes are available so that the student can use the program without continuous teacher intervention. The tapes introduce the skills, give directions for specific pages, and provide feedback.

## Personalized Reading Centers ▉ ✏                       (Xerox Education Publications)

Personalized Reading Centers are collections of paperback books and support materials for individualized reading. "Story cards" prepare a child for the vocabulary and concepts of the book of his or her choice. Creative activity cards suggest interesting follow-up activities. Each student has a log in which to make responses to the activity cards. The logs contain brief "mini-plots" to assist the student in selecting a book he or she really wants to read.

Personalized Reading Centers are available for grade levels 3–6, each with a range of reading levels represented. The grade 3 level has fewer story cards than the others but adds seven records to the support materials. A wall flow chart keeps the procedures for operating the program available for any student who might forget.

## Phonics Crossword Puzzles ✏                       (McCormick-Mathers)

Three levels of phonics crossword puzzles, *Book A* (Grades 1–2), *Book B* (Grades 3–4), and *Book C* (Grades 5–6), are an excellent supplement to a word attack skills and basic vocabulary development program. Each puzzle stresses a particular sound, sound pattern, or phonetic principle. Puzzles are fun. These are good for older remedial readers as well as children in the elementary grades. This series is available on duplicating masters as well as in workbooks.

## Phonics Is Fun Program ✏                       (Modern Curriculum Press)

*Phonics Is Fun* has three workbooks (Books 1, 2, and 3) for basic phonics skills. Four copies of each, prepared for lapboard use, make an inexpensive source of word attack skills exercises. Three copies of the Pre-Primers can be purchased to accompany the Book 1 workbook.

### The Phoenix Reading Series 🖉                          (Prentice-Hall)

The Phoenix Reading Series is a program designed for intermediate grade underachievers. There are three levels (A, B, and C), each with five pairs of books. In each pair there is a photo reader with contemporary newspaper-style stories and an action reader which develops a specific decoding skill and comprehension skills. Duplicating masters for additional skills practice and mastery tests are available. The program is primarily teacher-directed, but some of the materials could be modified and used for individualized instruction.

### Picto-Cabulary Basic Word Set 🖉                        (Barnell Loft)

The *Basic Word Set* of the Picto-Cabulary Series teaches 720 basic vocabulary words. The set contains 30 different titles, a teacher's manual, tests, a class record sheet, and duplicating masters for student response sheets, all in an attractive container.

This is an excellent product and a high-priority item which, like other Barnell Loft materials, is sold only to schools.

### Picto-Cabulary Series 🖉                                 (Barnell Loft)

On a higher level than the *Basic Word Set*, the Picto-Cabulary Series includes *Words to Eat, Words to Wear,* and *Words to Meet.* Designed for reading grade level 3–4, they actually seem to be functional at a much higher level.

For grades 5–9, Picto-Cabulary Sets are designed to develop interesting and exotic vocabulary. Unlike the *Basic Word Set,* which true to its name is basic, these higher-level kits seem to be enriching and enlarging rather than essential. We're not quite sure about presenting titles like "Succulent Steaks and Fragrant Flowers," and teaching words like *caviar,* to students whose families can't even afford to go to Burger King.

### Practicing Reading 🖉                                    (Random House)

*Practicing Reading* is a series of seven books, reading levels 2–8. Each book contains 40 short, high interest selections with multiple choice questions presented in standardized test format. The students record their answers on a structured response sheet called a "Skill Tracker," which enables them to keep track of the specific kinds of comprehension questions (main idea, detail, inference, sequence, vocabulary in context) being missed.

The selections are varied in content and were used in a number of different settings prior to publication. Kids seem to like them. The program is inexpensive and a good value for supplementary classroom materials. Of course, we do admit to being slightly less than perfectly objective in our evaluation of this program. We wrote it. Nevertheless, we think you'll like it.

### Practicing Vocabulary 🖉                                 (Random House)

*Practicing Vocabulary* can be used as a companion program to *Practicing Reading* or it can be used separately. There are seven levels, from 2 to 8. The words were selected from those that students need to know to do well in school and on tests.

The format of the lessons in *Practicing Vocabulary* is the same as that of Activity 381 in this book. The words are, of course, appropriate to the level of the particular book. The brief context selections used to teach the words are entertaining as well as instructive.

### Primary Reading Skills Program / (McCormick-Mathers)

Reinforcement exercises for beginning reading skills are available in three kits (Levels I, II, and III), each of which contains 150 duplicating masters, answer keys, and a teacher's guide. Certain of the pages are designated as tests, and correlations with other skills programs are provided.

### Puffin Books ▮ (Penguin Books)

Be sure to get the catalog of Puffin Books from the Penguin Division of Viking. Many excellent titles are available. The catalog identifies reading level and interest level for each book. Don't miss this fine collection of paperbacks. Many classics and wonderful works of fiction are included.

### RR / (Modern Curriculum Press)

*RR* is an inexpensive workbook designed to teach decoding to older remedial students. Its content is carefully chosen so it can be used from the upper elementary levels all the way up to adult illiterates. The word attack skills taught receive prompt application in short reading materials including some entertaining verse in cartoon format.

### Raintree Childrens Books ▮ (Macdonald-Raintree)

This publisher offers an excellent list of children's books, especially non-fiction titles. The books are colorful, sturdy, and informative. Among the sets we like best are Look At Science, Read About Science, Read About Animals, and the popular series from England, A Book About.

Raintree has some excellent reference sets for children. The *Raintree Illustrated Science Encyclopedia,* is especially interesting. Be sure to get the latest catalog. Other important series were in production when we went to press.

For a number of Raintree books, correlations to major classroom management systems and activities in *Reading Aids* are available, in the form of brief Skills Bulletins.

### Random House Reading Programs
### Orange and Yellow ▮ / ∩ (Random House)

Each of these two reading programs contains 50 different children's books and related support materials. For each book there is a series of self-directing, self-correcting skill cards for the student that pretest and preteach the vocabulary, guide the student in previewing the book, check comprehension, and present follow-up activities. A Teacher's Information Folder for each book provides a synopsis of the book and material for a student-teacher book conference. Questions on the book cards and in the book conference are coded so that the teacher can quickly tally a child's errors and prescribe the appropriate cards in Skilpacers units. Skilpacers, a skills kits with instruction and four practice cards for 15 different reading skills, can be ordered separately, as well.

*RHRP Orange* contains books at readability levels ranging from 1.5 to 3.0, with most of the books around grade 2 level. In addition, 20 of the books have a cassette lesson to assist the reader in working through the cards and to read the story aloud.

*RHRP Yellow* books are arranged in "interest centers" of 10 books each. There is a Picture Dictionary for each interest center, to aid the student in completing the word puzzle cards.

The major flaw, and it isn't really a flaw at all, is that these programs get little kids so hooked on reading that you'll run out of books. Like many other good things in this world, they are expensive.

### Random House Reading Programs Red, Blue, and Green

*Random House Reading Programs Red, Blue,* and *Green,* listed here in order of difficulty, are the higher-level units of the Random House Reading Program. The book cards are in small pockets right inside each book. The questions do not always seem to be as imaginative as those at the lower levels, but this is not a major problem. We frequently let students skip the vocabulary card and get right to the book. Many of the titles are excellent.

Information about each book is contained in the Teacher's Guide for each unit. Student response sheets and record folders come with the program. For each unit of the program there is a corresponding Skilpacers kit keyed to the items on the book cards and in the book conference.

Each of these units has 50 books in the basic package, arranged in "interest centers" of ten books each. Each level has two additional interest centers with special emphasis on contemporary themes and multi-ethnic interests. If you can't afford the entire program, or even a whole unit, these extra interest centers, together with the corresponding Skilpacers, are a good starting package.

### Random Reading Almanacs        (Random House)

This series of pamphlets (each only 16 pages) contains 24 titles, six topics at each of the levels 3–6. These books contain lots of interesting facts and trivia, but we don't feel they are of great value in a reading program. They don't really do very much, and most kids—even lousy readers—would do as well with the *Guinness Book of World Records.* However, that's just our opinion. You might have a different one.

### REACH        (Individualized Instruction Co.)

*REACH* (the acronym for *Reading Extravaganza of America Cycling and Hydroplane Show*) is an individualized remedial program for intermediate grade students. The audio cassette lessons use Pacer, a self-stopping cassette playback unit. Cassettes for standard playback units are available too. This program uses lingo from show business rather than the classroom, and addresses the student personally as "Trouper." A lesson is a "show"; a test is a "showstopper." Frankly, we find the whole thing a bit much. However, we admit to being somewhat over twelve years old.

### Read As You Listen  (Scott Education)

Read As You Listen is a series of large-type storybooks containing all-time favorites, each with a cassette (or record) to narrate the stories in the book.

### Read Along Libraries (Random House)

A number of excellent collections of young children's books (including Dr. Seuss titles, books by the Berenstains, and Richard Scarry) are available with read along cassettes. These items are expensive, but nice. Most of the titles are available singly as well as in sets. If you have money for audio materials, you should consider these for beginning readers.

### Read and Check (Scott, Foresman)

Read and Check is a plastic box with windows through which questions and answer choices appear. After selecting an answer, the student moves a button to check the response. These devices are inexpensive and useful.

### Read Better—Learn More (Ginn and Co.)

Read Better—Learn More is a series of three (Levels A–C) self-directing, self-correcting workbooks for reading skills in the content areas.

### Reader's Choice (Scholastic)

For an outstanding collection of paperback books at all grade levels, write for the Reader's Choice catalog. Books are available as special-interest collections by theme, level, or special-target population, or as separate titles. Records or cassettes are included in some of the collections.

Scholastic's high-quality books are an excellent value. Be sure to get the most recent catalog, because new titles are frequently added to the list.

### Reading Attainment Systems I and II  (Grolier)

These attractively packaged kits are designed for older readers who are in need of materials at a lower reading level. Kit I begins at approximately grade 3 level. The content of both kits is suitable for use from about grade 6 to adult interest.

Each kit contains Skill Cards (including a glossary of key words in the selection), reading selections with comprehension checks, and answer key cards. The cards are color coded by level and designed for convenient selection and correct replacement in the storage case.

Both the content and the procedures employed in the Reading Attainment Systems are pedagogically very sound. The student record booklets provide response pages with a place for self-checking and progress plotter graphs. Cassettes are available as an optional accessory for System I.

### Reading Awareness (J. B. Lippincott)

Reading Awareness is an introduction to learning to read for young children. It contains a dozen cassette lessons, each of which goes with a color-keyed section of the consumable student workbook *(My Book Book)*. The games, sing-alongs, listening exercises, and following directions tasks are designed to motivate the child in beginning reading instruction.

### Reading: Beginnings, Patterns, Explorations ▮⁄ (D. C. Heath Co.)

This is a beginning reading program, certain components of which do lend themselves well to individualized instruction. The "workshops" are workbooks, many pages of which can be modified for self-directing, self-correcting use. "Skill-shops" are duplicating masters to reinforce decoding skills. "Bookshops" are collections of paperback books.

### Reading Comprehension Programs ⁄↺ (Nystrom)

Nystrom offers three programs to develop reading comprehension. These programs are advertised as "companions" to basal readers. *Understand What We Read* is an audiovisual program for young children. It deals with comprehension, oral language, and listening skills. *Reading for Comprehension,* levels 3.5–6.5, provides practice in comprehension and thinking skills and encourages students to use the library. *Amazing Adventures* works on comprehension skills while encouraging elementary school children to become interested in reading science material.

### Reading Development Kits ⁄ (Addison-Wesley)

There are three *Reading Development Kits*—A, B, and C.

The selections in Kit A are aimed at mature interest level (grade 6 to adult) and reading level beginning at grade 2. The cards contain exercises on word attack skills, short selections to read, and comprehension questions on the selections. In addition, there are instruction cards on four different kinds of critical reading. The kit comes with alternative forms of a placement inventory and student record/answer-key booklets. The student booklets are mature in format and conceal the remedial nature of the materials. However, these pages may be a bit too complicated and busy for the reader in serious trouble. If so, you can provide response sheets with larger spaces in which to write the answers. Take at least one record booklet and paste the answer keys on index cards for the day when you run out of student booklets. Your kit will still be operative until the replacements arrive.

Kit B is organized like Kit A. However, most students who can use it will be able to use the student response booklets as directed. Keep one copy for a master key. Kit C reading level begins at about grade 7.

### Reading Enrichment Resources ▮⁄ (Allyn and Bacon)

*Reading Enrichment Resources* is a program to encourage independent, recreational reading. There are six boxes, one for each grade, 1 to 6. The program provides activities to accompany the reading of selected library books. Although the books are not included, most of the titles can be found in school and public libraries. The program is designed as enrichment material for *Pathfinder,* the publisher's basal reading series, but the activities could be used with other reading series or programs as well.

**Reading for Survival** 🖊 (Cambridge)

This series of four titles for reading levels 4–8, and three for levels 0–3 is aimed at a mature audience that is severely deficient in basic skills. the content deals with basic necessities of life—money, jobs, cars, being a good consumer, etc. The lowest level book, *Reading for Life,* is designed for the student who knows only the alphabet and a few sight words. It presents 300 new words, and work with 31 phonograms. This book works on getting the student up to a first grade competency level. There's so little out there that is suitable for the older nonreader, that this might be worth a try.

**Reading Improvement Series** 🖊🎧 (Educational Development Corp.)

Available in two levels, primary and intermediate, the Reading Improvement Series is a set of audio tape cassette lessons with activity sheets designed to supplement basal instruction or provide remediation of specific skill deficiencies.

**Reading Incentive Program**
**Gold Cup Reading Games** 📖🖊🎧 (Bowmar/Noble)

The *Reading Incentive Program* contains high-interest, easy-vocabulary books on topics such as motorcycle racing, ski-mobiles, horses, dogs, drag-racing, and mini-bikes. Each colorful book has a sound-filmstrip to go with it. For each title there is a set of eight self-directing duplicating masters for skills development. A classroom set for each title includes the filmstrip, a cassette or record, the duplicating masters, and seven copies of the book. Single copies of the books and the masters are available separately. Four titles are also available in Spanish.

Five Gold Cup Reading Games—*Horse Trail Ride, Bicycle Rally, The Great Balloon Race, Motorcycle Moto Cross,* and *Dune Buggy Rally*—give skills practice in game format.

**Reading Practice Program** 🖊 (Harcourt Brace Jovanovich)

The *Reading Practice Program* is a collection of word attack and comprehension skill exercises. Some of them are apparently the same as some that have appeared in earlier material, and some are apparently completely new. The cards are very plain and "mature" in format, making them quite suitable in appearance for the older retarded reader.

The design of the kit makes sense. There are listed behavioral objectives, pre- and post-tests for each section, and student record forms on which to track progress. Look carefully, however, at the exact content of the exercises. Certain of the tests are not behaviorally identical to the lessons they are designed to evaluate. In other words, the cards might provide practice on apples while the test measures oranges. Nevertheless, there are some worthwhile activities in the kit.

**Reading Skill Builders** 🖊 (Reader's Digest)

*Reading Skill Builders* from Reader's Digest have been popular for a long time— so popular, in fact, that some learners seem to have reached a saturation point with them. Optional audio lessons on cassette make the skill building completely self-directing and self-motivating. The audio lessons focus on vocabulary or comprehension skills, give the learner feedback, and explain why some answers are right and others wrong. Duplicating masters containing the skill building exercises are also available. The teacher's master manual outlines the entire skill building program by specific skill, level, and story content. This makes prescribing work in the skill builders easier than ever before.

### Reading Skills Practice Pads  ▱                          (Reader's Digest)
These are an excellent, inexpensive source of skills development material. There are six levels (A-F), each level corresponding approximately to an elementary grade reading level.

### Rolling Phonics  ▱                                      (Scott, Foresman)
*Rolling Phonics* is a set of blocks, some with consonants and blends, others with vowel phonograms. The student rolls the blocks and makes words. Engaging, inexpensive, and instructive.

### Rolling Readers  ▱                                      (Scott, Foresman)
*Rolling Readers* are a series of plastic blocks, each side of which shows a word. The student rolls the blocks, constructs a sentence, and reads it. There are three sets, each with ten blocks. They are inexpensive and fun.

### S.T.A.R.T. Reading Program  ▱                           (Spellbinder)
This program consists of ten skill kits, each of which contains 20 skill master cards, 40 word response cards, and 5 story booklets. Use of the program requires an electric console, the Spellbinder Star Console, which illuminates each correct response as the student decodes, manipulates words, and builds sentences.

This is not really a reading program, but more of a highly motivational electronic toy for reading skills reinforcement. If money is of no concern, the system might prove to be appealing. However, we would place it low on the list of priorities because fun as it might be, it's a gimmick that could become tiresome. We'd rather get kids hooked on books.

### SRA Reading Labs  ▱                         (Science Research Associates)
The *SRA Reading Labs* are so well known and widely used that to describe them here would be superfluous. If you and your students have reached the saturation point with the Labs, don't give up. Most of the kits have been revised. New content with the old effective pedagogy makes these kits a worthwhile purchase still.

### Satellite Books  ■                         (Holt, Rinehart and Winston)
The Satellite Books are paperbacks for independent reading. This attractive set of books includes both children's classics and works by outstanding contemporary authors. A study card for each book provides follow-up activities and suggestions for additional reading.

## Scholastic Bookshelf  (Scholastic)

*Scholastic Bookshelf* is a program for on-level or above level students in the intermediate grades. It uses whole books to teach important reading and literature skills. The program includes paperback books from Scholastic's excellent list, a workbook at each of the three levels, and ditto masters for additional skills exercises relating to the books. The quality of the materials is high. The demands on the teacher and students are also high. That is not a criticism, merely an observation.

## Scholastic's Elementary Skills Workbooks (Scholastic)

Scholastic publishes a number of excellent, economical (insofar as anything is these days) workbooks for a number of specific reading skills. The Reading Comprehension Series for Grades 3 to 6 has books at each level for Literal, Interpretive, and Critical Reading. A colorful set of six Phonics Workbooks can be used in the primary grades or with older remedial readers. Workbooks on Map Skills, Library Skills, Dictionary Skills, and Charts and Graphs are among the others available. Check the latest Scholastic catalog for a complete and current list.

## Scope Skills Books, Visuals, Activity Kits (Scholastic)

The Scope materials from Scholastic are high-interest items aimed at secondary school students with reading levels grades 4 to 6. The various skills books are an excellent and inexpensive source of reading practice materials. The visuals provide lessons on transparencies for overhead projector and accompanying dittos. The activity kits are mini-units containing readings related to a specific theme (e.g., monsters, families, mystery, frauds, and hoaxes, sports, love) and ditto masters for reinforcement of basic skills. There are many titles available for each of the Scope formats. Check the latest Scholastic catalog for the current list of what's available.

## Scoring High in Reading (Random House)

This program develops reading and test taking skills. The four books, Levels A-D, are designed to prepare students for standardized reading tests levels 2–8. Each workbook is organized into units commonly found on reading achievement tests— Word Study, Word Knowledge, Interpretation, Sentence Meaning, and Reading Comprehension.

If getting your students by the test is one of your required objectives, this program would be helpful.

## Scoring High in Survival Reading (Random House)

This program consists of three 32-page workbooks entitled *Earning and Spending, Taking Action,* and *Getting Around.* It is designed to prepare secondary age students for the real life reading demands they will meet. It's inexpensive and interesting.

## Scribner Book Fair Editions (Charles Scribner's Sons)

The Book Fair Editions are paperback picture and story books selected from Scribner's juvenile list. These books contain the same pictures and text as the original clothbound editions.

**Selections from the Black** ✎ (Jamestown Publishers)

Selections from the Black is a series of three Skilltexts (Olive, Brown, and Purple) which contain reading selections and vocabulary and comprehension skill exercises. These books are designed to be especially relevant to black students. The content of the materials is excellent and will appeal to the target audience and to others as well.

These books are intended to improve the reading skills of those who are already functionally literate. The reading levels begin at about grade 7 and are ideal for high school and junior college reading improvement courses.

**Sesame Street Prereading Kit** ✎ ∩ (Addison-Wesley)

This program uses the popular characters and content from the "Sesame Street" television series to develop skills in visual discrimination, auditory discrimination, and coding. The complete program is a rather expensive multimedia package. However, individual modules are available. The Teacher's Resource Book includes materials for record keeping, supplementary activities, and correlations to leading basal programs.

**Slow Reader Catalog** ■ (Follett Library Book Company)

Follett has compiled a very useful listing of high-interest, low-vocabulary titles from many different publishers. Reading level and interest level for each of the 2,700 volumes is included. Most of the books listed are fairly recent publications. Teachers of remedial classes will find this catalog a useful tool.

As far as we know, Follett still follows the practice of flagging books that they feel some customers might find objectionable in some way (e.g., controversial theme or mature content). We really don't like that practice, and suggest that you make your own decisions without that sort of help. Nevertheless, we still suggest Follett as a supplier because of their extensive list and generally good record of order fulfillment. You can request that they omit their little censorship flags from your order if you wish.

**Spacetalk** ∩ (Individualized Instruction Co.)

*Spacetalk* contains 40 cassette-based lessons on auditory discrimination of sounds in words. The pupil response folders are reusable plastic.

**Special Ed Materials from Book-Lab** ✎ (Book-Lab)

Book-Lab distributes a variety of materials designed to meet special education needs. Remedial reading teachers, learning disabilities specialists, and other teachers of difficult to reach students may find something of interest in the Book-Lab catalog.

**Specific Reading Skills (SRS)** ✎ ∩ (Jones-Kenilworth Co.)

SRS is a series of reading skills books for grades 1–8. For each grade level the hard-cover book contains three levels of difficulty. Each of these levels is also available separately in soft cover. The Pre-Pre, Pre, and Primer levels are available in soft cover only.

The series develops skills in word attack, comprehension, and content areas. Each level has a section devoted to social studies, science, math, and literature reading skills.

Also available with the series are placement tests and teaching cassettes for each level. For most students, the program is clear enough for use without the cassettes.

### Speech-to-Print Phonics  (Harcourt Brace Jovanovich)

The latest version of this popular phonics program by Durrell and Murphy retains the best pedagogical features of the first edition. The packaging is more attractive and convenient. Ten lessons on letter names begin the program, followed by 56 lessons on sound-symbol relationships.

Individual pupil response cards permit each student to participate actively, even in a group lesson. Because the teacher's manual has such complete instructions for each lesson, *Speech-to-Print Phonics* is excellent for use by volunteer tutors or aides.

### Spirit Duplicating Books (ESP, Inc.)

ESP has programs on ditto master available for levels K–8 in the areas of reading, phonics, and language arts. Also available is the *Jumbo Reading Cassette Program* for levels 2–6, with 96 audio lessons and worksheets for each level. ESP offers a reading program for Spanish-speaking children attending schools where English is the primary language.

### Sports Illustrated Books (J. B. Lippincott)

This series of more than twenty books covers the most popular spectator and participant sports. These books are suggested for junior high school students and up.

### Sports Star (Harcourt Brace Jovanovich)

Sports Star is a series of high-interest, low-vocabulary sports biographies written for beginning and hard-to-please older readers. The books are easy to read. They contain many photographs and much information.

### Spotlight on Literature (Random House)

This program is aimed at below level secondary school students. It contains adapted versions of material from traditional and contemporary classics. Exercises deal with comprehension and interpretive reading skills. Margin notes help guide the reader in developing these skills while calling attention to concrete examples.

Like all the Spotlight programs, this one is reasonably priced and worth a try if you happen to be teaching the intended target audience.

### Spotlight on Phonics (Random House)

This is an excellent new program that teaches decoding in a sequential, structured, and meaningful way. Some of the useful blending activities featured in the popular *Structural Reading Program* (same authors) are found here.

The program is well designed and easy to use. It is a good value.

### Spotlight on Reading  🖉 (Random House)

*Spotlight on Reading* is the Random House answer to Barnell Loft. There are eight Spotlight skills books for each of seven reading levels, 2–8. Each book concentrates on one skill. The skills covered include: Main Idea, Inference, Sequence, Details, Critical Reading, Maps, Charts and Graphs, Story Elements, and Vocabulary.

The catalog calls it "today's most affordable Mastery Learning Program." We think that might overstate the case slightly. The books are small, and might not contain enough to guarantee mastery of a particular skill. However, these items are very reasonably priced and worth having.

### Sprint Reading Skills Program  📖🖉 (Scholastic)

*Sprint* is a remedial reading program for students in the intermediate grades. The materials are extremely well prepared, high-interest items that deal with essential reading skills and content that can hold the attention of even the most reluctant readers. *Sprint Starter* is suitable for even nonreaders. It uses ten short workbooks to teach the 1,074 words in the Spache vocabulary list. Each of the higher levels of *Sprint* contain three Skills Books, a Story Book, a Play Book, and Spirit Masters for extra skills practice. The Sprint Libraries that accompany the program contain supplementary high-interest books and Spirit Masters. The Teacher's Guide provides plot summaries and suggested discussion questions. This is a program well worth looking at if you have students in the intermediate grades (or even higher) who are significantly below grade level in reading.

### Star Wars Attack on Reading  🖉 (Random House)

These colorful self-directing, self-correcting workbooks use the themes and characters—Artoo Detoo, See Threepio, Darth Vadar—from Star Wars to teach comprehension, word study, and study skills at reading levels 4–5. Interest level includes junior high school and above.

This is a solid program, although we do suspect that the theme is not quite as engaging as the publishers had hoped. Somehow it seems possible to turn kids onto reading without involving the entire galaxy, and we wonder if the content might become dated. Perhaps not. Maybe there will even be a remedial program called *The Empire Decodes Back* or something like that.

### STEP Language Board  🖉 (Cole Supply)

The *STEP Language Board* is a manipulative device which provides practice in the basic operations of encoding and decoding words. Letter and pictures pieces fit into the plastic board and provide immediate feedback. This is a sturdy support tool for beginning reading experiences. Make sure, however, that your students are responding to the letters and pictures directly, and not to the cut out puzzle shape at the bottom of each plastic piece.

**Story Go Round  ▪ ∩** (Bowmar/Noble)

*Story Go Round* is one of this publisher's Listening-Reading programs. This one, for the primary grades, has three levels. The package for each level contains four copies each of four children's books, cassettes, and a Teacher's Guide with suggestions for follow-up activities. Beginning readers will enjoy this program.

**Story Plays**
**Plays for Echo Reading  ▪ ∩** (Harcourt Brace Jovanovich)

Both of these programs develop purposeful oral reading skills. *Story Plays,* each of which has four parts, all at different reading levels (identified in the Teacher's Manual), permit the teacher to assign each child to a part at suitable reading level.

*Plays for Echo Reading* has records that the children listen to and follow, then read long with until they can read the parts on their own. Both of these programs provide pleasurable and meaningful oral reading experiences for children.

**Study Exercises for Developing Reading Skills  ∥** (Laidlaw Bros.)

*Developing Reading Skills* is a series of four workbooks for upper elementary or junior high school reading. Practice pages are presented in six general skill areas: comprehension and recall, vocabulary, dictionary use, story interpretation, organizational skills, and study skills. The books are simple in format and inexpensive. The exercises can be checked using the answer key, or the pages can be prepared for lapboard use.

**Study Skills for Information Retrieval  ∥** (Allyn and Bacon)

This is a series of four skillbooks (paper covers) to teach students to locate information, use libraries, and organize material. One book deals with student operation of A-V equipment commonly found in schools.

**Sunburst Materials  ▪ ∩** (Sunburst Communications)

Sunburst publishes a colorful assortment of high interest multi-media programs. The materials are high quality, and the content ranges from Newbery award winning literature to the survival skill of reading labels in the supermarket.

If you have a budget for audio-visual materials and you are looking for a place to start spending it, the Sunburst catalog is a good place to shop.

**Super Books  ▪ ∥** (J. B. Lippincott)

*SUPER Books (Stories Unique for Purposeful Extra Reading)* are a series of stories, each written to emphasize a specified set of sound-spelling correspondences. Each SUPER Kit contains five copies each of 40 titles and 40 duplicating masters of illustrated stories to read, color, and take home.

Considering the constraints of writing to a specified sound-symbol sequence, these little books aren't bad. However, great literature they are not.

### Supermarket Recall Reading Program   ✎       (Supermarket Recall)

*Supermarket Recall* is a program designed to improve visual memory and recall using work in real-life reading situations. Each supermarket reading label comes with a question sheet and an answer card. The program guide offers suggestions for follow-up activities. *Supermarket Recall* is suitable for intermediate grades through adult level in terms of interest. The program can also be used with the learning disabled. It lends itself to tutorial situations and pupil team learning.

### Super Products   ✎       (Trend Enterprises, Inc.)

Trend's catalog *Super Products for Super Teachers* presents a collection of games, bulletin board displays, activity cards, and similar devices. There are lots of unnecessary gimmicks in this catalog. There are also some very useful, colorful, and attractive materials. Get the catalog and see for yourself.

### Supportive Reading Skills   ✎       (Dexter and Westbrook)

*Supportive Reading Skills* is an excellent skills program by the author of the *Barnell Loft Specific Skills Series.* Each booklet focuses on a specific reading behavior, at a particular grade level. For the series, Level A corresponds approximately to grade 1, Level B to grade 2, and so on, through Level F and Advanced. The format and content are appealing to older remedial readers as well as to students on grade level.

The series seems to be expending all the time. You should consult Dexter and Westbrook's latest catalogue for an accurate up-to-date list.

### Survival Education   ✎       (Janus Book Publishers)

Survival Education is a series of kits designed for the mature, severely retarded reader. The average reading level is 2.5. The materials deal with real life topics such as job applications, buying a used car, and the like. These kits, because of their content and low reading level, are appealing to the struggling high school or adult illiterate.

### T-Scopes   ✎       (Jane Ward Co.)

*T-Scopes* are laminated devices which can be used for practice and reinforcement of basic phonics skills. A strip containing words or word parts slides through the "scope" (a laminated cardboard sleeve) and each item shows through a slot in the scope. As the strip is pulled through, answers appear for self-checking. You could make devices like this yourself, but these are inexpensive and colorful.

The catalog from Jane Ward Co. contains a number of other inexpensive items you might find useful. These include spirit masters, gameboards, flash cards, and the like. *Reading Warehouse* is a collection of the above items arranged by skill. We suspect that most teachers would prefer to assemble their own collections of such devices, but some of you might find this packaging appealing.

## Target Red, Target Yellow, Target Blue 🖉 🎧 (Addison-Wesley)

*Target Red* is the lowest level of the Target program. It deals with auditory and visual discrimination skills. *Target Yellow* contains lessons on grapheme-phoneme relationships (phonics). *Target Blue,* the third level in the series, concentrates on word structure.

The basic format of each of these programs is the same. Using cassettes and ditto master worksheets, the lessons are self-directing and self-correcting. Behavioral objectives for each lesson are clearly specified. The packaging is excellent. Each program has a bright, sturdy storage box for the cassettes, and stick-on labels for file folders in which to store the worksheets. Each material is color coded, of course, in red, yellow, or blue. The cassette storage boxes, when stacked, make an attractive chest of drawers.

When your students are using *Target Yellow* or *Blue,* be careful that they are attending to both the audio and the worksheet. On a few lessons, the student can complete the worksheet from visual clues only. However, this is a minor drawback, and all in all the materials are well designed. Because of their plain format, they can be used with older remedial readers as well as with younger learners.

## Target Green, Target Orange, Target Purple 🖉 🎧 (Addison-Wesley)

These are the higher levels in the Target series. *Target Green* and *Target Orange* deal with vocabulary. *Target Purple* contains lessons on skills for reading in the content areas.

*Targets Green, Orange, and Purple* are packaged in the same sturdy boxes that the lower levels come in—with, of course, the correct color coding.

Each Target program has, in addition to the cassettes for the student, a cassette to explain the program to the teacher.

These are beautifully designed materials. The objectives are clear and the materials do what they say they will do.

## Teaching Stuff for Reading 🖉 (Teaching Stuff)

Teaching Stuff offers a conglomeration of fairly inexpensive materials—workbooks, games, spirit masters—produced by teachers for teachers. The quality of content and appearance does vary. Some items are better than others, but in general these items are useful and reasonably priced.

## Teaching Resources 🖉 (Teaching Resources Corp.)

Teaching Resources offers a wide assortment of games, devices, and programs for early childhood, language development, and special education. Get the latest catalog to find out what's available. Reading and rhyming wheel devices are available in case you don't feel like making your own. Among our favorites from this catalog are *Sentence Sharpies* and *Phonics Puzzles and Games.* If reading is your objective, stay away from the many activities that appear attractive but do nothing for specific reading skills.

## Trade Books from Addison-Wesley ■ (Addison-Wesley, Juvenile Div.)

The Juvenile Division of Addison-Wesley has an excellent list. Try their science titles as well as their fiction. Get the complete catalogue.

**Text Extenders** ▇                                          (Scholastic)
Text Extenders are collections of paperback books chosen to correlate to a specific basal reading program. The Teacher's Guide for each level contains suggestions for using the books and additional activities.

**The Time Machine Series** ▇                              (Addison-Wesley)
The Time Machine Series is a series of books and records about Leonard, who has many interesting adventures, including a trip to outer space and a visit to dinosaur land. Excellent for the primary grades.

**Torchbearer Library** ▇                                  (Harper and Row)
Harper and Row is an excellent source of high-quality children's books. For intermediate grades try the Torchbearer I and Torchbearer II collections. Be sure to get the Harper and Row catalog and look at the entire list of available titles.

**Try This**
**Try This Too**
**Now Try This** ✐                              (Harcourt Brace Jovanovich)
*Try This* is a set of activities designed to go along with the first grade level of the Harcourt basal reading program. *Try This Too,* and *Now Try This* are designed to accompany the second and third levels of that program. The kits, however, can be used independent of the rest of the program. Self-directing, self-correcting activities in word attack skills and basic comprehension are provided on nonconsumable cards.

**Vocabulary Improvement Practice** ✐          (Harcourt Brace Jovanovich)
Teachers who have used Durrell's word-analysis cards will appreciate this attractive new packaging of an excellent old idea. Three intermediate grade levels plus a "Challenge" level for enrichment make up the kit. The cards can be used by pupil teams to improve vocabulary and classification skills.

**Ventures in Reading** ✐                                     (W. H. Sadlier)
These are skill packs intended for primary level children in need of work in basic phonics skills. The materials are an inexpensive addition to the beginning reading program.

**Vocabulary Workshop** ✐                                    (W. H. Sadlier)
*Vocabulary Workshop* is a program designed to improve vocabulary, and knowledge of synonyms, antonyms, and punctuation. Exercises include definitions, drills based on analogies, sentence completions, and analysis of word roots. The levels are from grade 6 to 12. Supplementary testing materials are also available. These materials may be useful preparation for standardized tests. The revision of this program is described as "modern, lively, and contemporary." We found parts of it more boring than lively, especially the work with definitions and word roots. The materials are useful, however, and not everything used in the classroom has to be absolutely fascinating.

## Voyager Books ▮         (Harcourt Brace Jovanovich)

Voyager Books are attractive, varied titles in children's paperbacks. These editions retain the text and illustrations of the original hard-cover editions. My special favorite is Saint-Exupéry's *The Little Prince*. There are other good books too, including some Caldecott and Newberry Award winners.

The trade sales department of Harcourt has a fine list of children's books in regular hard-cover editions.

## We Are Black ▱         (Science Research Associates)

*We Are Black* is a high-interest kit of reading selections and skill cards. The selections are about black people and can be of interest and benefit to all.

The reading selections are short, attractively presented, and engaging. The skill cards work on vocabulary in context and comprehension for each selection. There are 120 selections, each with a skill card. The range of reading levels is high grade 2 to grade 6.

## Webster Classroom Reading Clinic ▱         (Webster)

This kit contains a variety of reading materials including word wheels, reading skill cards, sight vocabulary cards, books that are rewritten classics, and 20 copies each of the workbooks *Dr. Spello* and *Conquests in Reading*. We've always been able to do without *Dr. Spello,* but over the years have found the other items in this kit to be quite useful. Kids seem to like the watered down classics, although most English teachers would cringe. Among our favorites are *Cases of Sherlock Holmes, Call of the Wild,* and a collection of stories by Edgar Allan Poe. These books, called the Everyreader Series, can be purchased separately.

## Webster Reading Centers ▱         (Webster)

These are two structured remedial reading programs. *Reading Center 1* is for students whose reading level is below 3.5. *Reading Center 2* is for those students whose level is above 3.5 but still below grade level. Included in each program are books, skill cards, tests, record keeping folders, dittos, and a teacher's handbook. Optional cassettes to present lessons are available, although the complete scripts are in the teacher's book. Center One contains Word Wheels and Snurk Cards as well as the other items. (Snurk Cards are to help students deal with sight words that violate the sound-symbol generalizations presented in the program.)

There is much that is useful in these two boxes. However, beware of the advertising claim that presents these programs as "everything you need for reading skills remediation." The programs are worth having, but there are certainly other things you'll want as well.

Some of the books in the program are rewritten, watered down classics. They would make most English teachers cringe, but kids who don't read well seem to like them.

## Weekly Reader Skills Books ▱         (Xerox Education Publications)

The Weekly Reader Skills Books are an excellent collection of inexpensive workbooks that cover many different reading skills, from phonics to using the library. Those of you who use the newpaper from Weekly Reader in your classroom probably need no introduction to these materials. If you aren't familiar with these skill workbooks, send for the catalog. The materials are well thought out and a good value.

### We Read Sentences ✐ (Dexter and Westbrook)

*We Read Sentences* are first grade reading level kits with cards that develop comprehension of sentences and words in context. These are excellent materials for use preceding the first level of the *Using the Context* books from Barnell Loft. These kits can be used with older remedial readers as well as with young children.

### Weird and Horrible Library ▮ (J. B. Lippincott)

The Weird and Horrible Library is a series of paperbacks (recommended for grades 5 and up) dealing with witches, vampires, werewolves, and the like. These are excellent titles to capitalize on the current interest in the occult.

### What Can She Be? ▮ (Lothrop, Lee and Shepard)

What Can She Be? is a series of books each of which describes a job or profession that has claimed relatively few women in the past. These books may interest girls who aspire to be veterinarians or lawyers, for instance.

### The Wildlife Adventure Series ▮ (Addison-Wesley)

The Wildlife Adventure Series is a set of eight books (levels 2.6–4.4) each about an interesting creature of nature—grizzly, alligator, dolphin, wolf, mountain lion, otter, moose, and jack-rabbit. These books maintain interest of students who are reading below grade level. A Teacher's Manual includes suggestions for art and writing activities.

### Wonder Starters ▮ (Grosset and Dunlap)

Wonder Starters are informative books for young children. They have controlled vocabulary and a picture dictionary in the back of each. They are well worth the reasonable price.

### Word Attack Series ✐ (Teachers College Press)

This is a set of three workbooks containing activities and games dealing with word structure. Workbook titles are *Learning About Words, Ways to Read Words,* and *More Ways to Read Words.* These are suited for intermediate grades and above. The plain format makes them usable for any age up to and including adult. This is an easy series to make into kit form.

### Wordcraft Vocabulary Programs ✐🎧 (Communicad)

This is a multi-media approach to vocabulary development. Words are introduced in context and are then defined. The student study manual for each level includes pretests and post-tests as well as the complete script of the lessons presented on the cassettes and filmstrips. An interesting feature is the Time Compressed Cassette for review, which contains the programs recorded at more than double speed to maintain involvement with words already taught. Wordcraft has three levels. They span a range of Grades 4 through 10 developmentally and can be used up through remedial adult programs as well.

## Wordpacers ✏ (Random House)

*Wordpacers* is a vocabulary development kit dealing with skills areas such as context clues, synonyms, antonyms, homonyms, prefixes, suffixes, roots, idioms, and origins of words. For each skill there is an instruction card and two levels of practice cards. A "Skilspotter" for each section of the kit can be used as a diagnostic and/or mastery test.

The cards are attractive and appropriate for achievers in intermediate grade or higher. Students with reading problems may find them confusing. The unmanageable box that housed the first edition of this program has been replaced by a more functional display rack for the cards. The Vocabulary Cards of *Random House Reading Program* are cross-referenced to the skills in *Wordpacers*.

## Word-Roll ✏ (McCormick-Mathers)

*Word-Roll* is a word game with blocks and picture cards that present fifteen beginning consonants and word families and forty-five new words. It's inexpensive and fun.

## Words are Important ✏ (Hammond)

This is a series of workbooks, grades 4–12. The materials use context to help the students discover the meanings of words. The easiest book in the series presents 108 words. The other levels present 180 words each. Because the books are not labeled by level, you can assign the appropriate book to each student without worrying about grade. These materials are relatively inexpensive. They are not the most fascinating items in the world, but they can be very useful.

## Wordshop ✏🎧 (Ideal School Supply Co.)

*Wordshop* is a reading cassette program with a number of different modules. Each unit contains cassettes, spirit masters, and a Teacher's Guide. The major objectives are word attack skills and phonetic analysis. Most of the units are for primary grades, but units for intermediate and remedial secondary are also available.

## Workshop Kits ✏ (Open Court)

These are kits of language arts games to supplement a reading program. These games are fun and they provide practice and reinforcement of basic skills. The materials are colorful and nicely presented.

**Yearling Individualized Reading Program**            (Bowmar/Noble)

The *Yearling Individualized Reading Program* consists basically of the Reading Centers, excellent classroom collections of paperback books ranging in difficulty from grade 3 to grade 6. The Yearling School Reading Center contains one each of the titles for all levels, 3–6. For each grade level there is a Skills Center, which contains placement inventories, reading comprehension checks, and multiple copies of a skills page to accompany each book.

The books are superb. However, the skills material is in some instances not ideally suited to the book. The selection of which activities go with which books appears at times to be completely arbitrary. If you keep the last two or three copies of the skills page for eachbook and laminate them, you can spend the replacement money for more books instead.

# Guide to Published Materials

| | Reading Readiness | Young Beginning Readers | Older Non and Beginning Readers | Middle Grade Remedial | Middle Grade Achievers | Junior High Remedial | Junior High Achievers | H.S. and Adult Remedial | Learning Disabilities | Minority Group Emphasis | Enrichment for Gifted |
|---|---|---|---|---|---|---|---|---|---|---|---|
| ABC Serendipity | • | • | | | | | | | | | • |
| Action, Double Action, and Triple Action | | | | | | • | | • | • | • | |
| Action Libraries | | | | | | • | | • | • | • | |
| AIMS | • | | • | | | | | | • | | |
| Americans All Reading Kit | | | | • | • | • | • | • | | • | |
| Associated Press Newspaper Reading Skills Kit | | | | | | | • | • | | | • |
| Audio Reading Progress Labs | • | • | • | • | • | • | • | • | • | | |
| A-V Materials from Troll | | | • | • | • | • | | • | • | | |
| Awareness Books and Read-alongs | | | • | • | | • | | • | | | |
| Barnell Loft Specific Skills Series | | • | • | • | • | • | • | • | • | | |
| Basic Living Skills Programs | | | | | | • | | • | | | |
| Be a Better Reader | | | | | • | • | • | • | | | |

| | Reading Readiness | Young Beginning Readers | Older Non and Beginning Readers | Middle Grade Remedial | Middle Grade Achievers | Junior High Remedial | Junior High Achievers | H.S. and Adult Remedial | Learning Disabilities | Minority Group Emphasis | Enrichment for Gifted |
|---|---|---|---|---|---|---|---|---|---|---|---|
| BEST | | | ● | ● | | ● | | ● | ● | | |
| Books from Garrard | | ● | ● | ● | ● | ● | | | | | |
| Books from Harcourt | | ● | | ● | ● | ● | | | | | ● |
| Books from Messner | | | | ● | ● | ● | ● | | | | |
| Breaking the Code | | | ● | ● | | ● | | | | | |
| Breakthrough | | | ● | ● | | ● | | ● | | ● | |
| Butterworth Books | | | | | | ● | | ● | | | |
| The Checkered Flag Series | | | ● | ● | ● | ● | | ● | ● | | |
| Choose and Check | | ● | ● | ● | | | | | ● | | |
| Clarion Books for Young People | | ● | | ● | ● | ● | | | | | ● |
| Clues to Reading | | | ● | ● | | ● | | ● | | ● | |
| The Codebook Series | ● | ● | ● | ● | | ● | | | | ● | |
| Content Readers | | | | ● | ● | ● | ● | ● | | | |
| Continental Ditto Masters | ● | ● | ● | ● | ● | ● | | | | | |
| The Cornerstone Readers | | ● | ● | ● | ● | | | | | | |
| Countries and Cultures | | | | | ● | ● | ● | ● | | ● | ● |
| Crane Reading System | | ● | ● | ● | | | | | | | |
| Creature Teachers | | ● | ● | | | | | | ● | | |
| Critical Reading | | | | | ● | | ● | | | | ● |
| Croft Comprehension Skillpacks | | ● | ● | ● | ● | ● | | ● | | | |
| Crowell Books | | ● | ● | ● | ● | | | | | | |
| CTP Materials | ● | ● | | ● | | | | | | | |

| | Reading Readiness | Young Beginning Readers | Older Non and Beginning Readers | Middle Grade Remedial | Middle Grade Achievers | Junior High Remedial | Junior High Achievers | H.S. and Adult Remedial | Learning Disabilities | Minority Group Emphasis | Enrichment for Gifted |
|---|---|---|---|---|---|---|---|---|---|---|---|
| The Deep Sea Adventure Series | | | • | • | | • | | • | | | |
| Developmental Reading Text Workbooks | • | • | • | • | • | • | | | • | | |
| Dolch Puzzle Books and Games | • | • | • | • | | | | | • | | |
| Duplicating Masters and Gameboards | • | • | • | • | | | | | • | | |
| Durrell-Murphy Phonics Practice Program | | • | • | • | | | | | • | | |
| Dutton Books | | • | | • | • | | | | | | • |
| Early Learning for Reading | • | • | | | | | | | | | |
| EARS | • | • | | | | | | | • | | |
| Easy Readers | • | • | | | | | | | • | | |
| EDL Study Skills Kits | | | | | • | • | • | • | | | • |
| Electric Company Sentence Comprehension Kit | | • | • | • | | | | | | | |
| Educational Materials | | • | • | • | | • | | | • | | |
| ETA Materials | | • | • | • | • | • | | | • | | |
| Extra Credit Reading | | | | | • | • | | | | | |
| Fantastic Fables | | • | • | | | • | | | | | |
| Fat Cats | | • | | | | | | | | | |
| Flash Gordon Remedial Reading Kits | | • | • | | | • | | | | • | |
| First Talking Alphabet | • | • | | | | | | | | | |
| Follett Library Books | | • | | • | • | • | • | • | | • | • |
| Ginn Word Enrichment Program | • | • | • | • | • | • | | | | | |
| Glazer Reading Involvement Program | | • | • | • | | | | | | | • |

| | Reading Readiness | Young Beginning Readers | Older Non and Beginning Readers | Middle Grade Remedial | Middle Grade Achievers | Junior High Remedial | Junior High Achievers | H.S. and Adult Remedial | Learning Disabilities | Minority Group Emphasis | Enrichment for Gifted |
|---|---|---|---|---|---|---|---|---|---|---|---|
| Globe Classroom Libraries | | | | ● | ● | ● | ● | ● | ● | ● | |
| Hammond Reading Skills | | | | ● | ● | ● | | | | | |
| Hastings House Trade Books | | | | ● | | | | | | | |
| High Interest Books | | | | ● | ● | ● | | ● | | | |
| The Hilltop Series | | | ● | ● | | | | | | | |
| Hip Pocket Stories | | | | ● | | ● | | ● | | ● | |
| HITS | | | | ● | ● | | | ● | | ● | |
| HITS Primary Reading System | | ● | | | | | | | | | |
| How and Why Wonder Books | | | | | ● | ● | ● | | | | ● |
| Humankind | | ● | | | ● | ● | | | | | ● |
| I Can Read Underwater Books | ● | ● | | ● | | | | | | | |
| I Can Read Books | ● | ● | ● | ● | | | | | ● | ● | ● |
| Ideal Instructional Materials | ● | ● | ● | ● | ● | ● | | | ● | | |
| Imperial A-V Materials | | ● | | ● | ● | ● | | | | | ● |
| The Incredible Series | | | | ● | ● | ● | | | ● | | |
| Instant Readers | ● | ● | | | | | | | | | ● |
| Instructor Curriculum Materials | ● | ● | | ● | ● | ● | | | | ● | |
| The Jim Forest Readers | | | ● | ● | | ● | | | | | |
| Joan Hanson Word Books | ● | ● | | | | | | | ● | | ● |
| The Kaleidoscope Readers | | | | | | ● | | ● | | ● | |
| Kinder-Fun Series | ● | ● | ● | | | | | | | | |
| King Comics Reading Library | | ● | ● | ● | ● | ● | | ● | ● | ● | ● |

| | Reading Readiness | Young Beginning Readers | Older Non and Beginning Readers | Middle Grade Remedial | Middle Grade Achievers | Junior High Remedial | Junior High Achievers | H.S. and Adult Remedial | Learning Disabilities | Minority Group Emphasis | Enrichment for Gifted |
|---|---|---|---|---|---|---|---|---|---|---|---|
| Learning Systems | | • | • | • | • | • | | | | | |
| Learning with Laughter | • | • | | | | | | | | | |
| Letters and Words | | • | | • | | | | | | | |
| Listening with a Purpose | | | | | • | • | | • | | | • |
| LOGOS | | • | • | • | • | • | | | | | |
| Magic Circle Books | • | • | | | | | | | | | |
| Mastering Basic Reading Skills | | | | • | • | • | | | | | |
| Match and Check | • | • | • | | | | | | • | | |
| McCall Crabbs Standard Test Lessons in Reading | | | | • | • | • | • | • | | | |
| McCall-Harby Test Lessons in Primary Reading | | • | • | | | | | | | | |
| MCP Phonics Program | • | • | • | | | | | | | | |
| Miller-Brody A-V Materials | • | • | | • | • | • | | | | | |
| The Morgan Bay Mysteries | | | | • | | • | | | • | | |
| Morrow Trade Books | | • | | • | • | • | | | | | |
| Milton Bradley Materials | • | • | • | • | • | • | | | • | | |
| Mini-Systems Programs for Individualized Instruction | • | • | | | | | | | | | |
| The New Linguistic Block Series | • | • | • | | | | | | • | | |
| Open Court Lit Kits | | • | | • | • | | | | | | |
| Our Book Corner | • | • | | | | | | | • | | |
| Owl Books | • | • | | | | | | | | | • |

| | Reading Readiness | Young Beginning Readers | Older Non and Beginning Readers | Middle Grade Remedial | Middle Grade Achievers | Junior High Remedial | Junior High Achievers | H.S. and Adult Remedial | Learning Disabilities | Minority Group Emphasis | Enrichment for Gifted |
|---|---|---|---|---|---|---|---|---|---|---|---|
| Oxford Children's Books | | | | | ● | | ● | | | | |
| Pal Paperback Kits | | | ● | ● | | ● | | ● | ● | ● | |
| Panorama Reading | | | | ● | | ● | | ● | | ● | |
| Paperbacks from Avon | | | | | | ● | ● | ● | | ● | ● |
| Paperbacks from Bantam | | | | ● | ● | ● | ● | ● | | ● | ● |
| Patterns, Sounds, and Meaning | ● | ● | ● | ● | | | | | ● | | |
| Personalized Reading Centers | | | | ● | ● | | | | | | ● |
| Phoenix Reading Series | | | | ● | ● | ● | | ● | ● | ● | |
| Phonics Crossword Puzzles | | ● | ● | ● | | | | | ● | | ● |
| Picto-Cabulary Basic Word Set | ● | ● | ● | ● | | | | | | | |
| Picto-Cabulary Series | | | | ● | ● | ● | ● | ● | | | ● |
| Practicing Reading | | ● | ● | ● | ● | ● | ● | ● | | | |
| Practicing Vocabulary | | ● | ● | ● | ● | ● | ● | ● | ● | | |
| Primary Reading Skills Program | | ● | ● | ● | | | | | | | |
| Puffin Books | | | | ● | ● | ● | | | | | |
| RR | | | ● | ● | | ● | | ● | ● | | |
| Raintree Children's Books | | ● | ● | ● | ● | ● | | | ● | | ● |
| Random House Reading Programs, Orange and Yellow | | ● | | ● | | | | | ● | | ● |
| Random House Reading Programs, Red, Blue, and Green | | | | ● | ● | ● | ● | ● | | ● | ● |
| Random Reading Almanacs | | | | ● | ● | ● | | | | | |
| REACH | | | | ● | ● | ● | | | | | |

| | Reading Readiness | Young Beginning Readers | Older Non and Beginning Readers | Middle Grade Remedial | Middle Grade Achievers | Junior High Remedial | Junior High Achievers | H.S. and Adult Remedial | Learning Disabilities | Minority Group Emphasis | Enrichment for Gifted |
|---|---|---|---|---|---|---|---|---|---|---|---|
| Read as You Listen | ● | ● | | | | | | | | | ● |
| Read Along Libraries | ● | ● | ● | | | | | | | | |
| Read and Check | | ● | ● | ● | | | | | | | |
| Read Better—Learn More | | | | ● | ● | | | | | | |
| Reader's Choice | ● | ● | ● | ● | ● | ● | ● | | ● | ● | ● |
| Reading Attainment Systems I and II | | | | ● | ● | ● | ● | ● | | ● | |
| Reading Awareness | ● | ● | | | | | | | | | |
| Reading: Beginnings, Patterns, Explorations | ● | ● | | ● | | | | | | | |
| Reading Comprehension Programs | | ● | | | ● | | | | | | |
| Reading Development Kits | | | | | | ● | ● | ● | | | |
| Reading Enrichment Resources | | ● | | ● | ● | ● | | | | | ● |
| Reading for Survival | | | ● | ● | ● | ● | | ● | | | |
| Reading Improvement Series | | ● | ● | ● | ● | | | | ● | | |
| Reading Incentive Program and Gold Cup Games | | ● | | | | ● | | ● | | | |
| Reading Practice Program | | ● | ● | | | ● | | ● | ● | | |
| Reading Skill Builders | | ● | ● | ● | ● | ● | ● | | | | |
| Reading Skills Practice Pads | | ● | ● | ● | ● | ● | | | | | |
| Rolling Phonics | ● | ● | ● | | | | | | ● | | |
| Rolling Readers | ● | ● | ● | | | | | | ● | | |
| S.T.A.R.T. Reading Program | | ● | ● | ● | | | | | | | |
| SRA Reading Labs | | ● | | ● | ● | ● | ● | ● | ● | | |

| | Reading Readiness | Young Beginning Readers | Older Non and Beginning Readers | Middle Grade Remedial | Middle Grade Achievers | Junior High Remedial | Junior High Achievers | H.S. and Adult Remedial | Learning Disabilities | Minority Group Emphasis | Enrichment for Gifted |
|---|---|---|---|---|---|---|---|---|---|---|---|
| Satellite Books | | • | | | • | | | | | | • |
| Scholastic Bookshelf | | | | | • | | | | | | • |
| Scholastic's Elementary Skills Workbooks | | • | • | • | • | • | | | • | | |
| Scope Skills Books, Visuals, Activity Kits | | | • | • | | • | | • | • | • | |
| Scoring High in Reading | | | | • | • | • | | • | • | | |
| Scoring High in Survival Reading | | | | | | • | | • | | | |
| Scribner Book Fair Editions | | • | | • | • | | | | | | • |
| Selections from the Black | | | | | | • | • | • | | • | |
| Sesame Street Prereading Kit | • | • | | | | | | | • | | |
| Slow Reader Catalog | | | | • | | • | | • | • | • | |
| Spacetalk | | • | | | | | | | • | | |
| Special Ed Materials from Book-Lab | | | • | • | | • | | • | • | | |
| Specific Reading Skills (SRS) | | • | | • | • | • | | | | | |
| Speech to Print Phonics | • | • | • | | | | | | • | | |
| Spirit Duplicating Books | • | • | • | • | • | • | | | | | |
| Sports Illustrated Books | | | | | | | • | • | | | |
| Sports Star | | | • | | | • | | • | | | |
| Spotlight on Literature | | | | | | • | | • | | | |
| Spotlight on Phonics | | • | • | • | | | | | | | |
| Spotlight on Reading | | • | | • | • | • | | • | • | | |
| Sprint Reading Skills Program | | | • | • | | • | | | | | |

| | Reading Readiness | Young Beginning Readers | Older Non and Beginning Readers | Middle Grade Remedial | Middle Grade Achievers | Junior High Remedial | Junior High Achievers | H.S. and Adult Remedial | Learning Disabilities | Minority Group Emphasis | Enrichment for Gifted |
|---|---|---|---|---|---|---|---|---|---|---|---|
| Star Wars Attack on Reading | | | | ● | ● | ● | | | | | |
| STEP Language Board | ● | ● | | | | | | | ● | | |
| Story Go Round | ● | ● | | | | | | | | | |
| Story Plays, Plays for Echo Reading | | | | ● | ● | ● | | | ● | | ● |
| Study Exercises for Developing Reading Skills | | | | ● | ● | ● | | | ● | | |
| Study Skills for Information Retrieval | | | | | ● | ● | ● | | | | |
| Sunburst Materials | | ● | ● | ● | ● | ● | ● | ● | ● | | ● |
| Super Books | ● | ● | | | | | | | ● | | |
| Supermarket Recall Reading Program | | | | ● | | ● | | | ● | | |
| Super Products | | ● | | ● | | | | | ● | | |
| Supportive Reading Skills | | ● | ● | ● | ● | ● | | ● | ● | | |
| Survival Education | | | | | ● | | ● | | ● | | |
| T-Scopes | | ● | ● | ● | | | | | ● | | |
| Target Red, Target Yellow, Target Blue | ● | ● | ● | ● | | | | | ● | | |
| Target Green, Target Orange, Target Purple | | | | ● | ● | ● | ● | ● | ● | | ● |
| Teaching Resources | ● | ● | | | | | | | ● | | |
| Trade Books from Addison-Wesley | | | | ● | ● | ● | ● | | | | ● |
| Text Extenders | | ● | | ● | ● | | | | | | |
| The Time Machine Series | ● | ● | | | | | | | | | |
| Torchbearer Library | | | | | ● | ● | ● | | | | |
| Try This, Try This Too, Now Try This | ● | ● | ● | | | | | | ● | | |

| | Reading Readiness | Young Beginning Readers | Older Non and Beginning Readers | Middle Grade Remedial | Middle Grade Achievers | Junior High Remedial | Junior High Achievers | H.S. and Adult Remedial | Learning Disabilities | Minority Group Emphasis | Enrichment for Gifted |
|---|---|---|---|---|---|---|---|---|---|---|---|
| Vocabulary Improvement Practice | | | | • | • | • | | | • | | • |
| Ventures in Reading | | • | | | | | | | | | |
| Vocabulary Workshop | | | | | | | • | • | | | |
| Voyager Books | | • | | • | • | • | | | | | • |
| We Are Black | | | | • | • | • | | | • | • | |
| Webster Classroom Reading Clinic | | | | • | • | • | | | • | | |
| Webster Reading Centers | | | | • | • | • | | | • | | |
| Weekly Reader Skills Books | | | | • | • | • | • | • | | | |
| We Read Sentences | | • | • | • | | • | | | | | |
| Weird and Horrible Library | | | | • | • | • | • | • | | | • |
| What Can She Be? | | | | • | • | | | | | | |
| The Wildlife Adventure Series | | | • | • | | • | | | • | • | |
| Wonder Starters | • | • | | | | | | | | | |
| Word Attack Series | | | | | • | • | • | | | | |
| Wordcraft Vocabulary Programs | | | | | • | • | • | • | | | |
| Wordpacers | | | | | • | • | • | • | | | • |
| Word-Roll | • | • | • | | | | | | | | |
| Words Are Important | | | | | • | • | • | • | | | |
| Wordshop | | • | • | • | • | • | | | • | | |
| Workshop Kits | | • | | • | • | | | | | | |
| Yearling Individualized Reading Programs | | | | • | • | • | | | | | • |

# PUBLISHERS' ADDRESS LIST

Addison Wesley Publishing Co.
Jacob Way
Reading, MA 01867

Allyn and Bacon
470 Atlantic Avenue
Boston, MA 02210

Ann Arbor Publishers
P.O. Box 388
Worthington, OH 43085

ARO Publishing Co.
P.O. Box 193
Provo, UT 84601

Avon Books
250 West 55 Street
New York, NY 10019

Bantam Books, Inc.
School Division
666 Fifth Avenue
New York, NY 10019

Barnell Loft, Ltd.
958 Church Street
Baldwin, NY 11510

The Bobbs-Merrill Co., Inc.
4300 West 62nd Street
Indianapolis, IN 46206

Book-Lab
1449 Thirty-Seventh St.
Brooklyn, NY 11218

Bowmar/Noble Publishers, Inc.
4563 Colorado Boulevard
Los Angeles, CA 90039

Cambridge Book Co.
488 Madison Avenue
New York, NY 10022

Children's Press
1224 West Van Buren Street
Chicago, IL 60607

Cole Supply
P.O. Box 1717
Pasadena, TX

Continental Press Publications
Elizabethtown, PA 17022

Communicad
The Communications Academy
Box 541
Wilton, CT 06897

Coronet Instructional Materials
65 East South Water Street
Chicago, IL 60601

Crane Publishing Co.
1301 Hamilton Avenue
P.O. Box 3713
Trenton, NJ 08629

Creative Teaching Press, Inc.
5305 Production Drive
Huntington Beach, CA 92649

Croft, Inc.
P.O. Box 15
Old Greenwich, CT

Thomas Y. Crowell
666 Fifth Avenue
New York, NY 10019

Davco Publishers
8154 Ridgeway Avenue
Skokie, IL 60076

Dexter and Westbrook
958 Church Street
Baldwin, NY 11510

E. P. Dutton
2 Park Avenue
New York, NY 10016

The Economy Co.
P.O. Box 25308
1901 North Walnut
Oklahoma City, OK 73125

Educational Development Corp.
202 Lake Miriam Drive
Lakeland, FL 33803

Educational Products, Inc.
1211 West 22 Street
Oak Brook, IL 60521

Educational Progress
P.O. Box 45663
Tulsa, OK 74145

Educational Teaching Aids
159 W. Kinzie Street
Chicago, IL 60610

ESP, Inc.
P.O. Box 5037
Jonesboro, AR 72401

Follett Library Book Co.
4506 Northwest Highway
Crystal Lake, IL 60014

Garrard Publishing Co.
1607 North Market Street
Champaign, IL 61820

Ginn and Co.
Education Center
P.O. Box 2649
Columbus, OH 43216

Globe Book Co.
175 Fifth Avenue
New York, NY 10010

Grolier Educational Corp.
845 Third Avenue
New York, NY 10022

Grosset and Dunlap, Inc.
51 Madison Avenue
New York, NY 10022

Hammond, Inc.
Maplewood, NJ 07040

Harcourt Brace Javanovich, Inc.
757 Third Avenue
New York, NY 10017

Harper and Row, Publishers
10 East 53 Street
New York, NY 10022

Hastings House Publishers, Inc.
10 East 40 Street
New York, NY 10016

D.C. Heath & Co.
125 Spring Street
Lexington, MA 02173

Holt, Rinehart and Winston
383 Madison Avenue
New York, NY 10017

Ideal School Supply Co.
11000 S. Lavergne Avenue
Oak Lawn, IL 60453

Imperial International Learning Corp.
P.O. Box 548
Kankakee, IL 60901

Individualized Instruction Co.
P.O. Box 25308
1901 North Walnut
Oklahoma City, OK 73125

Instructor Publications, Inc.
Instructor Park
Dansville, NY 14437

Interpretive Education
2306 Winters Drive
Kalamazoo, MI 49002

Jamestown Publishers
P.O. Box 6743
Providence, RI 02904

Janus Book Publishers
3514 Investment Boulevard
Suite 501
Haywood, CA 94545

Jones-Kenilworth Co., Inc.
8301 Ambassador Row
Dallas, TX 75247

King Features Syndicate
Education Division
235 E. 45 Street
New York, NY 10017

Laidlaw Bros.
Thatcher and Madison Streets
River Forest, IL 60305

Lerner Publications Co.
241 First Avenue N.
Minneapolis, MN 55401

J.B. Lippincott Co.
East Washington Square
Philadelphia, PA 19105

Lothrop, Lee & Shepard Co.
105 Madison Avenue
New York, NY 10016

Macdonald-Raintree, Inc.
205 West Highland Avenue
Milwaukee, WI 53203

McCormick-Mathers Publishing Co.
300 Pike Street
Cincinnati, OH 45202

McGraw-Hill
1221 Avenue of the Americas
New York, NY 10020

Julian Messner
Simon & Schuster Building
1230 Avenue of the Americas
New York, NY 10020

Milton Bradley
Materials are available from many
distributers, including:
Random House School Division
400 Hahn Road
Westminister, MD 21157

Modern Curriculum Press
13900 Prospect Road
Cleveland, OH 44136

ModuLearn, Inc.
P.O. Box 3178
Mission Viejo, CA 92690

William Morrow and Co.
105 Madison Avenue
New York, NY 10016

Nystrom
3333 Elston Avenue
Chicago, IL 60618

Oxford University Press
200 Madison Avenue
New York, NY 10016

Perma-Bound Division
Hertzberg-New Method, Inc.
Vandalia Road
Jacksonville, IL 62650

Penguin Books Division
The Viking Press
625 Madison Avenue
New York, NY 10022

Prentice-Hall, Inc.
Englewood Cliffs, NJ 07632

Prentice-Hall Learning Systems, Inc.
P.O. Box 527
San Jose, CA 95106

Random House, Inc.
School Division
400 Hahn Road
Westminster, MD 21157

Reader's Digest Association
Pleasantville, NY 10570

Frank E. Richards Publishing Co.
P.O. Box 66
Phoenix, NY 13135

Frank Schaffer Publications, Inc.
These materials are available
from a number of local distributors.
Check your nearest school
materials jobber.

W. H. Sadlier
11 Park Place
New York, NY 10007

Science Research Associates, Inc.
259 E. Erie Street
Chicago, IL 60611

Schloat Productions
150 White Plains Road
Tarrytown, NY 10591

Scholastic Book Services
904 Sylvan Avenue
Englewood Cliifs, NJ 07632

Scott Education
5 Lower Westfield Road
Holyoke, MA 01040

Scott, Foresman and Co.
1900 E. Lake Avenue
Glenview, IL 60025

Charles Scribner's Sons
Library Services Department
597 Fifth Avenue
New York, NY 10017

The Seabury Press, Inc.
815 Second Avenue
New York, NY 10017

Spellbinder, Inc.
33 Bradford Street
Concord, MA 01742

Steck-Vaughn Co.
807 Brazos
P.O. Box 2028
Austin, TX 78768

Sunburst Communications
Suite 84
41 Washington Avenue
Pleasantville, NY 10570

Supermarket Recall Reading Program
111 Roe Boulevard East
Patchogue, NY 11772

Teachers College Press
1234 Amsterdam Avenue
New York, NY 10027

Teaching Resources Corp.
100 Boylston Street
Boston, MA 02116

Teaching Stuff
801 Glenvista Drive
Glendale, CA 91206

Trend Enterprises, Inc.
St. Paul, MN 55164

Troll Associates
320 Route 17
Mahwah, NJ 07430

Jane Ward Co., Inc.
1642 So. Beech Street
Lakewood, CO 80228

Webster Division
McGraw-Hill Book Co.
1221 Avenue of the Americas
New York, NY 10020

Westinghouse Learning Corp.
5005 West 110 Street
Oak Lawn, IL 60453

Xerox Education Division
1250 Fairwood Avenue
Columbus, OH 43216

# Instructional Planning Index

| | Teacher Directed | Individual Self-Instruction | Peer Teams or Small Groups | Whole Class | Rainy Days or Friday Afternoons | Prepare in Advance | No Materials Needed |
|---|---|---|---|---|---|---|---|
| 1 | | ● | | | | ● | |
| 2 | | ● | | | | ● | |
| 3 | | ● | | | | ● | |
| 4 | | ● | | | | ● | |
| 5 | ● | | | ● | | | ● |
| 6 | | ● | | | | ● | |
| 7 | ● | | | ● | | | ● |
| 8 | | ● | | | | | |
| 9 | | ● | | | | | |
| 10 | | ● | | | | | |
| 11 | | ● | | | | | |
| 12 | | ● | | | | | |
| 13 | | ● | | | | | |
| 14 | ● | | | ● | | | ● |

| | Teacher Directed | Individual Self-Instruction | Peer Teams or Small Groups | Whole Class | Rainy Days or Friday Afternoons | Prepare in Advance | No Materials Needed |
|---|---|---|---|---|---|---|---|
| 15 | | ● | | | | ● | |
| 16 | | ● | | | | ● | |
| 17 | | ● | | | | ● | |
| 18 | | ● | | | | ● | |
| 19 | | ● | | | | ● | |
| 20 | | ● | | | | ● | |
| 21 | ● | | | ● | | ● | |
| 22 | ● | | | ● | ● | | ● |
| 23 | ● | | | ● | ● | | ● |
| 24 | ● | | | ● | | | ● |
| 25 | ● | | | ● | ● | | ● |
| 26 | ● | | | ● | | ● | |
| 27 | ● | | | ● | ● | | |
| 28 | ● | ● | | | | ● | |

| | Teacher Directed | Individual Self-Instruction | Peer Teams or Small Groups | Whole Class | Rainy Days or Friday Afternoons | Prepare in Advance | No Materials Needed |
|---|---|---|---|---|---|---|---|
| 29 | | • | | | | • | |
| 30 | | • | | | | • | |
| 31 | | • | | | | • | |
| 32 | | • | | | | • | |
| 33 | | • | | | | • | |
| 34 | | • | | | | • | |
| 35 | | | • | | | • | |
| 36 | | • | | | | • | |
| 37 | | • | | | | • | |
| 38 | | • | | | | • | |
| 39 | | • | • | | • | • | |
| 40 | | | • | | • | • | |
| 41 | | • | | | | • | |
| 42 | | • | | | | • | |
| 43 | | • | | | | • | |
| 44 | | • | | | | • | |
| 45 | • | | | • | • | • | |
| 46 | | • | | | | • | |
| 47 | | • | | | | • | |
| 48 | | • | | | • | • | |
| 49 | | | | • | | | • |
| 50 | • | | | | • | | • |
| 51 | • | | | | | | • |
| 52 | • | | | | | • | |

| | Teacher Directed | Individual Self-Instruction | Peer Teams or Small Groups | Whole Class | Rainy Days or Friday Afternoons | Prepare in Advance | No Materials Needed |
|---|---|---|---|---|---|---|---|
| 53 | • | | | • | | • | |
| 54 | | | | | | • | |
| 55 | | • | | | | • | |
| 56 | • | | • | • | | • | |
| 57 | | • | | | | • | |
| 58 | • | | | | | • | |
| 59 | | | | | | • | |
| 60 | | • | | | | • | |
| 61 | | • | | | | • | |
| 62 | • | | | | | • | |
| 63 | | | | | | • | |
| 64 | • | | | | | • | |
| 65 | | | | | | • | |
| 66 | • | | | • | | | |
| 67 | • | | | • | | • | |
| 68 | | • | | | • | • | |
| 69 | • | | | • | | • | |
| 70 | • | | | • | | | |
| 71 | • | | | • | | | |
| 72 | • | | | • | | • | |
| 73 | • | | | • | | • | |
| 74 | | • | | | | • | |
| 75 | | • | | | | • | |
| 76 | | | | | | • | |

| # | Teacher Directed | Individual Self-Instruction | Peer Teams or Small Groups | Whole Class | Rainy Days or Friday Afternoons | Prepare in Advance | No Materials Needed |
|---|---|---|---|---|---|---|---|
| 77 | | | | | | ● | |
| 78 | | | | | | ● | |
| 79 | ● | | | | | | |
| 80 | | ● | | | | ● | |
| 81 | | ● | | | | ● | |
| 82 | | ● | | | | ● | |
| 83 | | | | | | | ● |
| 84 | ● | | ● | ● | | | |
| 85 | ● | | ● | ● | | | |
| 86 | ● | | ● | ● | | | |
| 87 | ● | | ● | ● | | | |
| 88 | | ● | | | | ● | |
| 89 | | ● | | | | ● | |
| 90 | ● | | ● | ● | | | |
| 91 | | ● | | | | ● | |
| 92 | | ● | | | | ● | |
| 93 | | ● | | | | ● | |
| 94 | ● | | | | | ● | |
| 95 | | ● | | | | ● | |
| 96 | | ● | | | | ● | |
| 97 | | ● | | | | ● | |
| 98 | | ● | | | | ● | |
| 99 | | ● | | | | ● | |
| 100 | | ● | | | | ● | |
| 101 | | ● | | | | ● | |
| 102 | | ● | | | | ● | |
| 103 | | ● | | | | ● | |
| 104 | ● | | | ● | | | |
| 105 | | ● | | | | ● | |
| 106 | | ● | | | | ● | |
| 107 | | ● | | | | ● | |
| 108 | | ● | | | | ● | |
| 109 | | ● | | | | ● | |
| 110 | | ● | | | | ● | |
| 111 | | ● | | | | ● | |
| 112 | | ● | | | | ● | |
| 113 | | ● | | | | ● | |
| 114 | | ● | | | | ● | |
| 115 | ● | | | ● | | | ● |
| 116 | ● | | | ● | | | ● |
| 117 | | ● | ● | | | ● | |
| 118 | | ● | ● | | | ● | |
| 119 | | | | | | | |
| 120 | ● | ● | ● | ● | | | ● |
| 121 | ● | ● | ● | ● | | ● | |
| 122 | ● | | | ● | ● | | ● |
| 123 | ● | | | ● | ● | | ● |
| 124 | | | | | | ● | |

| | Teacher Directed | Individual Self-Instruction | Peer Teams or Small Groups | Whole Class | Rainy Days or Friday Afternoons | Prepare in Advance | No Materials Needed |
|---|---|---|---|---|---|---|---|
| 125 | | | ● | | | ● | |
| 126 | | | | | | ● | |
| 127 | | | | | | ● | |
| 128 | | | | | | ● | |
| 129 | | | ● | | | | |
| 130 | | ● | ● | | | | |
| 131 | | | ● | | | ● | |
| 132 | | ● | | | | ● | |
| 133 | | ● | | | | | |
| 134 | | ● | | | | | |
| 135 | ● | | | | ● | ● | |
| 136 | | | | | | ● | |
| 137 | ● | ● | ● | ● | ● | ● | |
| 138 | | ● | | | | ● | |
| 139 | ● | | ● | | | ● | |
| 140 | ● | | ● | | | ● | |
| 141 | | | ● | | | ● | |
| 142 | | | ● | | | ● | |
| 143 | | | ● | | ● | ● | |
| 144 | ● | | ● | ● | ● | ● | |
| 145 | ● | | ● | | ● | ● | |
| 146 | | | ● | | ● | ● | |
| 147 | | ● | ● | | | ● | |
| 148 | | | ● | | | ● | |

| | Teacher Directed | Individual Self-Instruction | Peer Teams or Small Groups | Whole Class | Rainy Days or Friday Afternoons | Prepare in Advance | No Materials Needed |
|---|---|---|---|---|---|---|---|
| 149 | | | ● | | ● | ● | |
| 150 | ● | | | | | ● | |
| 151 | | | ● | | ● | ● | |
| 152 | ● | | ● | ● | ● | ● | |
| 153 | ● | | ● | | ● | ● | |
| 154 | ● | | ● | ● | ● | ● | |
| 155 | ● | | ● | ● | ● | ● | |
| 156 | ● | | | | | | |
| 157 | | ● | | | ● | ● | |
| 158 | | ● | | | | ● | |
| 159 | | ● | | | | ● | |
| 160 | | ● | | | | | |
| 161 | ● | | ● | ● | | ● | |
| 162 | ● | | | | | | |
| 163 | ● | | | ● | ● | ● | |
| 164 | ● | | | ● | ● | ● | |
| 165 | ● | | | ● | ● | ● | |
| 166 | ● | | | | | | ● |
| 167 | | | | | | ● | |
| 168 | ● | | ● | ● | ● | | ● |
| 169 | ● | | ● | ● | ● | | ● |
| 170 | | | | | | | |
| 171 | ● | | ● | ● | ● | ● | |
| 172 | | ● | | | | | ● |

| # | Teacher Directed | Individual Self-Instruction | Peer Teams or Small Groups | Whole Class | Rainy Days or Friday Afternoons | Prepare in Advance | No Materials Needed |
|---|---|---|---|---|---|---|---|
| 173 | ● |  | ● | ● |  |  | ● |
| 174 |  | ● |  |  |  | ● |  |
| 175 |  |  | ● |  |  | ● |  |
| 176 |  | ● |  |  |  | ● |  |
| 177 | ● |  | ● | ● |  | ● |  |
| 178 |  | ● |  |  |  | ● |  |
| 179 | ● | ● |  | ● |  |  | ● |
| 180 |  |  |  |  |  | ● |  |
| 181 |  | ● |  |  |  |  |  |
| 182 |  | ● | ● |  |  | ● |  |
| 183 |  |  | ● |  |  | ● |  |
| 184 |  |  | ● |  |  | ● |  |
| 185 | ● |  |  | ● | ● | ● |  |
| 186 |  | ● | ● |  |  | ● |  |
| 187 |  |  |  |  |  |  |  |
| 188 |  |  |  |  |  | ● |  |
| 189 |  |  | ● |  |  | ● |  |
| 190 | ● |  | ● |  |  | ● |  |
| 191 | ● |  | ● |  |  | ● |  |
| 192 |  |  | ● |  | ● | ● |  |
| 193 |  | ● | ● |  |  | ● |  |
| 194 | ● |  |  | ● |  | ● |  |
| 195 | ● |  |  | ● |  | ● |  |
| 196 | ● |  | ● | ● |  | ● |  |

| # | Teacher Directed | Individual Self-Instruction | Peer Teams or Small Groups | Whole Class | Rainy Days or Friday Afternoons | Prepare in Advance | No Materials Needed |
|---|---|---|---|---|---|---|---|
| 197 |  |  |  |  |  | ● |  |
| 198 | ● |  |  |  |  |  | ● |
| 199 |  | ● |  |  |  | ● |  |
| 200 |  | ● | ● |  |  | ● |  |
| 201 |  | ● | ● |  |  | ● |  |
| 202 |  | ● |  |  |  | ● |  |
| 203 | ● |  |  | ● |  | ● |  |
| 204 |  | ● | ● |  |  | ● |  |
| 205 |  | ● |  |  |  | ● |  |
| 206 | ● |  | ● | ● |  | ● |  |
| 207 |  |  | ● |  |  | ● |  |
| 208 |  | ● |  |  |  | ● |  |
| 209 |  | ● |  |  |  | ● |  |
| 210 |  | ● | ● |  |  | ● |  |
| 211 |  | ● |  |  |  | ● |  |
| 212 |  | ● |  |  |  | ● |  |
| 213 |  | ● |  |  |  | ● |  |
| 214 | ● |  | ● | ● |  | ● |  |
| 215 |  | ● | ● |  |  | ● |  |
| 216 |  | ● | ● |  |  | ● |  |
| 217 |  | ● |  |  |  | ● |  |
| 218 |  | ● |  |  |  | ● |  |
| 219 |  | ● |  |  |  | ● |  |
| 220 |  | ● |  |  |  | ● |  |

| | Teacher Directed | Individual Self-Instruction | Peer Teams or Small Groups | Whole Class | Rainy Days or Friday Afternoons | Prepare in Advance | No Materials Needed |
|---|---|---|---|---|---|---|---|
| 221 | | ● | | | | ● | |
| 222 | | ● | | | | ● | |
| 223 | | ● | ● | | | ● | |
| 224 | | ● | | | | ● | |
| 225 | ● | | | | | | ● |
| 226 | | | ● | ● | | ● | |
| 227 | | | ● | | | ● | |
| 228 | ● | | ● | | | ● | |
| 229 | | | ● | | | ● | |
| 230 | ● | | ● | | | ● | |
| 231 | ● | | ● | | | ● | |
| 232 | | | ● | | | ● | |
| 233 | ● | | ● | ● | | | ● |
| 234 | | ● | | | | ● | |
| 235 | | ● | | | | ● | |
| 236 | | ● | | | | ● | |
| 237 | | ● | ● | | | ● | |
| 238 | | ● | | | | ● | |
| 239 | | ● | | | | ● | |
| 240 | | ● | | | | ● | |
| 241 | | ● | | | | ● | |
| 242 | | ● | | | | ● | |
| 243 | | ● | | | | ● | |
| 244 | | ● | | | | ● | |

| | Teacher Directed | Individual Self-Instruction | Peer Teams or Small Groups | Whole Class | Rainy Days or Friday Afternoons | Prepare in Advance | No Materials Needed |
|---|---|---|---|---|---|---|---|
| 245 | | ● | | | | ● | |
| 246 | | ● | | | | ● | |
| 247 | | ● | | | | ● | |
| 248 | | ● | ● | | | ● | |
| 249 | | ● | | | | ● | |
| 250 | | ● | | | | ● | |
| 251 | | ● | | | | ● | |
| 252 | | ● | | | | ● | |
| 253 | | | ● | | ● | ● | |
| 254 | | ● | | | | ● | |
| 255 | | ● | | | | ● | |
| 256 | | | | | | ● | |
| 257 | | | | | | | ● |
| 258 | | | | | | | ● |
| 259 | | ● | | | | ● | |
| 260 | | | | | | ● | |
| 261 | ● | | ● | ● | ● | ● | |
| 262 | ● | | | | ● | ● | |
| 263 | | | | | | ● | |
| 264 | ● | | | | | ● | |
| 265 | | ● | ● | | | ● | |
| 266 | | ● | ● | | | ● | |
| 267 | | ● | ● | | | ● | |
| 268 | | ● | ● | | | ● | |

| | Teacher Directed | Individual Self-Instruction | Peer Teams or Small Groups | Whole Class | Rainy Days or Friday Afternoons | Prepare in Advance | No Materials Needed |
|---|---|---|---|---|---|---|---|
| 269 | ● | ● | ● | ● | | ● | |
| 270 | | | | | | ● | |
| 271 | | | | | | ● | |
| 272 | | | | | | ● | |
| 273 | ● | | ● | ● | | ● | |
| 274 | | ● | | | | | |
| 275 | ● | | ● | ● | | | ● |
| 276 | | | | | | | ● |
| 277 | ● | ● | | | | ● | |
| 278 | | ● | | | | | ● |
| 279 | | | ● | | | | ● |
| 280 | ● | | ● | ● | ● | ● | |
| 281 | ● | | ● | ● | | ● | |
| 282 | | ● | | | | ● | |
| 283 | ● | | ● | ● | ● | | ● |
| 284 | | ● | | | | ● | |
| 285 | | ● | | | | ● | |
| 286 | | ● | | | | ● | |
| 287 | ● | | | | | ● | |
| 288 | | ● | | | | ● | |
| 289 | | ● | | | | ● | |
| 290 | ● | | ● | ● | | ● | |
| 291 | | ● | | | | ● | |
| 292 | | ● | | | | ● | |

| | Teacher Directed | Individual Self-Instruction | Peer Teams or Small Groups | Whole Class | Rainy Days or Friday Afternoons | Prepare in Advance | No Materials Needed |
|---|---|---|---|---|---|---|---|
| 293 | ● | ● | | | | ● | |
| 294 | ● | ● | | | | ● | |
| 295 | | | | | | ● | |
| 296 | ● | | | | | ● | |
| 297 | | | | | | ● | |
| 298 | ● | | | | | | ● |
| 299 | ● | | | | | ● | |
| 300 | ● | | | | | ● | |
| 301 | ● | | | | | | ● |
| 302 | | | ● | | ● | ● | |
| 303 | | ● | ● | | | ● | |
| 304' | ● | | | | | ● | |
| 305 | ● | | | | | ● | |
| 306 | ● | | | | | ● | |
| 307 | | ● | | | | ● | |
| 308 | ● | | | | | ● | |
| 309 | ● | | | | | ● | |
| 310 | ● | | | | | ● | |
| 311 | ● | | | | | ● | |
| 312 | | | | | | ● | |
| 313 | ● | | | | | | ● |
| 314 | ● | | | | | | ● |
| 315 | ● | | | | | ● | |
| 316 | | ● | | | | ● | |

| | Teacher Directed | Individual Self-Instruction | Peer Teams or Small Groups | Whole Class | Rainy Days or Friday Afternoons | Prepare in Advance | No Materials Needed |
|---|---|---|---|---|---|---|---|
| 317 | | ● | | | | ● | |
| 318 | ● | | | | | | |
| 319 | | | | | | ● | |
| 320 | | ● | | | | ● | |
| 321 | ● | | | | | ● | |
| 322 | ● | | | | ● | ● | |
| 323 | | | ● | | ● | ● | |
| 324 | ● | | ● | | ● | ● | |
| 325 | ● | | | | | | ● |
| 326 | ● | | | | | | ● |
| 327 | ● | | | | | | ● |
| 328 | | | | | | ● | |
| 329 | | ● | | | | | |
| 330 | | ● | | | | | |
| 331 | | ● | | | | | |
| 332 | | ● | | | | | |
| 333 | ● | | | | | ● | |
| 334 | | ● | | | | ● | |
| 335 | | ● | ● | ● | ● | ● | |
| 336 | | ● | ● | ● | ● | ● | |
| 337 | | ● | ● | ● | ● | ● | |
| 338 | | ● | ● | | | ● | |
| 339 | | ● | | | | ● | |
| 340 | | ● | ● | | | ● | |

| | Teacher Directed | Individual Self-Instruction | Peer Teams or Small Groups | Whole Class | Rainy Days or Friday Afternoons | Prepare in Advance | No Materials Needed |
|---|---|---|---|---|---|---|---|
| 341 | | | ● | | | | ● |
| 342 | | ● | | | | ● | |
| 343 | | ● | | | | ● | |
| 344 | | | ● | | | ● | |
| 345 | | ● | | | | ● | |
| 346 | | ● | | | | ● | |
| 347 | ● | ● | ● | ● | | ● | |
| 348 | | ● | ● | | | ● | |
| 349 | | ● | ● | | | ● | |
| 350 | | ● | ● | | | ● | |
| 351 | | ● | | | | ● | |
| 352 | | ● | ● | | ● | | |
| 353 | | ● | | | | ● | |
| 354 | | ● | | | | ● | |
| 355 | | ● | | | | ● | |
| 356 | | | ● | ● | | | |
| 357 | | ● | ● | ● | | | |
| 358 | | ● | ● | ● | | ● | |
| 359 | | ● | ● | | | ● | |
| 360 | | ● | | | | ● | |
| 361 | | ● | | | | ● | |
| 362 | | ● | | | | ● | |
| 363 | | ● | | | | ● | |
| 364 | ● | | | ● | | | |

| | Teacher Directed | Individual Self-Instruction | Peer Teams or Small Groups | Whole Class | Rainy Days or Friday Afternoons | Prepare in Advance | No Materials Needed |
|---|---|---|---|---|---|---|---|
| 365 | • | | | • | | | • |
| 366 | • | | | • | | | • |
| 367 | • | | | • | | | • |
| 368 | • | | | • | | | |
| 369 | | • | • | • | | | |
| 370 | | • | • | | | | |
| 371 | | • | | | | • | |
| 372 | | • | • | | | • | |
| 373 | | • | | | | • | |
| 374 | | • | • | | | • | |
| 375 | | • | • | | | • | |
| 376 | | • | | | | • | |
| 377 | | • | | | | • | |
| 378 | | • | | | | • | |
| 379 | | • | | | | • | |
| 380 | | | | | | • | |
| 381 | | • | | | | • | |
| 382 | | • | | | | • | |
| 383 | | • | | | | • | |
| 384 | | • | | | | • | |
| 385 | | • | | | | • | |
| 386 | | • | | | | • | |
| 387 | | • | | | | • | |
| 388 | | • | | | • | • | |

| | Teacher Directed | Individual Self-Instruction | Peer Teams or Small Groups | Whole Class | Rainy Days or Friday Afternoons | Prepare in Advance | No Materials Needed |
|---|---|---|---|---|---|---|---|
| 389 | • | | • | • | | • | |
| 390 | | • | | | | • | |
| 391 | | • | | | | • | |
| 392 | | • | • | | | • | |
| 393 | | • | | | | • | |
| 394 | | • | | | • | • | |
| 395 | | • | | | | • | |
| 396 | | • | | | | • | |
| 397 | | • | | | | • | |
| 398 | | • | | | | • | |
| 399 | | • | | | | • | |
| 400 | | • | | | • | • | |
| 401 | | • | | | | • | |
| 402 | | • | | | | • | |
| 403 | | • | | | | • | |
| 404 | | • | • | | • | • | |
| 405 | • | • | • | • | | | |
| 406 | | • | | | | • | |
| 407 | | • | | | | • | |
| 408 | | • | | | | • | |
| 409 | | • | | | | • | |
| 410 | • | • | • | • | | • | |
| 411 | • | • | • | • | | • | |
| 412 | | • | | | | • | |

| | Teacher Directed | Individual Self-Instruction | Peer Teams or Small Groups | Whole Class | Rainy Days or Friday Afternoons | Prepare in Advance | No Materials Needed |
|---|---|---|---|---|---|---|---|
| 413 | | ● | | | | ● | |
| 414 | | ● | | | | ● | |
| 415 | | ● | | | | ● | |
| 416 | | ● | | | | ● | |
| 417 | | ● | | | ● | ● | |
| 418 | | ● | | | | ● | |
| 419 | | ● | | | | ● | |
| 420 | | ● | | | | ● | |
| 421 | | ● | | | | ● | |
| 422 | | ● | | | | ● | |
| 423 | | ● | | | | ● | |
| 424 | | ● | | | | | |
| 425 | ● | | | | | | |
| 426 | ● | | ● | ● | | ● | |
| 427 | ● | | ● | ● | | ● | |
| 428 | | ● | | | | ● | |
| 429 | | ● | | | | | |
| 430 | | ● | | | | ● | |
| 431 | | ● | | | | ● | |
| 432 | | ● | | | | ● | |
| 433 | | ● | ● | | | ● | |
| 434 | | ● | | | | ● | |
| 435 | ● | ● | ● | ● | | | |
| 436 | ● | ● | ● | ● | | ● | |

| | Teacher Directed | Individual Self-Instruction | Peer Teams or Small Groups | Whole Class | Rainy Days or Friday Afternoons | Prepare in Advance | No Materials Needed |
|---|---|---|---|---|---|---|---|
| 437 | ● | | | | | | |
| 438 | | | | | | ● | |
| 439 | | | | | | ● | |
| 440 | | | ● | ● | | | |
| 441 | | ● | | | | ● | |
| 442 | | ● | | | | ● | |
| 443 | ● | ● | | | | ● | |
| 444 | | ● | | | | ● | |
| 445 | | ● | | | | ● | |
| 446 | | ● | | | | ● | |
| 447 | | | | | | ● | |
| 448 | | ● | ● | | | | |
| 449 | | | ● | | | ● | |
| 450 | | ● | ● | | | ● | |
| 451 | | ● | ● | | | ● | |
| 452 | | ● | ● | | | ● | |
| 453 | | ● | | | | ● | |
| 454 | | ● | ● | | | ● | |
| 455 | | ● | ● | | | ● | |
| 456 | | ● | ● | | | ● | |
| 457 | | ● | ● | | | ● | |
| 458 | | ● | | | | ● | |
| 459 | ● | ● | ● | ● | ● | ● | |
| 460 | ● | ● | ● | ● | ● | ● | |

| | Teacher Directed | Individual Self-Instruction | Peer Teams or Small Groups | Whole Class | Rainy Days or Friday Afternoons | Prepare in Advance | No Materials Needed |
|---|---|---|---|---|---|---|---|
| 461 | | ● | ● | | | ● | |
| 462 | ● | ● | ● | ● | ● | ● | |
| 463 | ● | ● | ● | ● | | ● | |
| 464 | ● | | ● | ● | | | ● |
| 465 | | ● | | | | ● | |
| 466 | | ● | | | | ● | |
| 467 | ● | | ● | ● | | | ● |
| 468 | ● | | ● | ● | | ● | |
| 469 | ● | | ● | ● | | ● | |
| 470 | ● | | ● | ● | | | ● |
| 471 | ● | ● | ● | ● | ● | ● | |
| 472 | ● | ● | ● | ● | ● | ● | |
| 473 | ● | ● | ● | ● | ● | ● | |
| 474 | ● | ● | ● | ● | ● | ● | |
| 475 | ● | ● | ● | ● | ● | ● | |
| 476 | ● | ● | ● | ● | ● | ● | |
| 477 | ● | | ● | ● | | | ● |
| 478 | ● | ● | ● | ● | ● | ● | |
| 479 | ● | ● | ● | ● | ● | ● | |
| 480 | ● | ● | ● | ● | ● | ● | |
| 481 | ● | | | ● | | ● | |

| | Teacher Directed | Individual Self-Instruction | Peer Teams or Small Groups | Whole Class | Rainy Days or Friday Afternoons | Prepare in Advance | No Materials Needed |
|---|---|---|---|---|---|---|---|
| 482 | ● | ● | ● | ● | | ● | |
| 483 | ● | ● | ● | ● | | ● | |
| 484 | ● | ● | ● | ● | | ● | |
| 485 | ● | ● | ● | ● | | ● | |
| 486 | ● | ● | ● | ● | ● | ● | |
| 487 | ● | ● | ● | | | ● | |
| 488 | ● | ● | ● | | | ● | |
| 489 | ● | ● | ● | | | ● | |
| 490 | ● | ● | ● | ● | | ● | |
| 491 | ● | ● | ● | ● | | ● | |
| 492 | ● | ● | ● | ● | | ● | |
| 493 | ● | ● | ● | ● | | | ● |
| 494 | | | | | | ● | |
| 495 | ● | | ● | ● | | | ● |
| 496 | | | | | | ● | |
| 497 | ● | | ● | ● | ● | ● | |
| 498 | ● | | ● | ● | ● | ● | |
| 499 | | | | | | | ● |
| 500 | | ● | | | | ● | |
| 501 | ● | | ● | ● | ● | ● | |